TOP **10**
NEW YORK CITY

ELEANOR BERMAN

D0324521

EYEWITNESS TRAVEL

Left **Brooklyn Bridge** Right **New York taxis**

LONDON, NEW YORK,
MELBOURNE, MUNICH AND DELHI
www.dk.com

Reproduced by Colourscan, Singapore
Printed and bound by South China Printing Co.
Ltd, China

First published in Great Britain in 2002 by Dorling
Kindersley Limited

80 Strand, London WC2R ORL

Reprinted with revisions 2004, 2005, 2006, 2007,
2008, 2009, 2010, 2011 (001)

**Copyright 2002, 2011 © Dorling Kindersley
Limited, London
A Penguin Company**

All rights reserved. No part of this publication
may be reproduced, stored in a retrieval system,
or transmitted in any form or by any means,
electronic, mechanical, photocopying, recording
or otherwise, without the prior written
permission of the copyright owner.

A CIP catalogue record is available from the
British Library.

ISBN 978 1 40535 848 4

Within each Top 10 list in this book, no hierarchy
of quality or popularity is implied. All 10 are, in
the editor's opinion, of roughly equal merit.

Throughout this book, floors are referred to in
accordance with American usage, ie the "first
floor" is at ground level.

MIX
Paper from
responsible sources
FSC
www.fsc.org   FSC™ C018179

Contents

New York's Top 10

The information in this DK Eyewitness Top 10 Travel Guide is checked regularly.
Every effort has been made to ensure that this book is as up-to-date as possible at the time of
going to press. Some details, however, such as telephone numbers, opening hours, prices,
gallery hanging arrangements and travel information are liable to change. The publishers
cannot accept responsibility for any consequences arising from the use of this book, nor for
any material on third party websites, and cannot guarantee that any website address in this
book will be a suitable source of travel information. We value the views and suggestions of
our readers very highly. Please write to: Publisher, DK Eyewitness Travel Guides,
Dorling Kindersley, 80 Strand, London, Great Britain WC2R ORL, or email travelguides@dk.com.

Cover: Front – **DK Images:** Dave King main; Rough Guides/Nelson Hancock clb. Spine – **DK Images:** Dave
King b. Back – **DK Images:** cl; Max Alexander c; Dave King cr.

Left **View of the Empire State Building** Right **Pier 17, South Street Seaport**

Contents

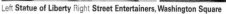
Left **Statue of Liberty** Right **Street Entertainers, Washington Square**

NEW YORK'S
TOP 10

NEW YORK'S TOP 10

TOP 10 New York Highlights

With its skyscrapers, great museums, and bright lights of Broadway, New York is a city of superlatives. There are countless sights that have to be seen, but a handful are truly definitive of the city. The following chapter illustrates the very best of these.

1 Empire State Building

This soaring Art Deco skyscraper is one of the most widely recognized symbols of the city, and star of countless movies. It offers unforgettable panoramas of New York from its 86th floor Observatory *(see pp8–9)*.

Hudson River

2 Fifth Avenue

A heady mix of fashionable shops and world-class architecture makes for an avenue of endless pleasures, and some of New York's best-known addresses *(see pp10–11)*.

Rockefeller Center 3

An urban wonder in the city's center, with gardens, restaurants, an underground shopping concourse, office space, a skating rink, and over 100 works of art, from murals to statues *(see pp12–15)*.

WISDOM AND KNOWLEDGE SHALL BE THE STABILITY OF THY TIMES

4 Statue of Liberty

The symbol of freedom for millions seeking a new life in America, the lady holding the torch of liberty is ensconced on her own island *(see pp16–17)*.

6 Times Square and the Theater District

An explosion of neon illuminates Broadway and Times Square, where more than 40 famous theaters play host to a changing parade of hit shows *(see pp22–5)*.

5 Ellis Island Immigration Museum

Carefully restored buildings bring to life the experience of the immigrants who have poured into New York over the years, helping to build the multiethnic city of today *(see pp18–21)*.

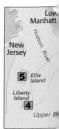

Lower Manhatt

New Jersey

Hudson River

5 Ellis Island

Liberty Island

4

Upper B

Harlem

Morningside
Heights

Central Park
The vast swath of green provides an 843-acre respite from the concrete of the city. The man-made park took 16 years and more than 500,000 trees to complete *(see pp26–7)*.

Metropolitan Museum of Art
It would take weeks to see all the treasures of this museum. It houses one of the greatest collections of the Western world and spans 5,000 years of culture *(see pp28–31)*.

Guggenheim Museum
This Frank Lloyd Wright building is a work of art in itself, and a fitting frame for a major collection of contemporary art *(see pp32–3)*.

American Museum of Natural History
Long famous for its dinosaurs, the museum moved into the space age with the dramatic Rose Center for Earth and Space *(see pp34–7)*.

Upper West Side

Upper East Side

Central Park

Midtown

Herald Square

Chelsea

Flatiron

Gramercy Park

Union Square

Greenwich Village

East Village

SoHo

Little Italy

TriBeCa

Chinatown

Civic Center

Lower East Side

South St Seaport

Lower Manhattan

Battery Park

Hudson River

East River

Harlem River

Roosevelt Island

1 ⌐—————— miles ⌐ 0 ⌐ km ————————⌐ 1

Empire State Building

The Empire State Building is the tallest and most famous skyscraper in New York. More than 120 million visitors, including the rock group Kiss and Queen Elizabeth II, have gazed down on the city from the Observatory since it opened in 1931. Planned in the prosperous 1920s by the architectural firm of Shreve, Lamb, and Harmon, this Art Deco classic was completed during the Depression and was largely vacant for several years, giving rise to the nickname "Empty State Building." It has been featured in countless movies; when King Kong returned to celebrate the 50th anniversary of the classic film in 1983, fans the world over cheered the triumphant ascent by a huge inflatable ape.

View of the Empire State Building

- There are a number of restaurants and shops on the ground level.

- Visit at the end of the day to watch the city lights go on.

- 350 5th Ave, at 34th St
- Map K3
- www.esbnyc.com
- Open 8am–2am daily (last ticket sold at 1:15am)
- Adults $20, seniors (62+) & youths (12–17) $18, children (6–11) $14, under 5 free, military in uniform free; Express Pass: $45, Audio Tour $7
- Be prepared for security screening; no bags larger than carry-on size allowed

Top 10 Features

1. The Building
2. Lobby Mural
3. 102nd Floor Observatory
4. 86th Floor Observatory
5. Spire
6. Elevators
7. Fifth Avenue Gallery Windows
8. Valentine's Day
9. New York Skyride
10. Empire State Run-up

The Building 1
A mooring mast for airships, now the base of a TV tower, was built to ensure the 102-story, 1,454-ft (443-m), building would be taller than the Chrysler Building.

Lobby Mural 2
The main lobby houses a 36-ft (11-m) Art Deco relief that showcases the Empire State Building image in steel, aluminum and gold leaf with dramatic impact.

102nd Floor Observatory 3
Visibility on a clear day from the 102nd floor deck is up to 80 miles (130 km). Tickets are sold only upon arrival at the Visitors' Center on the second floor ($15 extra).

For more New York Skyscrapers **See pp44–5**

Spire **5**

The spire is lit to honor holidays, seasons, and the many ethnic groups of New York: red, white, and blue for national holidays; green for St. Patrick's Day, blue and white for Chanukah.

4 86th Floor Observatory

Breathtaking views from the 86th floor's glass-enclosed pavilion 1,050 ft (320 m) above the city attract more than 3.5 million visitors each year.

6 Elevators

Visitors can ride to the 86th floor in 45 seconds – 1,400 ft (427 m) per minute – in one of 73 Art Deco elevators. The last elevator leaves at 1:35am.

7 Fifth Avenue Gallery Windows

Five display windows in the lofty marble-clad Fifth Avenue lobby exhibit art and memorabilia from New York City's many museums, galleries, and artists. The exhibits are changed on a regular basis.

8 Valentine's Day

Weddings have been an Empire State Building tradition since 1994. Every year, 14 lucky, romantic couples are specially selected to get married on the only day that the ceremony is conducted here.

Building the Empire State

The Empire State Building was designed by William F. Lamb following a brief to "make it big." It took only 410 days to build this 102-story, 365,000-ton limestone and granite skyscraper, with an average of four and a half stories added every week. However, in one outstanding ten-day period, the 3,500-strong construction team completed no fewer than ten stories. Due to the building's relatively shallow foundations, 60,000 tons of steel beams were used to support the tower.

New York Skyride **9**

A virtual reality, big-screen simulation of a helicopter ride takes viewers over, under, and through some of the city's best-known landmarks.

10 Empire State Run-up

Each February, following a tradition dating to 1978, 150 runners race up the 1,576 steps from the lobby to the 86th floor. The record is 9 minutes, 33 seconds.

Fifth Avenue

Midtown Fifth Avenue is New York's best-known boulevard and home to three of its most famous buildings. In the late 1800s, it was lined with mansions belonging to prominent families, but as retailers moved north in the 1900s, society fled uptown. One of the former mansions that remains is the Cartier building, reputedly acquired from banker Morton F. Plant in 1917 in exchange for a string of pearls. Although commercial enterprises now share the avenue, it has remained a mecca for luxury goods. Fifth Avenue is at its best on Easter Sunday when traffic is barred and the street is filled with New Yorkers in elaborate hats.

Cartier façade, decorated for Christmas

⏺ Free tours of the New York Public Library: 11am and 2pm Mon–Sat, and 2pm on Sun; there's no need to book for groups of less than 10 people.

St. Patrick's Cathedral is open to visitors 6:30am–8:45pm daily.

• The heart of Fifth Avenue is from the Empire State Building (see pp8–9) on 34th St, to the Grand Army Plaza, 59th St, an easily walkable stretch of just over one mile (1.6 km)
• Map H3–K3
• Tourist Information: 212 484 1222
• New York Public Library: 212 930 0800

Top 10 Exhibits

1. Grand Army Plaza
2. Bergdorf Goodman
3. General Motors Building
4. Tiffany and Company
5. Trump Tower
6. Cartier
7. St. Patrick's Cathedral
8. Saks Fifth Avenue
9. New York Public Library
10. Lord and Taylor

Grand Army Plaza 1
This ornamented plaza is presided over by the 1907 Plaza Hotel and Augustus Saint-Gaudens' statue of General William T. Sherman. Hansom cab rides through Central Park can be boarded here.

Bergdorf Goodman 2
Founded in 1894 as a small ladies' tailoring and fur shop, the most élite department store has been here since 1928. A separate shop for men was opened in 1990 across Fifth Avenue.

General Motors Building 3
Edward Durrell Stone's 1968 marble skyscraper is of interest not for its architecture but for the CBS studio in the plaza area and the F.A.O. Schwarz toy store adjacent.

Tiffany and Company 4
Truman Capote's 1958 *Breakfast at Tiffany's* made this the most famous jewelry store in New York. The window displays are works of art.

Sign up for DK's email newsletter on traveldk.com

5 Trump Tower
A six-story open interior space, the Trump Tower Atrium is graced by hanging gardens and a spectacular 80-ft (24-m) water wall.

Cartier 6
Look up to admire what remains of the fine 1905 Beaux Arts mansion housing this famous luxury jeweler. During the Christmas season, the whole building is wrapped in a giant red ribbon.

7 St. Patrick's Cathedral
In 1878 James Renwick, Jr. designed New York's grandest religious building in French Gothic style (above). The bronze doors, the baldachin over the high altar, the Lady Chapel, and the rose window are among its notable features.

8 Saks Fifth Avenue
One of New York's most attractive stores, Saks is famous for the changing seasonal decor on the main floor of its 1924 building, as well as for its exclusive fashions for men and women.

New York Public Library 9
The epitome of Beaux Arts elegance, this 1911 landmark features vaulted marble halls and a paneled reading room that glows with light from great arched windows.

Public Library's guardian lion

10 Lord and Taylor
Retailing on Fifth Avenue since 1914, Lord and Taylor offers a mix of fashions for budgets low and high. The store is known for its animated Christmas windows.

Millionnaires' Row
From its inception in the early 19th century, Fifth Avenue has been the territory of New York's well-heeled society, with homes costing the princely sum of $20,000 after the Civil War. As retail and commercial ventures, albeit exclusive ones, encroached on the wealthy's patch toward the end of the 19th century, they moved their palacial residences further north along Fifth Avenue. This trend was set by Mrs Astor who moved up to 65th Street after her nephew, William Waldorf Astor, built the Waldorf Hotel next to her former home.

For more on New York shopping See pp64–5

11

Rockefeller Center

A city within a city and a National Historic Landmark, this is the largest privately owned complex in the world. Begun in the 1930s, it was the first commercial project to integrate gardens, dining, and shopping with office space. Rockefeller Center is the hub of midtown New York, alive with activity day and night. The number of buildings has grown to 19, though the newer buildings do not match the Art Deco elegance of the original 14 structures. Over 100 works of art lie within the complex, including a major mural in each building. Still growing, this site contains one of the most outstanding public art collections in America.

Starting on 5th Ave, walk through the Channel Gardens to the Sunken Garden.

Pick up a self-guided tour leaflet from the lobby of the G.E. Building while looking at the Sert Murals.

For stunning, 360-degree views of Manhattan, visit the Top of the Rock observation deck on the 67th–70th floors.

- Rockefeller Center extends from 5th to 6th Aves, between 48th and 51st Sts
- Map J3
- www.rockefeller center.com
- NBC Studios: 30 Rockefeller Plaza, 212 664 7174, tours: Open 8:30am–4:30pm Mon–Fri, 9:30am–5:30pm Sat, 9:30am–4:30pm Sun, admission charge, reservations advised
- Today Show: Rockefeller Plaza at 49th St, open 7–9am Mon–Fri
- Top of the Rock: 30 Rockefeller Plaza, 212 698 2000, open 8am–midnight daily (last lift 11pm), adm charge, www.topoftherocknyc. com

Top 10 Exhibits

1. Channel Gardens
2. Sunken Garden
3. Prometheus Statue
4. Atlas Statue
5. G.E. Building
6. NBC Studios
7. Today Show Studio
8. Shopping Concourse
9. Radio City Music Hall
10. Top of the Rock

Channel Gardens
Named after the English Channel because they separate the French and British buildings, the gardens change with the calendar and are lined with glowing angels at Christmas. The six fountainhead figures are by René Chambellan *(below)*.

Sunken Garden
A skating rink in winter and leafy outdoor café in summer, the Sunken Garden is a bright spot year round. It is surrounded by colorful flags that represent the members of the United Nations.

Prometheus Statue
An 18-ft (5.5-m) gold-leafed bronze statue *(below)* by Paul Manship presides over the Sunken Garden. The pedestal represents Earth and the circle containing the signs of the zodiac represents the heavens.

Atlas Statue 4
Sculpted by Lee Lawrie, this 14,000-lb (6,350-kg), 15-ft (4.5-m) figure is perched on a 9-ft (3-m) pedestal. One of 15 works by Lawrie at the Center, it stands at the entrance to the International Building.

Rockefeller Center Plan

G.E. Building 5
The centerpiece of Rockefeller Center is a slim, 70-story limestone tower. The design features gradual setbacks as the building rises to ensure that no office is more than 27 ft (8 m) from a window.

NBC Studios 6
Backstage tours of a major television network's studios are popular. Visitors can buy tickets online or write ahead for shows (see p166); tickets are also available in the lobby of the G.E. building.

Today Show Studio 7
This morning TV show can be viewed live every weekday morning from the sidewalk in front of the studio. A camera often films the fans watching the show.

Shopping Concourse 8
A variety of stores is found in the underground concourse, also known as the catacombs, of the G.E. Building, including a branch of the Metropolitan Museum shop.

John D. Rockefeller, Jr.

The legendary philanthropist and multimillionnaire, John D. Rockefeller, Jr. (1874–1960) was son and heir to Ohio oil magnate John Davison Rockefeller's fortunes and took over the family oil business in 1911. Rockefeller, or John D., as he was known, strongly believed his inheritance should be used for the public good. Among his philanthropic donations were contributions to the building funds of the United Nations Headquarters (see pp124–5), the Cloisters (see p31), and the Riverside Church (see p145).

Radio City Music Hall 9
Tours of this Art Deco masterpiece and former movie palace are a chance to admire the decor, the stage, and the legendary Wurlitzer organ (see p51).

Top of the Rock 10
Here visitors are treated to breathtaking, unobstructed views – and even space to move about – on the observation deck's three levels.

Left **Lee Lawrie's Winged Mercury** Right **Gaston Lachaise's panel**

Rockefeller Center Artworks

1 American Progress
Jose Maria Sert's (1876–1945) mural depicts America's development over 300 years by uniting two forces, brain and brawn. Sert's *Time* mural adorns one of the ceilings.

2 Wisdom
The striking central figure of *Wisdom* by Lee Lawrie (1877–1963) grasps a compass pointing to light and sound waves and is carved on a screen made of 240 glass blocks.

3 Gaston Lachaise's panels
This two-panel work by the noted American sculptor (1882–1935) honors the contribution made by workmen to the Rockefeller Center's construction, depicting them at their labors.

4 News
This heroic sculpture by Isamu Noguchi (1904–88) is cast in stainless steel. The 10-ton panel illustrates the tools of the press, including camera, telephone, pad, and pencil.

News, Isamu Noguchi

5 Industries of the British Empire
Cast in bronze and finished in gold leaf, this panel by Carl Paul Jennewein (1890–1980) depicts nine major industries of the British Commonwealth, including sugar cane, salt, and tobacco.

6 Intelligence Awakening Mankind
Some one million tesserae (pieces of glass enamel) in more than 250 shades create Barry Faulkner's (1881–1966) mosaic representing spoken and written words.

7 Portals
Josef Albers' 1961 work of thin, highly polished, milky-white and ivory Carrara glass creates a surface of receding squares that gives the mural a sense of depth.

8 Winged Mercury
Lee Lawrie's stunning 1933 relief of Mercury, the Roman god of trade, profit and commerce, celebrates the British Empire. The golden classical figure wears a helmet – a sign of protection.

9 The Story of Mankind
Another Lawrie is a bold 15-block history accented in gold, scarlet and blue-green. The history is topped with a clock, signifying the passage of time.

10 Wall Drawing 896
The newest mural, a site-specific, geometric design created in 1999 by Sol Lewitt, covers four walls of the entrance to the headquarters of Christie's on 48th St.

Top 10 Statistics

1. Tallest building: 850 ft (259 m), 70 floors
2. Elevators: 388
3. Passenger rides per day: more than 400,000
4. Fastest elevator speed: 1,400 ft (427 m) per minute (37 seconds non-stop to 65th floor)
5. Number working in the complex: 65,000
6. Telephones: 100,000
7. Office windows: 48,758
8. Restaurants: 45
9. Shops: 100
10. Daily visitors: 250,000

The Building of Rockefeller Center

John D. Rockefeller driving in final rivet

When the Depression made John D. Rockefeller Jr.'s original plan for a new opera house impractical, he instead developed a large, creative-commercial complex. The innovative Art Deco design, led by Raymond Hood, included a mid-block street (Rockefeller Plaza) and an underground concourse. The 14 buildings constructed in 1931–40 provided 225,000 jobs during the worst of the Depression. Artworks were an essential element; over 30 artists contributed work for foyers, façades, and gardens as part of the "New Frontiers" program.

Early Radio Broadcast

The young network-broadcasting industry, made up of RCA, RKO, and NBC, became the primary tenants of the Rockefeller Center. The entire complex was originally named "the Radio City."

Rockefeller Center construction workers, 1932

Statue of Liberty

The figure presiding over New York harbor, officially titled "Liberty Enlightening the World," has been a harbinger of freedom for millions since her inauguration by President Grover Cleveland in 1886. The statue, a gift of friendship from the French to mark the U.S.'s 100th birthday in 1876, was designed by the French sculptor Frédéric-Auguste Bartholdi, who devoted 21 years to the project. Slow fundraising on both sides of the Atlantic delayed the unveiling by 10 years, but no problem was encountered financing the $100 million restoration for the statue's 100th birthday. Her unveiling on July 3, 1986, was the occasion for the largest fireworks display ever seen in the U.S.

Restoration celebrations, July 3, 1986

🐧 Crowds can be heavy, so an early departure is advised. A cafeteria is available on site.

For the best photos, sit on the right of the boat going out, the left coming back.

• Take the 1 train to South Ferry, 4 or 5 train to Bowling Green, or the R or W train to Whitehall St to get to Battery Park by subway.
• Ferries leave from Castle Clinton, Battery Park, every 30–45 mins between 8:30am–4pm daily (winter from 9:30am)
• www.nps.gov/stli

Top 10 Features

1. Castle Clinton National Monument
2. Battery Park
3. Boat Ride
4. Close-up View of the Statue
5. Pedestal
6. Crown
7. Torch and Book
8. Frame
9. Views
10. Historical Exhibits

Close-up View of the Statue

A close-up view reveals the awesome size of the Statue of Liberty. Dominating New York harbor, she stands 305 ft (93 m) tall and weighs 200 tons. Her right arm carrying the symbolic torch is 42 ft (13 m) long while her index finger measures 8 ft (2.4 m) and dwarfs most men.

Battery Park

With statues and monuments honoring everyone from New York's first Jewish immigrants to the U.S. Coast Guard, the park is also a great spot for sea-gazing.

Boat Ride

The views from the ferries that carry a constant stream of visitors from Manhattan and Jersey City to the Statue of Liberty and on to Ellis Island are dramatic.

Pedestal

Richard Morris Hunt, one of America's most prestigious architects, was chosen to design the 89-ft (27-m) pedestal of the Statue of Liberty. The pedestal sits on a concrete foundation within the 11-pointed, star-shaped walls of Fort Wood, a fortress erected for the War of 1812.

Castle Clinton National Monument

Built as a fort in 1807, it now serves as a visitor center for Statue of Liberty and Ellis Island visitors. The building exhibits panoramas of New York history.

Sign up for DK's email newsletter on traveldk.com

Crown

Legend says that Bartholdi's mother was the model for Liberty, but the face was actually based on his early drawings for a never-commissioned statue in Egypt. The seven rays of her crown represent the seven seas and seven continents.

Torch and Book

The new torch, with its 24-carat gold leaf-coated flame, was added during a 1984–86 restoration. The original is on display in the main lobby. The book in the statue's left hand is inscribed July 4, 1776, in Roman numerals.

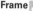

Frame

Gustave Eiffel, best known for his Paris tower, created the inner framework. The copper sheeting shell, weighing 31 tons, is hung on bars from a massive central iron pylon that anchors the statue to the base.

Views

The observation decks in the pedestal and crown of the Liberty Statue, offer spectacular views of Manhattan. The crown reopened to limited numbers of visitors in 2009 following its closure due to the events of September 11.

Historical Exhibits

The museum inside the base documents the complete history of the Statue of Liberty using photos, prints, videos, oral histories, and full-scale replicas of the face and foot. A pass is required to visit the base and observation platform.

Gateway to the New World

The Statue of Liberty has symbolized the beginning of a new way of life for millions of immigrants fleeing poverty and hardship. She is an enduring symbol of the freedom and hope offered by the U.S. and the subject of Emma Lazarus's poem *The New Colossus:*
" *...Give me your tired, your poor, Your huddled masses yearning to breathe free... Send these, the homeless, tempest-tost to me, I lift my lamp beside the golden door".*

Ellis Island Immigration Museum

Ellis Island is the symbol of America's immigrant heritage. From 1892 to 1954, it was the arrival point for over 12 million people fleeing religious persecution, poverty, or unrest in their homelands. Their descendants, more than 100 million people, comprise almost 40 percent of today's population. First and second class passengers were processed for immigration on board ship, but the poor traveling in steerage class were ferried to the crowded island for medical and legal examinations. It was a frightening prospect after an exhausting journey to a land where few newcomers could speak the language. As many as 5,000 passed through in a day. The museum not only retraces their experience here, but is a picture of the total immigrant experience in America.

The vast interior of the Great Hall

🍴 The island's cafeteria and picnic areas are great for lunch or snacks.

⏰ Catch an early ferry from Battery Park to avoid crowds on the island.

Stop at the museum information desk for tickets to the free 30-minute film "Island of Hope, Island of Tears."

• For a map of Ellis Island see Lower Manhattan to Midtown inset on p6
• 212 363 3200
• www.nps.gov/elis
• Ferries from Battery Park: 866 STATUE4
• Ferry rides to Statue of Liberty and Ellis Island: adults $12, seniors $10, children (4–12) $5, children under 4 free • Open Jun–Aug: 9am–6pm daily; Sep–May: 9am–5:15pm daily
• Free

Top 10 Features

1. Arrival Area
2. Great Hall
3. Medical Examining Line
4. Dormitory
5. Railroad Ticket Office
6. Baggage Room
7. The Peopling of America
8. Immigration History Center
9. American Immigration Wall of Honor
10. Immigrants' Living Theater

Arrival Area
Crowds of steerage passengers *(below)* entered through the original gateway here after being ferried from arrival vessels. Instructions were given by interpreters in a babel of languages.

Great Hall
Huddled on benches, immigrants awaited examinations that would determine whether they would be granted entry. A doctor watched as they ascended the stairs and marked letters in chalk on those who showed signs of conditions needing special inspection.

Medical Examining Line
Interpreters guided immigrants through their medical examinations. The most dreaded were the "eye men," looking for symptoms of trachoma, a disease that caused blindness. It was the reason for more than half the medical detentions and meant sure deportation.

For more on New York's history See pp48–9

Dormitory
4 Immigrants who were detained for further examinations slept here in separate quarters for men and women. Although the process was nerve-wracking, only two percent of those seeking refuge were sent back.

Railroad Ticket Office
5 Those traveling beyond New York were ferried to railroad terminals in New Jersey to continue their journeys. Agents could sell as many as 25 tickets per minute.

Key to Floor Plan

☐	First Floor
☐	Second Floor
■	Third Floor

Baggage Room
6 Here newcomers checked the boxes, trunks, and baskets that held the meager belongings they carried, now all their worldly possessions.

The Peopling of America
7 400 years of immigration history are displayed in more than 30 galleries. Exhibits such as *The Peopling of America* have artifacts, heirlooms, posters, maps, and photos donated by immigrants' families.

American Family Immigration History Center
8 Using computer and multimedia technology, visitors can access passenger arrival records of more than 22 million people entering New York between 1892 and 1924.

American Immigration Wall of Honor
9 To honor their forebears, Americans pay to have their names inscribed on this list. Including the families of John F. Kennedy and Barbra Streisand, this is the world's largest wall of names; over 600,000.

New Jersey's Ellis Island

Although federal property, a long-fought battle over territorial jurisdiction of Ellis Island was settled in 1998. Originally a 3-acre site, Ellis Island's landmass was increased in the 1900s with landfill to more than nine times its original size, to over 27 acres. A US Supreme Court ruling in 1998 decided the added landfill to be in the territory of New Jersey, and the original portion to be in New York. New Jersey officials launched a restoration program that included saving the derelict hospital buildings

Immigrants' Living Theater
10 Daily theatrical productions that are based on actual immigrant accounts are given by actors who recreate the experiences of Ellis Island. The museum has two movie theaters, a Library and an Oral History Studio with taped reminiscences.

For more museums **See pp40–41**

Left **Italian immigrants** Center **Arrivals to the island** Right **French West Indian arrivals**

Milestones in Immigration History

1624
First Dutch arrived in New Amsterdam, which thrived as a trading center, attracting settlers from many other nations. By 1643, the 500-strong population spoke 18 different languages.

1664
The dislike of Dutch governor Peter Stuyvesant and unpopular tax demands by the Dutch West India Company meant little resistance to the ousting of the Dutch by the British, who renamed the city New York.

1790
For the first U.S. Census, New York's population of 33,131 was the second largest in the Colonies. The make-up was mostly British and Dutch.

Mid-1800s
Ireland's 1845–8 Great Famine and economic hardship in Germany led many to seek new lives in New York, where rapid growth as a seaport and manufacturing center opened many jobs.

Polish woman at Ellis Island c.1910

1880–1910
Thousands of Russian and Polish Jews and Italians arrived, fleeing persecution or hard economic times.

1892
When Castle Island, an immigrant depot set up in 1855, could no longer handle the inflow, Ellis Island took over. "Settlement Houses" were set up in the city to help those living in squalid tenements, and "Americanization" programs encouraged assimilation.

1924
Nearly 40 percent of New York's population was foreign-born. U.S. laws set national quotas on immigration; Great Britain's Caribbean colonies benefited from the British quota and arrived in large numbers.

Asian women in a garment factory in Chinatown

1965
The Hart-Cellar Act ended discrimination based on national origin; a new wave of immigration began.

1980s
One million mainly Asian and Latin American newcomers arrived. The Chinese population topped 300,000, Koreans became visible elements in the city, and Dominican numbers grew.

1990–present
Over 1.2 million newcomers entered, swelling the foreign-born population to over 40 percent of the total population – the highest since 1910. Queens is classified as the most ethnically diverse county in the U.S.

Top 10 Nationalities Entering Ellis Island

1. Italy: 2,502,310
2. Austria and Hungary: 2,275,852
3. Russia: 1,893,542
4. Germany: 633,148
5. England: 551,969
6. Ireland: 520,904
7. Sweden: 348,036
8. Greece: 245,058
9. Norway: 226,278
10. Ottoman Empire: 212,825

(Between 1892–7, 1901–31)

The Restoration of Ellis Island

Laws defining immigration quotas enacted in 1924 drastically curtailed the numbers of foreigners coming into the U.S., and Ellis Island was no longer needed as an immigration depot. It became a detention and deportation center for undesirable aliens, a training center for the U.S. Coast Guard, and a hospital for wounded servicemen during World War II. In 1954 the U.S. government closed the island. It remained abandoned until 1984, when a $156 million renewal project replaced the copper roof domes, cleaned the mosaic tiles, and restored the interior, preserving any surviving original fixtures in the largest historic restoration in U.S. history.

The restoration included the establishment of the Ellis Island Immigration Museum (see pp18–19), telling the immigrant story through displays and more than 2,000 artifacts. The museum also has an oral history archive of taped interviews and an interactive children's gallery, both available to visit by appointment. Reopened to the public in 1990, Ellis Island receives almost 2 million visitors every year.

Restoration

Preservation of Ellis Island began in 1965 with the rebuilding of the seawall, but the biggest task was the restoration of the main building, which had deteriorated severely. The period of 1918–24 was chosen for reconstruction because this coincided with a peak time for immigration.

Glass canopy marking the restored main entrance to Ellis Island

For more New York museums **See pp40–41**

21

TOP 10 Times Square and Theater District

Known as the "Crossroads of the World," Times Square is New York's most famous intersection and the symbol of the lively surrounding theater district that includes Broadway. It was called Longacre Square until 1904, when the New York Times built a 25-story tower on the site. Its occupancy on New Year's Eve was marked with fireworks, a celebration that continues today. Currently, a giant crystal ball descends the building at midnight to herald the new year, cheered by the millions packed into the square. The reputation of Times Square was sullied when the adjacent 42nd Street grew seedy in the 1970s. The 1990s saw the peep shows and X-rated movie houses closed, and with a massive government and private effort, the street and neighborhood have again been transformed.

News Ticker, Times Square

Go to the TKTS booth in Times Square at Broadway and 47th (212 221 0013/www.tdf.org) for half-price tickets to all kinds of Broadway shows.

Discount coupons for shows are often available at the Times Square Information Center, 1560 Broadway between 46th and 47th streets.

Try to see Broadway at night, when the lights are on.

- Times Square is located where Broadway and 7th Ave intersect at 42nd St
- Map J3
- www.timessquare nyc.org
- Madame Tussaud's New York: 234 West 42nd Street, 1 800 246 8872, open 10am–8pm Sun–Thu, 10am–10pm Fri–Sat, admission charge, www.nycwax.com

Top 10 Exhibits

1. Broadway Lights
2. Times Square News Ticker
3. Nasdaq Headquarters
4. MTV Headquarters
5. Brill Building
6. Condé Nast Building
7. New 42nd Street
8. Madame Tussaud's, New York
9. Duffy Square
10. Off-Broadway

1 Broadway Lights
The city's longest street is known best for the section north of 42nd Street dubbed the "Great White Way" for its dazzle of neon.

2 Times Square News Ticker
In 1928, the *New York Times* erected the world's first moving electronic sign to post news, a fixture that remains although the *Times* has moved to 8th Avenue.

3 Nasdaq Headquarters
The headquarters of this over-the-counter stock market dominates its corner with a screen that regularly broadcasts financial news.

For more entertainment venues See pp50–51

4 MTV Headquarters

The occasional crowd of teenagers gathered beneath the second-floor studios of this music TV network hope to spot an idol on the way in, or a camera crew descending to tape crowds in the street.

5 Brill Building

Everyone from Cole Porter to Phil Spector has produced hits in this legendary music industry building, a long-time home to famous music publishers and arrangers.

6 Condé Nast Building

The 48-story skyscraper opened in 2000 to house this magazine empire is a sign of the resurgence of Times Square.

7 New 42nd Street

The renovation of the new Amsterdam Theater in the 1990s uplifted 42nd Street. Today, the New 42nd Street Studios and several theaters line the block.

8 Madame Tussaud's, New York

Barack Obama, Brangelina and Madonna are among the wax inhabitants of this 42nd Street's tenant. The museum has exterior glass elevators and a huge hand holding the illuminated sign.

9 Duffy Square

The block was revitalized with the unveiling of the TKTS area in 2008, a dramatic wedge of red overlaid with a set of stairs to nowhere.

10 Off-Broadway

Before the rest of 42nd Street was rejuvenated, this block between 9th and 10th Avenues was resurrected by Off-Broadway companies needing inexpensive homes. New plays are premiered at Playwrights Horizons, one of the better-known tenants.

Theater District

It was the move by the Metropolitan Opera House to Broadway in 1883 that first drew lavish theaters and restaurants to this area. In the 1920s, movie palaces added the glamour of neon to Broadway. After World War II, the popularity of movies waned and sleaze replaced glitter. Now a redevelopment program has brought the public and bright lights back to this area.

Left **Lyceum** Center **Hilton Theater** Right **Hudson Theater**

Theaters

Lyceum
The oldest playhouse boasts a vaulted ceiling, murals, and elaborate plasterwork. Often used as an auxiliary for Lincoln Center *(see p139)*. ⊗ *149–157 West 45th St • Map J3*

New Victory Theater

New Victory Theater
Built for Oscar Hammerstein in 1900, this had resorted to X-rated films until restored in 1995 to present family entertainment. ⊗ *209 West 42nd St • Map K3*

Hilton Theater
The rundown Lyric and Apollo were combined to form this showcase for musicals in 1998, marking the arrival of corporate sponsorship for theaters. ⊗ *214 West 42nd St • Map K3*

Shubert Theater
Built in 1912–13 as a lavish site for musicals and headquarters for the Shubert Organization. The Booth, opposite, was built at this time. ⊗ *221–33 West 44th St • Map J3*

New Amsterdam Theater
This Art Nouveau beauty housed the famous Ziegfeld Follies. Restored by Disney, it is now home to the popular *Mary Poppins*. ⊗ *214 West 42nd St • Map K3*

Hudson Theater
A restrained façade belies the lavish interior, including an inner lobby with a classical arcade and domes of Tiffany glass. ⊗ *139–141 West 44th St • Map J2*

Belasco Theater
A 1907 monument to impresario David Belasco, who supervised the unusual Georgian Revival design. The rooftop duplex was his personal residence. ⊗ *111–121 West 44th St • Map J3*

Lunt-Fontaine Theater
Originally the Globe (finished in 1910); part of the roof of this venue could be removed to create an open-air auditorium. ⊗ *203–217 West 46th St • Map J3*

Palace Theater
Sarah Bernhardt inaugurated the stage, and playing the Palace became the ultimate assignment. Now restored as a venue for musicals. ⊗ *1564 Broadway • Map J3*

Winter Garden Theater
Originally the American Horse Exchange in 1885, this was acquired by the Shuberts in 1910 and remodeled in 1922. Until 2000, it was the home of *Cats*. ⊗ *1634 Broadway • Map J3*

For more New York theaters See pp50–51

Top 10 Broadway Shows

A Brief History of New York Theater

Oscar Hammerstein

The first of countless theaters built in New York is thought to have been the New Theater, erected in lower Manhattan in 1732. The city's theatrical center steadily moved uptown to the Bowery, then Astor Place, Union Square, and Herald Square, until it settled for good around Longacre Square (now Times Square), following the opening of Oscar Hammerstein's Olympia Theater on Broadway in 1895. Some 85 theaters were built over the next three decades, many with grand Beaux Arts interiors by architects such as Herbert J. Krapp, and Herts and Tallant, the latter responsible for designing cantilevered balconies that eliminated the need for columns. Impresarios like the Shuberts and the Chanins made theater-going more democratic by blurring the class distinction between orchestra and balconies, using a single entrance for all. As modern theaters replaced them, more than 40 of these beauties have been demolished. Fortunately, the rest have now been designated landmarks.

Show stoppers

Although recent economic woes have seen a number of shows close, favorites such as *The Lion King* still draw crowds. Broadway's longest-running show of all time, *Phantom of the Opera*, is still going, more than 20 years after its debut.

Kiss Me Kate (above) and 42nd Street, former Broadway shows

🔟 Central Park

New York's "backyard," an 843-acre swathe of green, provides recreation and beauty for over two million visitors each year. Designed by Frederick Law Olmsted and Calvert Vaux in 1858, the park took 16 years to create and involved the planting of over 500,000 trees and shrubs, the hauling in of vast amounts of stone and earth to form hills, lakes, and meadows, and the building of 30 stone-and-iron bridges and arches.

Bethesda Terrace
Overlooking the lake and Ramble, the ornate terrace and its fountain are the focal point of the park. On the adjacent tree-lined Mall inline skaters often show off acrobatic stunts.

The Beresford apartments on Central Park West

🍴 Refreshments and light lunches are available at the Boat House snack bar; The Boat House restaurant serves gourmet meals.

📍 Make your first stop The Dairy, a Victorian Gothic building housing the Visitor Center. Ask about the free nature workshops and guided walks.

Rent bicycles, row-boats, and gondolas from the Boathouse, and skates at the Wollman Rink.

• From Central Park South to 110th St & between 5th Ave and Central Park West.
• Map D3–H3
• www.centralparknyc. org
• Open dawn–dusk

Top 10 Features

1. Great Lawn
2. Bethesda Terrace
3. Belvedere Castle
4. The Ramble
5. Reservoir
6. Strawberry Fields
7. Conservatory Garden
8. Hans Christian Andersen Statue
9. Central Park Zoo
10. Delacorte Theater

Great Lawn
This is a 13-acre oval of green lawn. In summer, free concerts by the Metropolitan Opera and New York Philharmonic draw as many as 100,000 people.

Belvedere Castle
A 19th-century stone castle atop a rock, complete with towers and turrets, offers peerless views in all directions. Inside is the Henry Luce Nature Observatory with exhibits covering the surprisingly diverse wildlife found in the park.

The Ramble
This wooded 37 acres of land is crisscrossed by paths and streams and is a paradise for bird-watchers. Over 270 species have been spotted in Central Park, which is on the Atlantic migration flyway.

The Visitor Center is open 10am–5pm Tue–Sun, and can be contacted on: 212 794 6564

5 Reservoir
The 106-acre lake is rimmed by a 1.6-mile (5-km) running track used by joggers. It is the largest of the park's five lakes and ponds, which include Conservatory Water, where model boat races are held each Saturday.

6 Strawberry Fields
This peaceful garden area *(above)* was created by Yoko Ono in memory of John Lennon, who lived in the nearby Dakota apartments. Gifts for the memorial came from all over the world.

7 Conservatory Garden
An elegant 6-acre formal garden with fountains and beautiful displays of flowering trees, bulbs, annuals, and perennials is at its best in the spring, when crabapples, tulips, and azaleas are in bloom.

8 Hans Christian Andersen Statue
Children's storytelling sessions are held here in the summer. Other activities for youngsters include nature workshops, a vintage carousel, and a marionette theater.

9 Central Park Zoo
This conservation center and children's zoo has three climate zones. The space features a rainforest and over 100 species, including seals, monkeys, and penguins.

Creating Central Park
Central Park was the first landscaping project for Frederick Law Olmsted, who was already 43 years old. Rejecting the usual formal plantings, he created passages of contrasting scenery, calm and pastoral against the rugged and picturesque. Areas for active and passive recreation were separated, and dense raised plantings shut out the surrounding city. The park brought Olmsted high praise and set a pattern for landscapes that followed. He went on to become America's most prolific designer of parks.

10 Delacorte Theater
The New York Public Theater presents two "Shakespeare in the Park" productions in July and August. Free tickets are available on the day, but get in line early. Other free park entertainment includes a SummerStage series of popular music and dance.

Central Park Zoo is open daily, for more information call 212 439 6500 or visit www.centralparkzoo.com

Metropolitan Museum of Art

One of the world's great art museums, the Metropolitan "Met" is a veritable collection of museums, spanning 5,000 years of culture from every part of the globe. Each of its specialized galleries holds an abundance of treasures. It was founded in 1870 by a group who wanted to create a great art institution in America, and began with three private European collections and 174 paintings. The present holdings number over two million. The original 1880 Gothic Revival building by Calvert Vaux and Jacob Wrey Mould has been expanded many times. Recent additions include courts with huge windows overlooking Central Park.

Entrance, Metropolitan Museum of Art

🖢 There is a cafeteria, bar (Fri & Sat), and two cafés inside. The Roof Garden Café is accessed from the first floor.

✒ If time is short, the European Paintings on the second floor, Egyptian Art on the first, and the American Wing will give you a sense of the greatness of this enormous institution.

Weekend evenings are less crowded and offer the advantage of bar service and live music.

• 1000 5th Ave at 82nd St
• Map F3
• 212 535 7710
• www.metmuseum.org
• Open 9:30am–5:30pm Tue–Thu & Sun, 9:30am–9pm Fri & Sat (galleries cleared 15 mins before closing time)
• Adults $20, seniors $15, students $10, children under 12 and members free

Top 10 Exhibits

1. European Painting
2. Egyptian Art
3. Michael C. Rockefeller Wing
4. American Wing
5. Robert Lehman Collection
6. Costume Institute
7. Asian Art
8. Lila Wallace Wing
9. European Sculpture and Decorative Arts
10. Roof Garden

Egyptian Art

The largest collection of Egyptian art outside Cairo includes masks, mummies, statues, jewelry, the Tomb of Perneb, and the spectacular Temple of Dendur, c.15B.C., re-assembled as it appeared on the banks of the Nile.

Key to Floor Plan

Ground Floor

First Floor

Second Floor

European Painting

The museum's 2,500 Old Master and 19th-century European paintings form one of the greatest collections in the world and include many instantly recognizable masterpieces. Special strengths include the Rembrandts and Vermeers, and the many Impressionist and Post-Impressionist canvases.

Michael C. Rockefeller Wing

Masks, wooden sculpture, gold and silver ornaments, Pre-Columbian gold, ceramics and stone from Mexico and Peru, and art from the Court of Benin in Nigeria are highlights among 1,600 objects from Africa, Oceania, and the Americas covering 3,000 years.

For more New York museums See pp40–41

Robert Lehman Collection
5 This extraordinary private collection, includes Renaissance masters, Dutch, Spanish and French artists, Post-Impressionists and Fauvists, plus ceramics and furniture.

American Wing
4 Tiffany glass, paintings, and period rooms from the 17th to 20th centuries. The galleries for American Paintings reopen during 2011.

Costume Institute
6 Women's fashions from ballgowns to miniskirts, and menswear from the French courts to the present day; annual shows draw the crowds.

Asian Art
7 The most comprehensive collection in the West features paintings, sculpture, ceramics, and textiles.

Lila Wallace Wing
8 The Metropolitan has a growing display of art from 1900 to the present day, with works from Picasso to Jackson Pollock.

European Sculpture and Decorative Arts
9 One of the museum's largest collections reflects the development of art in Western Europe, and includes architectural settings, French and English period rooms, tapestries, and sculptures by Rodin and Degas.

Roof Garden
10 From May to October the Iris and B. Cantor Roof Garden boasts outstanding annual displays of 20th-century sculpture. The garden also offers a fine opportunity to enjoy a drink with a peerless view of Central Park and the surrounding skyline.

Gallery Guide

The Costume Institute and Robert Lehman Collection are on the ground floor. The 1st floor includes the American Wing, European Sculpture and Decorative Arts, Egyptian Art, and Greek and Roman galleries; the 2nd floor has European Paintings, and 19th-Century European Paintings and Sculpture.

🌟
8

Left *The Card Players*, 1890 Center *Garden at Sainte-Adresse*, 1867 Right *Gertrude Stein*, 1905

🔟 Paintings in the Met

1 Self-portrait
Rembrandt (1606–1669) painted a self portrait each decade of his career. In this moving study from 1660, when he was 54, he portrayed age very honestly.

2 View of Toledo
Darkening clouds set an eerie mood for one of El Greco's (1541–1614) most memorable paintings, depicting the capital city of the Spanish empire until 1561.

3 Young Woman with a Water Pitcher
Painted between 1660 and 1667, this is a classic example of the subtle and sensitive use of light that has made Vermeer (1632–75) one of the most revered Dutch masters.

4 The Harvesters
One of five remaining panels of the months of the year, painted in the 1500s, this is Bruegel (1551–1569) at his realistic best, an example of the use of light and detail that set him apart.

5 Madame X
Part of the excellent American art collection, this canvas by John Singer Sargent (1856–1925) is of an American woman who married a French banker, becoming a notorious Paris beauty in the 1880s.

6 Garden at Sainte-Adresse
This resort town on the English Channel where Monet spent the summer of 1867 is portrayed with sparkling color and intricate brushwork. The work combines illusion and reality, showing why Monet (1840–1926) was considered one of the greatest Impressionists.

7 Gertrude Stein
This portrait, created when Picasso (1881–1973) was 24 years old shows the influence of African sculpture and a shift from the slender figures of his early years to Cubist forms.

8 The Card Players
Better known for landscapes and still lifes, Cézanne (1839–1906) was intrigued by a scene of peasants intent on their card game. This ambitious project emphasizes the somber concentration of the participants.

Cypresses, 1889

9 Cypresses
Painted in 1889, soon after Van Gogh's (1853–90) voluntary confinement at an asylum in Saint-Remy, it shows the swirling and heavy brushwork typical of his work from this period.

10 Autumn Rhythm
This work by Jackson Pollock (1912–1956), the Abstract Expressionist famous for his drip paintings, is part of the Met's modern collection.

30 *For more New York art galleries* **See pp42–3**

The Cloisters

Stained-glass window detail

In addition to the medieval treasures in the main building, the Met oversees a spectacular branch, The Cloisters, built in medieval architectural style and overlooking the Hudson River in Fort Tryon Park in northern Manhattan. Opened in 1938, the complex consists of elements from five medieval cloisters and other monastic sites in southern France. The collections are noted for Romanesque and Gothic architectural sculptures and include illuminated manuscripts, tapestries, stained glass, enamels, ivories, and paintings. The Cloisters' gardens are a serene escape from the city. John D. Rockefeller, Jr. (see p13), who gave items from his own collection, is largely responsible for funding the complex. To reach The Cloisters, take the A train to 190th St.

The Unicorn in Captivity, 1495

Cloisters Arcades
These arcades are from the Bonnefont-en-Comminges Cloister in southern France. They date back to the late 13th and early 14th century.

Annunciation altarpiece by Robert Campin, 1425

Solomon R. Guggenheim Museum

One of the great architectural achievements of the 20th century, Frank Lloyd Wright's 1959 spiral design alone would make this museum a must. Solomon Guggenheim's core collection of Abstract art has been widened by donations of several important collections. The museum owns a host of work by Brancusi, Calder, Klee, Chagall, Miró, Leger, Mondrian, Picasso, Oldenberg, and Rauschenberg. Only a small portion, changed periodically, is displayed, as the main gallery is used for temporary exhibits. Sections of the Thannhauser collection, which includes masterpieces by Cézanne, Gauguin, van Gogh, and Picasso, are always on view. The Guggenheim has the largest collection of Kandinsky's works in the U.S. The Kandinsky Gallery contains permanent displays.

Façade of the Guggenheim Museum

🄮 The café on the main floor is a good spot to rest your feet.

🄲 The best way to see the museum is to take the elevator to the skylighted top and wind your way back down.

Free audio tours cover Frank Lloyd Wright architecture and the permanent collection.

There is a regular daily program of interpretive tours. Check the main desk for current schedules.

- 1071 5th Ave at 89th St • Map E4
- 212 423 3500
- www.guggenheim.org
- Open 10am–5:45pm Sat–Wed, 10am–7:45pm Fri
- Adults $18, students and seniors (with valid ID) $15, children under 12 and members free, 5:45–7:45pm Sat donation only.

Top 10 Exhibits

1. *Woman Ironing* (Thannhauser Collection)
2. *Woman with Yellow Hair* (Thannhauser Collection)
3. *Mountains at Saint-Remy* (Thannhauser Collection)
4. *Before the Mirror* (Thannhauser Collection)
5. *Haere Mai* (Thannhauser Collection)
6. *Still Life: Flask, Glass, and Jug* (Thannhauser Collection)
7. *Bibémus* (Thannhauser Collection)
8. *The Hermitage at Pontoise* (Thannhauser Collection)
9. *Black Lines*
10. *Paris Through the Window*

Woman Ironing
Picasso's early paintings showed sympathy for the working class. This striking 1904 canvas uses angular contours and a bleak palette of whites and grays to make the subject a symbol of the misfortunes of the poor.

Woman with Yellow Hair
In this memorable portrait from 1931, Picasso portrays the supple body and golden tresses of his mistress, Marie-Thérèse, one of his favorite subjects. He employed the continuous arched line from forehead to nose that he would often repeat in the many paintings of his young muse.

For more New York museums See pp40–41

Before the Mirror
Edouard Manet scandalized Paris with his paintings of prostitutes and courtesans. This private scene is of a partially undressed woman, an actress perhaps, contemplating her image.

Mountains at Saint-Remy
Van Gogh was recovering from an attack of mental distress when he painted this scene in July 1889, one year before his suicide. The subject was the low range of the Alpilles mountains in southern France, visible from his hospital grounds. The bold brush strokes are characteristic of van Gogh's later work.

Still Life: Flask, Glass, and Jug
Paul Cézanne's later style, based on the interplay of surface and depth, is shown in this 1077 painting. His mastery of space and depth, as seen in the mottled apples in the foreground, make him the foremost precursor of Cubism.

The Hermitage at Pontoise
This unsentimental rendering *(above)* of the village where Pisarro lived on and off from 1866–83 emphasizes the use of light and shade. The depiction of villagers was thought vulgar by some painters of the day.

Black Lines
Kandinsky wanted the undulating, richly-colored ovals and animated black brushstrokes to elicit specific reactions from viewers. *Black Lines* (1913) is one of his best-known nonobjective works.

Paris Through the Window
Painted after Chagall moved to Paris from Russia in 1910, the scene reflects the latest avant garde styles. The Eiffel Tower seen in the distance is a metaphor for Paris and for modernity.

Haere Mai
Gauguin made his first trip to Tahiti in 1891 in search of a paradise untainted by Western culture. This idyllic village landscape *(below)* was painted during that trip; the rich hues and flattened forms show the simplicity he sought. The phrase "Haere Mai," ("Come Here") is painted into the left corner.

Bibémus
In Bibémus, the abandoned quarries outside Aix-en-Province, France, Cézanne found a man-made landscape that suited his increasingly geometric style. He painted many variations of this scene from 1895–9.

Frank Lloyd Wright
Though Wright (1867–1959) designed many public buildings, he was best known for residential designs, "organic architecture" that followed the natural contours of the land, and tradition-breaking open interior spaces that have had lasting worldwide influence. The Guggenheim, one of his last projects, was a complete departure. So intent was Wright on his spiral design that when told some walls were too short for large works, he reportedly responded, "cut the paintings in half."

For more on New York's art scene **See pp42–3**

American Museum of Natural History

Few city children grow up without visiting the dinosaurs, the life-size dioramas of animal life, and other natural wonders in this popular museum patronized by over 4 million people each year. Since its founding in 1869, the museum has grown to 45 permanent exhibition halls spanning four city blocks, 13 of them opened in the past 10 years. Holdings include 30 million specimens and cultural artifacts, many unique in the world. Newer exhibition areas such as the Hall of Biodiversity, the Fossil Halls, and the Rose Center (see pp36–7), bring constantly updated research to visitors through multimedia installations.

Museum seen from 77th Street

🍴 Eat at the lower-level food court, or one of the three cafés.

🔄 Visit the great dinosaurs, African mammals, and minerals and gems collection.

Join a free tour of the museum's highlights or enjoy free jazz concerts on the first Friday of each month.

• Central Park West, be-tween 77th and 81st Sts
• Map F2
• 212 769 5100
• www.amnh.org
• Open 10am–5:45pm daily; Rose Center open until 8:45pm on first Fri of month
• Adults $16, students and seniors $12, children $9, members free; Museum & Hayden Planetarium Space Show $24/$18/$14; Super Saver (includes IMAX films & special exhibitions) $32/$24.50/$20

Top 10 Exhibits

1. Dinosaurs and Fossils
2. Mammals
3. Ocean Life
4. Hall of Biodiversity
5. Hall of Asian Peoples
6. Hall of African Peoples
7. Meteorites, Minerals, and Gems
8. Northwest Coast Indians
9. Human Biology and Evolution
10. Birds of the World

Mammals
Dramatic dioramas of life-size animals are divided by continents and shown in accurate natural habitats. The wildlife ranges from colossal African elephants to endangered Asian species such as lions and leopards.

Key to Floor Plan

- First Floor
- Second Floor
- Third Floor
- Fourth Floor
- Rose Center

Ocean Life
The Milstein Hall of Ocean Life ex-plores the waters of the earth and their inhabitants in skillful dioramas of ocean life. The hall is presided over by a 94-ft (29-m) life-size model of a blue whale.

Dinosaurs and Fossils
The best-known hallmark of the museum, the collection of dinosaur fossils is the world's largest. The giant Barosaurus in the rotunda is the highest free-standing exhibit.

Mid-Oct–mid-May: walk through the Butterfly Conservatory where 500 species flutter around you (admission charge)

4 Hall of Biodiversity
Opened in 1998 to encourage conservation, the hall contains a rainforest with accurate sounds, plants, and inhabitants. The 100-ft (30-m) long Spectrum of Life wall displays 1,500 specimens from bacteria to mammals, as well as a giant squid overhead.

5 Hall of Asian Peoples
Exquisite artifacts, artwork, costumes, and dioramas of daily life show the different religions and lifestyles of Chinese, Korean, Indian, and other Asian cultures.

Third Floor includes the Hayden Planetarium (see pp37).

6 Hall of African Peoples
These depictions of tribes living in various environments reflect 100 years of research. The displays include dwellings, clothing, masks, textiles, weapons, and tools.

7 Meteorites, Minerals, and Gems
Wonders include the 563-carat Star of India, a 596-lb (270-kg) topaz crystal from Brazil, and the Cape York meteorite, 4.5 billion years old and weighing 34 tons.

8 Northwest Coast Indians
This area features Native American totem poles showing the woodworking skills of tribes living from Washington state to southern Alaska. Also on show is a 63-ft (19-m) canoe built in 1878.

9 Human Biology and Evolution
This display of human origins and physical characteristics includes reconstructed heads of early hominids that bring you face to face with your predecessors.

10 Birds of the World
The museum has the world's largest collection of birds – more than a million specimens. The collection is organized geographically, with separate halls displaying dioramas of oceanic, North American, and other birds of the world.

Museum Guide

Enter from Central Park West onto the 2nd floor to view the Barosaurus exhibit, and African, Asian, and Central and South American peoples and animals. The Hall of Biodiversity, ocean life, and minerals and gems are on the 1st floor. North American Indians, birds, and reptiles are on the 3rd floor, and dinosaurs and fossils on the 4th.

To obtain advance tickets to the Rose Center's Space Show, call 212 769 5200

Left **Cosmic Pathway** Center **Scales of the Universe** Right **Cosmic Pathway**

🔟 Rose Center for Earth and Space

1 The Building
Opened in 2000 to explore inner earth and the outer universe, the dramatic exhibit building is a huge glass cube enclosing a three-story, 87-ft-wide sphere containing the Hayden Planetarium.

Hall of the Universe

2 Hall of the Universe
Exhibits, divided into the universe, galaxies, stars, and planets, show the discoveries of modern astrophysics. Digital scales measure your weight on Saturn, Jupiter, and the Sun.

3 Ecosphere
A sealed spherical aquarium in the Hall of the Universe holds a complete ecosystem of plants and animals that recycle nutrients and obtain energy solely from sunlight.

4 AstroBulletin
This high-definition screen displays the latest imagery from telescope observations worldwide and current NASA missions.

5 Hall of Planet Earth
Geological samples from around the world and videos explain the processes that formed the earth and continue to shape it.

Hayden Planetarium

6 Dynamic Earth Globe
This globe, suspended above an amphitheater in the Hall of Planet Earth uses a projection system to re-create views of a rotating earth as seen from space.

7 Earth Event Wall
Events such as earthquakes or volcanoes are broadcast on a screen as they unfold. Other video stations show scientists at work.

8 Scales of the Universe Walkway
Models show the relative size of cosmic, human, and microscopic objects, from galaxies, stars, and planets, to the human brain and the smallest atom.

9 Big Bang
Glass flooring around a circular opening lets visitors look down into a multisensory interpretation of the first movements of the universe. Explanatory narration is by Jodie Foster.

10 Cosmic Pathway
The Big Bang exits to this sloping 360-ft pathway with astronomical images tracing landmarks through 13 billion years of cosmic evolution.

For more New York museums See pp40–41

Top 10 Features

The Hayden Planetarium

The Hayden Planetarium, a remarkable advance in the study of astronomy and astrophysics, boasts a highly sophisticated Digital Dome System that is the most advanced high-resolution virtual reality simulator ever built. The space shows take place in a 429-seat Space Theater and are virtual flights through a scientifically accurate universe. It is advisable to order tickets for the space shows in advance, or to pick them up early in the day to secure a spot. Also showing is "Sonicvision", hypnotic visuals set to a range of music, where digital technology is also used to illuminate the planetarium's dome.

Virtual Nebula
The planetarium presents a virtual representation of every star and nebula in a 3D map of the galaxy. The state-of-the-art, multisensory technology creates such a realistic environment that all sense of being in a theater is lost.

The Hayden Planetarium within the Rose Center for Earth and Space

Following pages **Times Square by night**

Left **Solomon R. Guggenheim Museum** Right **Frick Collection**

Museums

1 Metropolitan Museum of Art

It would take weeks to take in all the treasures of this mammoth, ever-changing museum that includes a collection of more than 3,000 European paintings. The Greek, Roman, Cypriot, and Asian halls attract many of the museum's visitors, and the Joyce and Robert Menschel Hall for Modern Photography is also well attended *(see pp28–31)*.

Museum of Modern Art

2 Museum of Modern Art

After a $425 million expansion program, MoMA reopened in 2004. The renovation marked the museum's 75th anniversary and doubled the building's capacity. MoMA has one of the world's most comprehensive collections of modern art, including works by Picasso, Van Gogh, and Warhol. ◉ *11 West 53rd St • Map J3 • Open 10:30am–5:30pm Wed–Mon (to 8pm Fri) • www.moma.org • Admission charge*

3 American Museum of Natural History

The largest museum of its kind in the world exhibits everything from dinosaurs to Chinese costumes and rare gems. In addition to the planetarium show in the Rose Center, there are films in a giant IMAX theater *(see pp34–7)*.

4 Solomon R. Guggenheim Museum

The Guggenheim has expanded its collection with several major donations, including Justin Thannhauser's Impressionist masters, Peggy Guggenheim's Cubist, Surrealist, and Abstract Expressionist works, a collection of American Minimalist and Conceptual art, and the most extensive collection of Kandinsky's works in the U.S. *(see pp32–3)*.

5 Whitney Museum of American Art

The entire range of 20th-century American art can be seen in the permanent collection housed in this striking Marcel Breuer building, along with changing exhibitions of contemporary art. ◉ *945 Madison Ave at 75th St • Map G4 • Open 11am–6pm Wed–Thu, 1–9pm Fri, 11am–6pm Sat & Sun • www.whitney.org • 1-800-WHITNEY • Admission charge*

6 Frick Collection

The mansion of industrialist Henry Clay Frick, with indoor garden court and fountain, is the setting for his exceptional collection of Old Masters, French furniture, and Limoges enamels. Look for Rembrandt, Vermeer, and Hals in the West Gallery; Holbein, Titian, and Bellini in the Living Hall. ◈ *1 East 70th St at 5th Ave • Map G4 • Open 10am–6pm Tue–Sat, 11am–5pm Sun • www.frick.org • Admission charge*

Brooklyn Museum
Housed in a fine Beaux Arts building, this museum presents a wide range of special exhibitions alongside permanent collections of Asian, Egyptian, African, and American art. The Elizabeth A. Sackler Center for Feminist Art, opened in 2007, is the first public space of its kind in the country. ◈ *200 Eastern Pkwy, Brooklyn • Subway 2, 3 to Eastern Pkwy • Open 10am–5pm Wed–Fri, 11am–6pm Sat & Sun, 11am–11pm first Sat of month (except Sep) • www.brooklynmuseum.org • Admission charge*

Morgan Library & Museum
This *palazzo* was designed in 1902 to hold the collection of billionaire J. Pierpont Morgan, an extraordinary assemblage of rare manuscripts, books, and prints, and galleries with changing exhibits. His original opulent study and library are highlights. ◈ *225 Madison Ave at 36th St • Map K4 • Open 10:30am–5pm Tue–Thu (to 9pm Fri), 10am–6pm Sat, 11am–6pm Sun • www.themorgan.org • Admission charge*

Museum of the City of New York
The toy collection is a highlight and the rotating exhibitions explore fashion, architecture, entertainment, cultural identity, ethnic traditions, and social history. The museum also features a film that documents the evolution of the city. ◈ *1220 5th Ave at 103rd St • Map D3 • Open 10am–5pm Tue–Sun • www.mcny.org • Admission charge*

Museum of the City of New York

American Folk Art Museum
The first New York museum built from the ground up in 30 years, the eight-level, innovative, skylit structure shows off a great collection of whimsical, all-American paintings, sculptures, quilts, weathervanes, and furniture. ◈ *45 West 53rd St between 5th and 6th Aves (Branch: 2 Lincoln Square at Columbus Ave) • Map J3 • 10:30am–5:30pm Tue–Sun, 10:30am–7:30pm Fri • www.folkartmuseum.org • Admission charge*

Left **Mary Boone Gallery** Right **Paula Cooper Gallery**

TOP 10 Art Galleries

1 Gagosian

Expect big names and equivalent price tags at this blue-ribbon gallery with three locations, one uptown and two Chelsea addresses, with the lofty spaces necessary for exhibiting large-scale art. Damien Hirst, Anselm Kiefer, Richard Serra, and Cy Twombly are among the contemporary artists represented. ◈ *980 Madison Ave (& Chelsea: 555 West 24th St & 522 West 21st St) • Map E4 • Open 10am–6pm Tue–Sat • www.gagosian.com*

2 Marlborough

This top-of-the-art-world gallery, representing the estates of artists including Larry River, Red Grooms, and R.B. Kitaj, has opted for two locations. The Midtown gallery has shown work by sculptors such as Anthony Caro and Jacques Lipschitz. New sculpture and paintings are found at the Chelsea location. ◈ *40 West 57th St, Floor 2 (& Chelsea: 245 West 25th St) • Map H3 • Open 10am–5:30pm Mon–Sat • www.marlboroughgallery.com*

3 Mary Boone

One of the art world's big names has deserted SoHo for a sleek Chelsea gallery where work on show still has a downtown edge and talented newcomers share space with established artists. Occasional intriguing group shows, assembled by independent curators, include sculpture, photography, and painting. ◈ *541 West 24th St between 10th & 11th Sts (& uptown: 745 5th Ave) • Map L2 • Open 10am–6pm Tue–Sat (by appointment only on Sat in summer) • www.maryboonegallery.com*

Contemporary works at the Pace Wildenstein Gallery

4 Pace Wildenstein

Expect the likes of Picasso, Rothko, Chuck Close, or Agnes Martin at this ultra-prestigious gallery showing modern masters of the 20th century and living artists. At 57th Street the galleries are for photographs, prints, and fine art. The gallery in Chelsea shows large-scale pieces.

◈ *32 East 57th St, Floor 4 (& Chelsea: 534 West 25th St & 545 West 22nd St) • Map H4 • Open 10am–6pm Tue–Fri, 10am–6pm Sat • www.pacewildenstein.com*

5 Sperone Westwater

This is an excellent place to see some of the most creative work being produced today. The gallery was set up in 1975 to showcase European artists who had little recognition in the US. Exhibitions have included works by many notable international artists, including Bruce Nauman, Donald Judd, and William Wegman. ◈ *415 West 13th St • Map M3 • Open 10am–6pm Tue–Sat (open Mon in summer) • www.speronewestwater.com*

The spacious Paula Cooper Gallery

The Drawing Center
Formed in 1977 to promote the art of drawing, this non-profit center has displayed the drawings of more than 2,500 emerging artists, including the early work of Kara Walker and Sikander Shahzia, as well as the work of the Old Masters. The Center also hosts monthly readings to present new writing. ⊗ 35 Wooster St • Map P4 • Open noon–6pm Wed, Fri–Sun, noon–8pm Thu, closed Nov 25–26, Dec 24–Jan 1 • www.drawingcenter.org

Deitch
Deitch, with exhibits of paintings, photography and sculpture, is one of the best sites for authentic contemporary works. It also features site-specific performance art, and gained notice when artist, Oleg Kulik, "transformed" himself into a dog and lived in the space for two weeks. It also has ties to established artists like Julian Schnabel and the estates of Keith Haring and Jean-Michel Basquiat. ⊗ 18 Wooster St • Map P3 • Open noon–6pm Tue–Sat • www.deitch.com

Matthew Marks
This was the first commercial gallery to open in Chelsea, in a converted garage, in 1994. Marks specializes in displaying the work of big-name artists such as Ellsworth Kelly, Jasper Johns, Nan Goldin, and Brice Marden. There are three other Chelsea locations, which show new works by painters, photographers, and sculptors (see p120).

Paula Cooper
This vast, creatively designed space filtering natural light through a cathedral ceiling is a superb setting for conceptual and minimalist art by Donald Judd, Sol Lewitt, Sophie Calle, and others. Paula Cooper, the first gallery to open in SoHo in 1968, deserted in 1996 to move to Chelsea (see p120).

Paul Kasmin
Kasmin is the son of a bohemian London dealer and continues the family tradition of taking chances on new artists. He usually features these artists in group shows. More established names, including those of sculptors and photographers, regularly appear in solo exhibitions (see p120).

Left **Chrysler Building** Right **View of the World Financial Center from the yacht harbor**

New York Skyscrapers

1 Empire State Building

The Empire State Building (1930–31) is the tallest structure in New York. For 28 years its dominance was eclipsed by the World Trade Center, which was destroyed in the September 2001 terrorist attack. With an 86th-floor observatory, the building receives some 3.5 million visitors each year *(see pp8–9)*.

Empire State Building

2 G.E. Building

Soaring 70 stories into the sky, this dramatic skyscraper *(see p13)*, designed by Raymond Hood and erected between 1931 and 1933, has shallow setbacks that recede into the distance. Part of the greatness of Hood's design is the contrast between the building's height and surrounding Rockefeller Center. ⊗ *30 Rockefeller Plaza, between 50th & 51st Sts • Map J3 • Closed to public*

3 Chrysler Building

The gleaming, stainless steel, tiered spire of the Chrysler Building adds grace to the city skyline. William Van Alen fashioned this Art Deco classic in 1928–30 as a tribute to the automobile. The building has a decorative frieze of stylized hubcaps and silver gargoyles, much like the winged radiator caps of a Chrysler automobile *(see p123)*.

4 Flatiron Building

This 21-story, triangular-shaped building has intrigued New Yorkers since it was built by Daniel Burnham in 1902; the shape was so unusual that people took bets on whether it would topple. The secret of this successful design was in the steel frame support, which was used instead of traditional heavy stone walls: a precursor of skyscrapers to come *(see p112)*.

5 Woolworth Building

Architect Cass Gilbert was responsible for this flamboyant 1913 Neo-Gothic building, the tallest in the world for two decades after it was completed. The rich terracotta ornamentation accentuates the structure's steel frame, which soars to a crown 60 stories above Broadway. The small lobby boasts one of the most luxurious marble interiors in Manhattan. ⊗ *233 Broadway, between Park Pl & Barclay St • Map Q4 • Free*

6 Lever House

Gordon Bunshaft's 24-story Lever House, completed in 1952, was revolutionary; it was New York's first skyscraper built in the form of a soaring glass and steel vertical slab. It began the eventual transformation of Park Avenue into an avenue of glass towers. ⊗ *390 Park Ave, between 53rd and 54th Sts • Map J4 • Open during office hours*

7 Seagram Building

The first New York building by Mies van der Rohe is this landmark "glass box" with slender bands of bronze amid walls of smoked glass rising from the horizontal open plaza. The materials in the glass-walled lobby by Philip Johnson help blur the division between indoor and outdoor space. The Four Seasons Restaurant, offering American cuisine, lies within. ✆ *375 Park Ave, between 52nd & 53rd Sts • Map J4 • Open during office hours*

Citigroup Center

8 Citigroup Center

The 59-story Citigroup Center, built in 1978, was New York's first Postmodern skyscraper. The rakish, triangular top never served its original purpose as a solar panel, but it did make the building instantly recognizable. An open base on four tall columns and a reflective aluminum-and-glass exterior give the building an airy quality despite its huge size. ✆ *153 East 53rd St at Lexington Ave • Map J4 • Closed to public*

9 World Financial Center

Cesar Pelli's Postmodern complex, comprising four tall towers around a glorious palm-filled Winter Garden, gave the city an elegant business center when it was completed in 1985. In addition, there are public spaces for concerts and special events and an outdoor plaza on the water complete with boat marina and Statue of Liberty views *(see p74).*

The Winter Garden, World Financial Center

10 World Wide Plaza

The copper roof and crown of frosted glass atop a 48-story tower by Skidmore, Owings & Merrill bring some traditional romance to a 1989 Postmodern building. There is a wraparound arcade that acts as another entrance. The building of the World Wide Plaza complex, which includes two apartment buildings, a theater, and a large open plaza, transformed a decaying neighborhood. ✆ *Between 8th & 9th Aves and 49th & 50th Sts • Map J2*

Left **Grand Central Station** Right **U.S. Custom House**

Historic Buildings

1 St. Paul's Chapel
Completed in 1766, this church has a glorious Georgian interior lit by Waterford chandeliers. The pew where George Washington prayed after his inauguration as president has been preserved (see p80).

2 City Hall
Built in 1803–12, this Georgian building with French Renaissance influences is one of New York's finest. The interior features a rotunda circled by 10 Corinthian columns, opening to twin spiral marble staircases (see p80).

City Hall's imposing façade

3 Trinity Church
This lovely, square-towered church has bronze doors designed by Richard Morris Hunt. Built in 1839–46, the spire, once the tallest in Manhattan, is now dwarfed by Wall Street towers. Alexander Hamilton (see p48) and Robert Fulton are buried here (see p73).

Trinity Church

4 St. Patrick's Cathedral
James Renwick, Jr. designed America's largest Catholic cathedral (opened in 1879) in French Gothic style with twin 330-ft (100-m) towers. The interior has side altars dedicated to saints and holy figures, chapels, and stained-glass windows (see p124).

5 Carnegie Hall
Philanthropist Andrew Carnegie financed the city's first great concert hall, built in 1891. Major renovation in 1996 restored the wonderful interior bronze balconies and ornamental plaster, and added a museum. Corridors are lined with memorabilia of the great artists who have performed here (see p50 & p125).

6 Cathedral of St. John the Divine
The world's largest cathedral was begun in 1892 and is still a work in progress. The part-Romanesque, part-Gothic building is impressive for its stonework, enormous nave, bay altar windows, and rose window. The seat of New York's Episcopal archdiocese, the church is the scene of many avant-garde musical and theatrical events (see p145).

7 New York Stock Exchange
Opened in 1903, the façade of this 17-story edifice is appropriately monumental for the building at the center of the U.S. economy. The figures on the pediment represent the "sources of American prosperity". "Black Thursday," the start of the Depression, began here in 1929 *(see p73)*.

8 U.S. Custom House
One of the city's best Neo-Classical buildings, this eight-story structure, built in 1907, features an elaborate mansard roof and fine sculptures, including tour by Daniel Chester French. A 1927 nautical mural by Reginald Marsh adorns the huge, oval rotunda *(see p74)*.

New York Public Library

9 New York Public Library
This white marble, 1911 Beaux Arts edifice is magnificent inside and out. Imposing stairways, terraces, and fountains inspire awe; reading rooms invite repose. Events and talks are also held here *(see p124)*.

10 Grand Central Terminal
This 1913 public facility is remarkable for its beauty; the main concourse is suffused with natural light and the vaulted ceiling is decorated with twinkling constellations *(see p123)*.

Top 10 Churches and Temples

1 Zion St. Mark's Evangelical Lutheran Church
Built in 1892, it is a reminder of the Upper East's German past. ✪ *339 East 84th St • Map F5*

2 St. George's Ukrainian Catholic Church
A contemporary church built in Byzantine style. ✪ *30 East 7th St • Map M4*

3 St. Nicholas Russian Orthodox Cathedral
Five onion domes mark this Russian Baroque church. ✪ *15 East 97th St • Map E4*

4 St. Sava Serbian Orthodox Cathedral
Byzantine windows were added to this 1856 church. ✪ *16–20 West 26th St • Map L3*

5 St. Vartan Armenian Cathedral
The goldleaf dome was inspired by the churches of Armenia. ✪ *630 2nd Ave • Map K4*

6 St. Elizabeth of Hungary Church
This Neo Gothic church has a painted vaulted ceiling. ✪ *211 East 83rd St • Map F4*

7 Greek Orthodox Cathedral of the Holy Trinity
Built in 1931 in Byzantine style as the seat of the Diocese. ✪ *319 East 74th St • Map G5*

8 Temple Emanu-El
The world's largest synagogue was built in 1929. ✪ *1 East 65th St • Map G4*

9 First Chinese Presbyterian Church
The stone sanctuary dates from 1819. ✪ *61 Henry St • Map P5*

10 Islamic Cultural Center
Ninety bulbs hang by brass rods from the dome. ✪ *1711 3rd Ave (at 96th St) • Map E4*

Left **Alexander Hamilton** Center **DeWitt Clinton** Right **John D. Rockefeller, Jr. (left)**

10 Figures in New York History

1 Peter Minuit
Sent from the Netherlands in 1626 to govern New Amsterdam, Peter Minuit (1580–1638) was so disliked by his subjects that they welcomed British occupation.

2 Alexander Hamilton
Revolutionary leader and first Secretary of the Treasury, Hamilton's (1755–1804) business-friendly policies were instrumental in New York's emergence as the financial center of the U.S. He lost his life in a duel with political opponent Aaron Burr and is buried in Trinity Church graveyard.

3 William "Boss" Tweed
The political leader of Tammany Hall, Tweed (1823–78) became the living embodiment of political corruption, kickbacks, and payoffs. It is estimated that he and his associates took up to $200 million from the city. To hide his crime, he did good works, building orphanages, public baths, and hospitals, but died in prison.

William "Boss" Tweed

4 DeWitt Clinton
Mayor of the city, governor of the state, and U.S. senator, Clinton (1769–1828) is best remembered for negotiating the construction of the Erie Canal in 1817–25. By connecting the Great Lakes to the Hudson River, he helped to secure New York's future as a predominant seaport.

Jacob Riis

5 Jacob Riis
Appalled by immigrant living conditions, Riis (1849–1914), a social reformer, writer, and photographer, used photos taken in tenements to illustrate his stories, shocking the middle class and motivating them to act. His 1888 article, *Flashes from the Slums*, and his book, *How the Other Half Lives*, brought national attention.

6 John D. Rockefeller, Jr.
The largess of John D. Rockefeller, Jr. (1874–1960) helped support housing in Harlem, the Bronx, and Queens, created Fort Tryon Park and the Cloisters, and provided land for the United Nations. The construction of Rockefeller Center *(see pp12–15)* employed thousands at the height of the depression and gave the city an enduring landmark.

7 Fiorello LaGuardia
Considered the city's best mayor, after his election in 1933 LaGuardia (1882–1947) modernized and centralized a chaotic city government, eliminated waste, unified the transit system, and obtained federal funds to help the city. A man of the people, he is remembered for reading the comics on the radio during a city newspaper strike.

Robert Moses

Robert Moses

As construction supervisor and parks commissioner from the 1930s–1950s, Moses (1888–1981) vastly enlarged and upgraded the city's recreational areas, but he also covered the city with highways rather than develop a public transport system and was responsible for urban renewal projects that razed many neighborhoods in favor of high-rises.

Donald Trump

"The Donald" (b. 1946), the flamboyant real estate wheeler-dealer, has left an indelible mark on New York. The huge Trump Place development overlooks the Hudson River, while the cheapest condo in the world's highest residential building, Trump World Tower, costs close to $1 million.

Rudolph Giuliani

Rudolph Giuliani

Mayor Rudy Giuliani (b. 1944) is widely credited with reducing crime, making the city cleaner, and upgrading quality of life for most New York citizens during his tenure, 1993–2001. Once controversial for his strong personality, his leadership following the attack on the World Trade Center rallied a stunned city and won praise at home and abroad.

Top 10 Dates in New York History

1 1626
Peter Minuit buys Manhattan from the natives. Beads and trinkets worth about $24 accomplished this ultimate real estate deal.

2 1664
The British take Manhattan from the Dutch. New Amsterdam becomes New York.

3 1789
George Washington is inaugurated as first president and takes his oath of office in Federal Hall. New York serves as the first U.S. capital.

4 1792
New York Stock Exchange opens; 24 traders sign an agreement beneath a tree on Wall Street, and the city becomes a financial center.

5 1859
Central Park opens and the city gains a green center enjoyed by millions every year.

6 1886
The Statue of Liberty is unveiled, becoming the symbol of freedom for millions of immigrants, who form a "melting pot" of nationalities.

7 1898
The five boroughs unite to form New York, the world's second largest city.

8 1931
The Empire State Building establishes New York as the world's skyscraper capital.

9 1952
The city becomes home to the United Nations headquarters.

10 2001
Terrorists use hijacked planes to destroy the towers of the World Trade Center.

Left **Madison Square Garden** Center **Radio City** Right **Brooklyn Academy of Music**

Performing Arts Venues

Carnegie Hall

1 Carnegie Hall

This historic concert hall opened in 1891 with Tchaikovsky making his U.S. debut on the podium. A campaign led by violinist Isaac Stern saved the hall from demolition after Lincoln Center *(see p139)* was completed in 1969, and it entered its second century with old-world style intact after lavish renovation *(see p125).*

Metropolitan Opera House

2 Metropolitan Opera House

Lincoln Center's most elegant performance venue shows off glorious oversize murals by Marc Chagall inside great arched windows. The interior boasts exquisite starburst chandeliers that are raised to the ceiling

before each performance. The theater presents the American Ballet Theater and many traveling groups, as well as its famous opera company *(see p139)*.

3 Avery Fisher Hall

Thanks to the generosity of benefactor Avery Fisher, the hall is now, after early acoustics problems, worthy of the New York Philharmonic, the oldest symphony orchestra in the U.S. A bust by Rodin of composer and former Philharmonic Music Director Gustav Mahler, on the west side of the building, is one of the best pieces of public sculpture in Lincoln Center *(see p139)*.

4 New York State Theater

The stage was built in 1964 to the specification of legendary choreographer George Balanchine, the founder of the New York City Ballet company, which dances here in winter and spring. The New York City Opera Company is also based here, presenting laudable productions that are far more affordable than the neighboring Metropolitan *(see p139)*.

5 Alice Tully Hall

Originally built in 1969 for the Chamber Music Society of Lincoln Center, the hall was renovated in 2009. Besides chamber and vocal concerts, it is used for shows by the Julliard School students and faculty, many of which are free to the public *(see p139)*.

For more entertainment venues **See pages 24 and 52–3**

City Center Theater
The ornate, Moorish-style building with a dome of Spanish tiles was opened in 1923 as a Shriner's Temple. Saved from developers by Mayor LaGuardia (see p48), it survived after losing its companies to Lincoln Center, and has become a major venue for touring dance companies.
⊗ 131 West 55th St, between 6th & 7th Aves • Map H3 • 212 581 1212
• Admission charge • www.citycenter.org

City Center Theater

Joyce Theater
A 1941 Art Deco movie theater was converted (in 1982) to become an intimate home for dance. Small and medium-sized modern dance companies from around the world present an exciting range of work that can't be seen elsewhere in Manhattan. Question-and-answer sessions with the artists follow some Wednesday night performances.
⊗ 175 8th Ave at 19th St; Joyce Soho: 155 Mercer St • Map L2 • 212 242 0800
• Admisson charge • www.joyce.org

Radio City Music Hall
Opened in 1932, the largest theater in the U.S. has an opulent, Art Deco interior. Once a movie palace, it now hosts musical performances and special events. The annual Christmas show starring the Rockettes, a troupe of long-legged dancers, is a New York tradition.

⊗ 1260 6th Ave at 50th St • Map J3 • 212 247 4777 • Tours: 11am–3pm Mon–Sat
• Admission charge • www.radiocity.com

Brooklyn Academy of Music (BAM)
This stately, Neo-Italianate 1908 building draws city-wide audiences for New York's most avant garde program of international music, theater, and dance, most notably the Next Wave Festival, a fixture since 1981. ⊗ 30 Lafayette Ave, Brooklyn • Subway 2, 3, 4, 5, B, Q to Atlantic Ave • 718 636 4100 • Admission charge • www.bam.org

Madison Square Garden
Home court for New York Knicks basketball and New York Rangers hockey, the 20,000-seat Garden is also used for rock concerts, ice shows, tennis, boxing, dog shows, and the circus. ⊗ 7th Ave at 32nd St • Map K3 • 212 465 6741
• Admission charge • www.thegarden.com

Left **Birdland** Center **Blue Note** Right **Iridium Jazz Club**

🔟 Music Venues

Beacon Theatre

1 Beacon Theatre
Name the stars and they've probably been on stage at the Beacon, where the likes of Bob Dylan, Sting, and B.B. King have performed. Shows range from pop music and light rock to gospel and world music.
◈ Broadway at West 74th St • Map G2 • Open 1 hour before show • Admission charge

2 Village Vanguard
Since 1935, this basement club has featured a "who's who" of jazz. The early years were eclectic, launching folk singers like Harry Belafonte. Since the 1950s it has been all jazz. ◈ 178 7th Ave South • Map M3 • Open 8pm–late • Cover charge

Jackie McLean at the Vanguard

3 Birdland
Another legend, although no longer in the location opened by Charlie Parker in 1949. Now near Times Square, the venue is built in three tiers to ensure good sightlines. Birdland Big Band plays on Mondays. ◈ 315 West 44th St, between 8th & 9th Aves • Map J2 • Open 5pm–3am Mon–Sun • Cover charge

4 Blue Note
Tony Bennett, Natalie Cole, and Ray Charles have all played this Greenwich Village venue. The emphasis is on jazz, but blues, Latin, R&B, soul, and big band also feature. ◈ 131 West 3rd St, between MacDougal St & 6th Ave • Map N3 • Open 7pm–2am Sun–Thu, 7pm–4am Fri & Sat • Admission & cover charge

5 S.O.B.s
The initials stand for Sounds of Brazil, but the music ranges from African to reggae via soul or jazz. The beat is contagious, and the dance floor gets crowded. Friday is salsa night.
◈ 204 Varick St at West Houston St • Map N3 • Opening times vary • Cover charge

6 Highline Ballroom
This industrial-look space on the edge of the meatpacking district offers an intimate experience. Mos Def, Lou Reed, Jonatha Brooke, and Lady Sovereign have all graced the stage here.
◈ 431 West 16th St between 9th & 10th Aves • Map M2 • Admission charge

7 Iridium Jazz Club
Opened in 1994, Iridium has funky decor, good food, and excellent established and new jazz groups. The great guitarist Les Paul plays here on Monday nights.
◈ 1650 Broadway at West 51st St • Map J3 • Open 7pm–2am Fri–Sat, 5pm–midnight Sun–Thu • Admission charge

For more New York entertainment venues See pp50–51

Dizzy's Club Coca Cola

8 Part of Jazz at Lincoln Center, this dazzling club features changing line-ups of top jazz groups. The cover is steep, but "after hours sets" are $10 maximum, and the food is reasonably priced. ◈ *Broadway at 60th St • Map H2 • Sets at 7.30, 9:30, & 11:30pm daily • Admission & cover charge*

Jazz Standard

Jazz Standard

9 First-rate acoustics and traditional to avant garde music. The restaurant, Blue Smoke, offers barbequed food. The Mingus Big Band plays most Monday nights. ◈ *116 East 27th St, between Park Ave Sth & Lexington Ave • Map L4 • Open 7pm–3am Tue–Sat (from 6pm Sun) • Adm*

Bowery Ballroom

Bowery Ballroom

10 The opening of Bowery Ballroom in 1998 helped spearhead a Lower East Side renaissance. The venue boasts great acoustics and sightlines. Well-known touring acts, mid-scale indie rockers, and local bands feature. ◈ *6 Delancey St, between Bowery and Chrystie St • Map N4 • Opening times vary • Admission charge*

Top 10 Dance Clubs

1 **Bar 13**
Three floors plus a roof deck and rocking DJs. ◈ *35 East 13th St • Map M4*

2 **Element**
Drink in the downstairs vault, then dance away at this club in a one-time bank. ◈ *225 East Houston St • Map N5*

3 **Lotus**
A mix of dining room, bars, lounges, and dance floor. ◈ *409 West 14th St • Map L2*

4 **APT**
Great setting and sound in a Meatpacking District favorite. ◈ *419 West 13th St • Map M2*

5 **Marquee**
Tough to get in if you're not with a model – but worth it. House and hip hop. ◈ *289 Tenth Ave • Map L2*

6 **Club Shelter**
Dance until dawn at this Soho standby; Saturday is the big night. ◈ *150 Varick St • Map N3*

7 **The Sullivan Room**
Draws the cream of techno talent to this intimate venue. ◈ *218 Sullivan St • Map N3*

8 **The 40/40 Club**
Rapper Jay-Z's swanky sports bar-cum-R&B dance spot also boasts a cigar bar and three VIP sections. ◈ *6 West 25th St • Map L3*

9 **Cielo**
The beautiful set come for soulful and deep house. ◈ *18 Little West 12th St • Map M2*

10 **Pacha New York**
Dance music and urban style spread over four floors from the Ibiza superclub. ◈ *618 West 46th St • Map J2*

Left **Flute** Center **Salon de Ning** Right **Monkey Bar**

TOP 10 Bars and Lounges

1 King Cole Bar and Lounge

Maxfield Parrish's famous mural of Old King Cole, rich mahogany paneling, and sumptuous seating set the stage for New York's most famous hotel bar, which has only been admitting women since 1950. Lush, luxurious, and very expensive, the soft piano music sets a mood that makes it easy to clinch a deal or spark a romance. ⊗ *St. Regis Hotel, 2 East 55th St, between 5th and Madison Aves • Map H4 • 212 753 4500*

King Cole Bar

2 Bar 44 at the Royalton

Located in the heart of Manhattan's Midtown, the Royalton launched a legion of boutique-style imitations when it first opened in 1988. A $17.5 million renovation to the lobby, bar and restaurant in 2007 bid adieu to the post-modern Philippe Starck interior. Bar 44 is now cozy, with elements of brass, steel, wood, velvet, suede, and fur, while Brasserie 44 is a light, airy space with teak banquettes and cream-colored leather. ⊗ *Royalton Hotel, 44 West 44th St • Map J3 • 212 944 8844*

3 Monkey Bar

A sophisticated spot with a whimsical theme – monkey murals and light fixtures, even a Purple Monkey cocktail. Monkey Bar is a long-time favorite, which serves Chinese food with a modern twist. The bar attracts a well-heeled, well-dressed crowd. ⊗ *Hotel Elysee, 60 East 54th St, between Madison and Park Aves • Map J4 • 212 308 2950*

4 Flute

Proudly stocking over 150 types of champagne, several available by the glass, this former speakeasy blends high-end opulence and a sumptuous menu with a romantic atmosphere and friendly service. There's a second branch in Gramercy. ⊗ *205 West 54th St, between 7th Ave and Broadway, 212 265 5169; 40 East 20th St, 212 529 7870 • Map H3 & L4 respectively*

5 Campbell Apartment

This is a gem hidden in Grand Central Terminal. Housed in the richly paneled, luxurious former offices of 1920s railroad tycoon John W. Campbell, this bar features leaded glass, a beautifully painted beamed ceiling, and a carved wood balcony, all inspired by a Florentine palazzo. Single-malt scotches and vintage wines complement this elegant setting. The dress code is business-casual. ⊗ *West balcony, Grand Central Terminal, 15 Vanderbilt Ave at 42nd St • Map J4 • 212 953 0409*

Salon de Ning

The former Pen-Top Bar is now decorated with an Asian theme, but the views of city lights needed no improvement at this 23rd-floor oasis. The outdoor terrace is an unbeatable spot on a balmy summer night. Devotees say it is well worth the steep tab. ❧ *Peninsula Hotel, 700 5th Ave at 55th St • Map H3 • 212 956 2888*

Plunge

Enjoy superb views of the New York skyline and the Hudson River from this rooftop bar at the trendy Gansevoort Hotel, in the Meatpacking District. Although a little on the expensive side, this is a great spot to hang out in the summer months. ❧ *Gansevoort Hotel, 18 9th Ave at 13th St • Map M2 • 212 206 6700*

Boathouse Bar

Watch the sun set and the lights come on across the skyline at this outdoor bar beside the lake in Central Park, a location worthy of a movie set. The setting is particularly romantic on warm nights when rowboats and gondolas glide by. ❧ *Central Park near East 72nd St • Map G2 • 212 517 2233*

Park View at the Boathouse

Hudson Bar

With a backlit glass floor, elaborate, hand-painted ceiling, and unusual Louis XV meets Star Wars decor, the bar at the Hudson Hotel draws a stylish crowd. Punters love the vibe here despite the high price of drinks, and those looking for a quieter spot can always head for the hotel's Library Bar. ❧ *Hudson Hotel, 356 West 58th St • Map H2 • 212 247 0769.*

Ñ

Head for this out-of-the-way block in SoHo to discover an absolute gem: a raffish bar with polka dot walls, reasonably priced drinks, and Spanish tapas to be enjoyed with a choice of sherries, fruity sangria, or Spanish wines. Live flamenco music in the evenings adds to the atmosphere. This place is small and extremely popular so get there early to ensure a seat. ❧ *33 Crosby St, between Broome and Grand Sts • Map P4 • 212 210 0856*

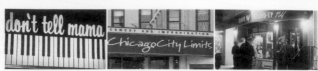

Left **Don't Tell Mama** Center **Chicago City Limits** Right **Stand Up New York**

🔟 Cabarets

Café Carlyle

Look around the Algonquin too, a hotel famous for the "round table" of writers who met here in the 1920s. ⬉ *Algonquin Hotel, 59 West 44th St, between 5th & 6th Aves • Map J3 • Cover charge*

Café Carlyle
Chic and classy Café Carlyle is New York at its best and is well worth the steep cover charge; Eartha Kitt was a regular, and Woody Allen is often part of Monday night jam sessions. Bemelmans Bar features pianists like Barbara Carroll, and a cheaper tab. ⬉ *Carlyle Hotel, 35 East 76th St at Madison Ave • Map G4 • Cover charge*

Café Pierre
An elegant setting for talented singers performing Broadway and pop favorites. The food, while pricey, is first rate. Jackets are required in the evenings. ⬉ *Pierre Hotel, 5th Ave at 61st St • Map H3 • No cover*

The Oak Room
Settle into a banquette and look forward to top entertainers like Maureen McGovern or Julie Wilson. The repertories usually favor American classics, such as Gershwin, Berlin, or Cole Porter.

The Oak Room

Don't Tell Mama
No telling who will be at this fun spot in the Theater District – singers, comics, or magicians. There are no big names, and abilities range from amateur to destined-for-stardom. Sometimes even the waiters get into the act. ⬉ *343 West 46th St, between 8th & 9th Aves • Map J2 • Cover charge*

Feinstein's at Loews Regency
This is a fashionable spot to hear artists like guitarist John Pizzarelli and Grammy-nominated vocalist and song writer, co-owner Feinstein. ⬉ *Loews Regency Hotel, 540 Park Ave at 61st St • Map H4 • Cover charge*

Café Sabarsky
On Thursday nights, this Viennese café in the Neue Galerie becomes the city's most beautiful setting for contemporary cabaret. Shows are at 9pm; a prix-fixe dinner is available at 7pm. Check for dates and book tickets at the museum. ⬉ *Neue Galerie, 1048 5th Ave at 86th St • Map F3 • 212 628 6200 • No cover*

7 Joe's Pub

This intimate oasis, attached to the Public Theater in the East Village, hosts an eclectic range of arty performers, from beginners to big names. Without dinner reservations, seating or standing is on a first come, first served basis. ⊗ *425 Lafayette St, between East 4th & Astor Place • Map N4 • Cover charge*

8 The Metropolitan Room

Opened in 2006, this sleek venue has won ample praise for its warm vibe and top performers, including jazz legends Annie Ross, Marilyn Maye, and Billy Stritch. ⊗ *34 West 22nd St, between 5th & 6th Aves • Map L3 • Cover charge*

The Duplex

9 The Duplex

The oldest cabaret in town features a broad range of entertainment, from early versions of *Nunsense* or *Mark Twain Tonight*, to singers, comedians, drag diva Lady Bunny, or the troupe Funny Gay Males. The raucous shows attract straight and gay. ⊗ *61 Christopher St at 7th Ave South • Map N3 • Cover charge*

10 Laurie Beechman Theater at the West Bank Café

The room here hosts regular cabaret series. Some performances are open, which means the headliners may ask audience members to help out on a song or two. ⊗ *407 West 42nd St between 9th and 10th Aves • Map K2 • Admission charge*

Top 10 Comedy Clubs

1 The Comic Strip Live

A leading venue for up-and-comers; Eddie Murphy and Jerry Seinfeld are alumni. ⊗ *1568 2nd Ave • Map E4*

2 Caroline's Comedy Club

In the heart of the theater district, Caroline's features big names as well as beginners. ⊗ *1626 Broadway • Map J3*

3 Dangerfield's

One of the oldest and best; former testing ground of the legendary Rodney Dangerfield. ⊗ *1118 1st Ave • Map G5*

4 Gotham Comedy Club

A spacious setting for top talent from Comedy Central and other sources. ⊗ *208 West 23rd St • Map L3*

5 Comix

This ambitious upscale newcomer is a massive hit with comedy fans. ⊗ *335 West 14th St • Map M2*

6 People's Improv Theater

You can laugh here, and take a comedy class too. ⊗ *154 West 29th St • Map N3*

7 Stand-up New York

Novices and pros feature in this intimate space. ⊗ *236 West 78th St • Map F2*

8 NY Comedy Club

Top NYC comics and a low cover charge. ⊗ *241 East 24th St • Map L4*

9 Upright Citizens Brigade Theater

Mainly improv; their regular Sunday night show, *Asssscat 3000*, is hilarious. ⊗ *307 West 26th St • Map L2*

10 Chicago City Limits Theater

Timely improvization in this long-running review. ⊗ *318 West 53rd St • Map H2*

Left **Carriage rides through Central Park** Right **Staten Island Ferry**

🔟 Romantic Settings

1 Carriage Ride through Central Park

The horse-drawn hansom cabs lined up at the edge of Central Park are romance personified. The driver, appropriately attired in fancy dress and top hat, will help you up as you nestle in for a 20-minute trot past park landmarks (see pp26–7).

2 Dinner at the River Café

The Manhattan skyline is never more dazzling than when seen from this barge restaurant just across the East River in Brooklyn. The food is worthy of the setting; the package is worth the price (see p157).

River Café, nestling beneath Brooklyn Bridge

3 View from the Empire State Building at Twilight

It has been the setting for dozens of romantic movies and countless proposals have taken place here. At dusk you can watch the sun set over the city as a million lights go on in its towers (see pp8–9).

Beekman Tower Hotel

4 Drinks at the Top of the Tower

The 26th floor of this Art Deco landmark building affords unsurpassed views of the city lights and the East River from its wraparound terraces. Order champagne and enjoy the scene and each other. 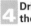 Beekman Tower Hotel, 3 Mitchell Place at 1st Ave & 49th St • Map J5

5 Gondola Ride on Central Park Lake

Relax aboard the authentic, Venetian gondola as you glide out on the water and revel in the beauty of the park reflected in the lake and the city buildings ringing the park like a crown. 🅢 Loeb Boat House, Central Park at East 74th St • Map G3 • Charge

6 Walk in the Cloisters' Gardens

This branch of the Met is an oasis of serene beauty, a chance to glory in the past while planning the future. More than 250 kinds of plants grown in the Middle Ages are found in these gardens. Trie Cloister features plants shown in the Unicorn Tapestries (see p31).

For more special days out in New York **See pp62–3**

7 Dinner at One if by Land...

A restored 18th-century Greenwich Village carriage house, candlelight, and soft piano music make for Manhattan's most seductive setting. ◈ *17 Barrow St, between 7th Ave South & West 4th St • Map N3 • 212 228 0822 • www.oneifbyland.com*

8 Staten Island Ferry Ride

Stand on the top deck to watch Manhattan's skyscrapers recede as you sail past Liberty, Ellis, and Governors Islands. Take the car deck coming home for close-up photos of the skyline *(see p155)*. ◈ *Whitehall Terminal, Whitehall and South Sts • Map R4 • Boats every 15 mins–1 hr, 24 hours daily • Free*

Brooklyn Bridge

9 Brooklyn Bridge Stroll

The walk across Brooklyn Bridge yields thrilling vistas of skyscrapers through the intricate bridge cable work. Bring the camera to record unparalleled views. ◈ *The bridge begins behind City Hall, Broadway and Park Row • Map Q4*

10 Concert at St. Paul's Chapel

Just to walk into this chapel, New York's oldest public building, is to enter a world of grace and reverent serenity. The concerts held on Mondays at 1pm offer visitors a chance to revel in the setting and the music *(see p80)*.

Top 10 City Oases

1 Samuel Paley Plaza
Respite from Midtown bustle with its own waterfall. ◈ *3 East 53rd St • Map J4*

2 Greenacre Park
A "vest pocket" park donated by the daughter of John D. Rockefeller, Jr. ◈ *217–21 East 51st St • Map J4*

3 Bryant Park
A swath of green with formal plantings behind the Public Library. ◈ *6th Ave, between 41st & 42nd Sts • Map K3*

4 Metropolitan Museum Roof Terrace
Have a drink or just admire the prime views of Central Park and city towers beyond. ◈ *5th Ave and 82nd St • Map F3 • Open May–late fall*

5 High Line
An elevated train track turned stylish park. ◈ *Ganesvoort St at 10th Ave • Map M2*

6 Theodore Roosevelt Park
A shady patch of green behind the American Museum of Natural History. ◈ *Columbus Ave, between 77th & 81st Sts • Map F2*

7 John Jay Park
Past the playgrounds is a placid seating area with East River views. ◈ *East 77th St and FDR Drive • Map F5*

8 Wave Hill
Former estate with gardens and greenhouses. ◈ *675 West 252nd St, Bronx*

9 Grace Church
A Renwick masterpiece, this beautiful 1846 church is a calm respite in the Village. ◈ *802 Broadway • Map M4*

10 St. John the Baptist Church
Sanctuary and Prayer Garden with statuary and fountain. ◈ *210 West 31st St • Map K3*

Left **Lucky Cheng's drag show** Center **Christopher Street** Right **Next**

Gay and Lesbian New York

Stonewall Pub

Stonewall Pub
Next door to the Stonewall Inn, where a police raid on June 27, 1969, turned into a riot as gays rose up against constant police harassment, the present bar is far more peaceful. Photographs on the walls are reminders of its history. ⚓ *53 Christopher St • Map N3*

Christopher Street
The profusion of bars, shops, and cruisers between 6th and 7th avenues is the epicenter of gay Greenwich Village. The crowd is a bit older since many younger gay men have defected to Chelsea. ⚓ *Map N3*

Chelsea
This neighborhood is where it all happens these days. Gay revellers pack the bars and spill onto the sidewalks at the weekend, and a scene of some sort can be found in every café. ⚓ *8th Ave between West 14th and West 23rd St • Map M2/L2*

Bluestockings Book Store
Named after an 18th-century feminist group, this Lower East Side lair is not only a comprehensive source for women's literature but a social center with an organic café, gallery, readings, and events. Women of all ages and races are welcome. ⚓ *172 Allen St at Stanton St • Map N5*

Lesbian and Gay Community Services Center
A nucleus of the gay community; headquarters for organizations and event notices; active in public education, health, and emotional counseling; and a hub for social events, the Center also maintains history archives and an extensive library. An informative welcome pack is available for tourists.
⚓ *208 West 13th St • Map M2 • Open 9am–11pm daily*

HX and Time Out magazines

Publications
HX and *Next* are weeklies reviewing the club and entertainment scene. Other publications include *Gay New City News*, a newspaper covering politics, health, and arts; the *New York Blade*, a free tabloid; and *Metro-Source*, a glossy lifestyle magazine. *Time Out New York*, a general entertainment weekly sold at all newsstands, has a big section on gay and lesbian events from lectures to clubs.

7 Club Nights
Many bars and clubs have party nights. For example, Thursdays at Happy Ending, Saturdays at HK, and Sundays at The Monster. The Cock and Splash Bar are lively most nights. New York night life is under pressure from rising rents and complaining neighbors and venues frequently change.
◈ *Check listings publications for details*

8 Lesbian Herstory Archive
The world's largest and oldest lesbian archive, founded in 1973, is located in Park Slope, a popular lesbian neighborhood. The volunteer-run archive houses art, books, photos, periodicals, video, and films recording lesbian lives and holds events supporting lesbian writers and artists in all media.
◈ *484 14th St, Brooklyn • Subway (F) 15th St, Prospect Park • 718 768 3953 • Open by appointment*

9 David Barton Gym
The muscle boys in Chelsea flock to this upscale gym in the historic 23rd St Y space, owned by gym titan David Barton. Besides yoga, steam rooms, and Russian baths, you will find a DJ and a Bumble & Bumble hair salon. ◈ *215 West 23rd St, near 7th Ave • Map L3 • Open 5:30am–midnight Mon–Fri, 8am–9pm Sat & Sun • Admission charge*

10 Drag Shows
A transgender waitstaff and drag shows in the basement make Lucky Cheng New York's most unusual Chinese restaurant, drawing tour buses as well as gay patrons. Also check out the drag queens lipsynching songs at Lips, and performing to a Latin beat at La Nueva Escuelita. ◈ *Check listings publications for details.*

Top 10 Eating and Meeting Places

1 View Bar
Coffee house by day, bar by night, and a bustling sidewalk café in summer.
◈ *232 8th Ave • Map L2*

2 Gym
This friendly, casual site is home to New York City's first true gay sports bar.
◈ *167 8th Ave • Map L2*

3 Therapy
Chic two-level lounge with cabaret shows, nightly DJs, and great drinks. ◈ *348 West 52nd St • Map H2*

4 G
Trendy lounge with a live D.J., round stainless steel bar, and conversation pit. ◈ *225 West 19th St • Map L3*

5 SBNY
Enjoy the go-go guys working on the shower stage and erotic videos above the urinals.
◈ *50 West 17th St • Map M3*

6 Phoenix
An East Village hangout with an old-school vibe. Unpretentious, with cheap drinks.
◈ *447 East 13th St • Map M5*

7 Cattyshack
Popular lesbian bar with a rooftop patio. ◈ *249 4th Ave, Park Slope, Brooklyn*

8 Posh Bar
An elegant, laid-back bar with half-price drinks from 4–8pm. ◈ *405 West 51st St • Map J2*

9 Henrietta Hudson
Warm, down-to-earth, lesbian lair in Greenwich Village.
◈ *438 Hudson St • Map N3*

10 The Cubby Hole
Cozy, unpretentious lesbian bar where regulars sing along to the jukebox. ◈ *281 West 12th St • Map M2*

Left **Easter Parade** Right **Feast of San Gennaro**

TOP 10 Festivals and Events

1 St. Patrick's Day Parade
People wear Irish green for this big day when marching bands, politicos, and lovely lasses march down 5th Avenue to proclaim their love of the Emerald Isle. Millions come to watch and the celebrations last way into the night.
⊗ *5th Ave • 11am Mar 17 • Check press for exact route*

2 Easter Parade
Following a long-time tradition, 5th Avenue closes to traffic in Midtown, and New York families in their Sunday best stroll up the avenue, with ladies sporting amazing hats, both traditional and outrageous. ⊗ *5th Ave • Map H3–J3 • 11am Easter Sunday*

3 9th Avenue Food Festival
New York's biggest food extravaganza began in 1974. Vendors come from all over and thousands of people jam the streets to sample a United Nations of food from burritos to samosas.
⊗ *9th Ave, 37th to 57th Sts • Map H2–K2 • Mid-May*

4 4th of July Fireworks
River drives close to traffic and huge crowds come out to see this pyrotechnic spectacular over the East River. Macy's spends over $1 million for this salute to the red, white, and blue.
⊗ *East River • Map R3 • 9:30pm Jul 4*

4th of July fireworks over the East River

5 West Indian Day Carnival
Brooklyn's West Indian population celebrates its heritage with a parade of enormous floats, lavish, feathered costumes in rainbow hues, and contagious Caribbean music. Street stands offer Caribbean specialties. ⊗ *Eastern Parkway, Brooklyn • Subway C to Franklin Ave • Labor Day (1st Mon in Sep)*

West Indian Day Carnival

6 Feast of San Gennaro
The patron saint of Naples is carried through the streets of Little Italy, and Mulberry Street is packed day and night with music, game booths, and tons of tasty, traditional food. Sausage and pepper sandwiches are the trademark of this 10-day event, but there is an Italian treat for every taste. ⊗ *Mulberry St • Map P4 • 3rd week in Sep for 10 days*

7 New York City Marathon

An amazing 30,000 entrants run the 26.2-mile (42-km) marathon that starts on Staten Island, takes in all five boroughs, and finishes in Central Park. New Yorkers line the route, cheering and offering water to the runners.

1st Ave above 59th St is a good viewpoint • Map H5 • 10:45am 1st Sun in Nov

8 Macy's Thanksgiving Day Parade

New Yorkers take to the streets and America watches on television as cartoon character balloons, marching bands, lavish TV and movie star-laden floats, and the dancing Rockettes announce the start of the Christmas season.

Central Park West at 77th St along Broadway to 34th St • Map G2 • 9am Thanksgiving Day

9 Christmas Tree Lighting Ceremony

America's tallest Christmas tree, festooned with miles of lights, stands next to the skating rink in Rockefeller Center. Trumpeting angel decorations in the Channel Gardens and animated windows in 5th Avenue department stores add to the holiday spirit.

Rockefeller Center • Map J3 • 1st week in Dec

10 New Year's Eve Ball Drop

Crowds begin gathering hours before, ready to cheer when a giant, illuminated, Waterford crystal ball lowered at midnight marks the official start of the New Year. Other "First Night" events include dancing at Grand Central Station or the Empire State Building and a midnight run, with fireworks, in Central Park. *Times Square • Map K3 • Midnight Dec 31*

Top 10 Sports Events

1 U.S. Open Tennis Championships
The last Grand Slam of the year. *USTA National Tennis Center, Queens • Aug–Sep*

2 New York Yankees and Mets Baseball
Perennial rivals compete in America's favorite pastime. *Yankee Stadium, Bronx; Citi Field, Queens • Apr–Sep*

3 New York Knicks Basketball
Fast-paced games that always sell out. *Madison Square Garden, 7th Ave • Oct–Apr*

4 New York Liberty
Women's professional basketball. *Madison Square Garden, 7th Ave • Jun–Aug*

5 New York Jets and Giants Football
Both teams play in New Jersey; tickets are scarce. *Giants Stadium, New Jersey • Sep–Dec*

6 New York Rangers Hockey
Played on ice, requiring speed and skill. *Madison Square Garden, 7th Ave • Sep–Apr*

7 Millrose Games
America's fastest runners compete in this indoor track meet. *Madison Square Garden, 7th Ave • Feb*

8 Wood Memorial
Race featuring Kentucky Derby contenders. *Acqueduct Raceway, Queens • Mid-Apr*

9 Belmont Stakes
The last of racing's "triple crown." *Belmont Park, Long Island • 2nd Sat in Jun*

10 New York Red Bulls
The growing popularity of soccer draws devoted fans. *Giants Stadium, New Jersey. • Apr–Oct*

New York's Top 10

Left **Bloomingdale's** Center **Barney's** Right **Henri Bendel**

New York Stores

Macy's

Macy's
What can you say about the world's largest store? Food to futons, the selection is vast. And Macy's is a major part of the New York scene, from the spring flower show to Tap-O-Mania, when thousands of tap dancers converge on Herald Square *(see p119)*.

Bloomingdale's
After Macy's, this is New York's best-known department store, renowned for high fashion for men and women. The main floor with cosmetics, jewelry, and accessories is a mob scene, but don't be discouraged; upper floors are more manageable. ◈ *1000 Lexington Ave at 59th St • Map H4*

5th Avenue Department Stores
Bergdorf Goodman, Saks Fifth Avenue, and Lord and Taylor have a full range of well-known brand clothing for men, women, and children, as well as an upscale selection of home accessories. All have ultra-stylish seasonal window displays. ◈ *Bergdorf Goodman, 754 5th Ave (at 57th St); Saks Fifth Avenue, 611 5th Ave (at 50th St); Lord and Taylor, 424 5th Ave (at 38th St) • Map H3–K3*

Saks Fifth Avenue

Barney's New York
If you have the wherewithal, here's the place to find the latest designer labels to please a well-heeled, young and trendy clientele. Their semi-annual clearance sales are legendary and draw hordes of shoppers after chic on the cheap. ◈ *660 Madison Ave at 61st St • Map H4*

Henri Bendel
Set up like a series of boutiques, Bendel's displays innovative, fun women's fashions for glamorous shoppers. The sales staff are particularly friendly. The signature brown and white shopping bag is such a status symbol that the pattern is used for accessories. ◈ *712 5th Ave at 55th St • Map H3*

Takashimaya
In a sleek, five-story Postmodern building, this outpost of the Japanese department store sells clothing, art, linens, *objets d'art*, and furniture. All have Eastern influence, are expensive, and are chosen for their excellent

For more on New York shopping See p165

design. Visit the serene Tea Box for bento box lunches and beautiful desserts. ◈ *693 5th Ave, between 54th & 55th Sts • Map H3*

Midtown H&M

H&M
Hennes & Mauritz, a Swedish retailer, was a smash success when the 5th Avenue store opened in New York in 2000. Their secret? Kicky, young designs for men, women, and children at rock bottom prices, creating a look that belies the price tag. ◈ *640 5th Ave at 51st St; 34th St and Herald Square; 558 Broadway • Map J3, K3, & N4 respectively*

Madison Avenue Designers
The epicenter of designer boutiques in New York used to be 57th Street between 5th and Madison avenues, where shops such as Burberry are still found. But as stores like Nike and Levi's have invaded this territory, the designers, Giorgio Armani to Yves Saint Laurent, have moved to Madison Avenue, where the exclusive shops and boutiques now run from 59th almost to 79th Street. ◈ *Giorgio Armani, 760 Madison Ave; Yves Saint Laurent, 855–859 Madison Ave • Map F4–H4*

SoHo Boutiques
The 20–30-something crowd does its shopping in trendy SoHo boutiques such as Anna Sui, A.P.C., Miu Miu, and Cynthia Rowley.

Shops are between Thompson Street and Broadway, between Prince and Greene streets, though any block in this area may yield a special find. This is also prime hunting ground for home furnishings at stores such as Portico and Armani Casa. ◈ *Anna Sui, 113 Greene St; A.P.C., 131 Mercer St; Miu Miu, 100 Prince St; Cynthia Rowley, 376 Bleecker St; Portico, 139 Spring St; Armani Casa, 97 Greene St • Map N3–N4*

6th Avenue Superstores
Around 18th Street, the cast-iron buildings that comprised the late-1800s "Fashion Row" are another shopping mecca. Current occupants include superstores like Bed, Bath, and Beyond for homewares, Old Navy for casual clothing, and bargain fashion outlets such as T.J. Maxx and Filene's Basement. ◈ *Bed, Bath & Beyond, T.J. Maxx and Filene's Basement all at 620 6th Ave; Old Navy, 610 6th Ave • Map L3*

Left **Coney Island** Center **Central Park's carousel** Right **Children's Museum of Manhattan**

🔟 Places for Children

1 Central Park
Myriad activities for kids include storytelling, carousel rides, bike riding, boating, ice skating, nature workshops, and guided walks. The Central Park Zoo is excellent, not too large in size, and the Tisch Children's Zoo allows petting and feeding of farm animals (see pp26–7).

Polar Bear in Central Park Zoo

2 Bronx Zoo
America's largest city zoo offers authentic environments for exhibits such as the Himalayan Highlands, African Plains, Jungle World, the Congo Gorilla Forest, Tiger Mountain, and popular attraction Madagascar! All enclosures are easily reached via shuttle trains and elevated rides (see p151).

3 Children's Museum of Manhattan
Five floors of educational hands-on fun with exhibits like Body Odyssey, exploring a giant crawl-through body; Inventor Center, using scanners and digital images; and a TV studio where kids produce their own shows. Under-fours have their own play area (see p140).

4 American Museum of Natural History
Join throngs of New York parents introducing children to the world-famous dioramas of wild animals in realistic natural habitats and the fascinating dinosaur exhibits. The totem and giant canoe in the Northwest Coast Indian exhibit and the enormous meteorites and mineral rock specimens are also favorites. The Rose Center will intrigue older children and teens (see pp34–7).

5 New Victory Theater
The "New Vic," a 1900 landmark, has been transformed into New York's first major theater devoted to family entertainment. Troupes from around the world offer plays, circus acts, and other diversions to delight young audiences. Pre-performance family workshops with staff and cast are scheduled, offering interesting insights into how a theater works. ⓢ 209 West 42nd St, between 7th & 8th Aves • Map J3 • Box office open noon–7pm Tue–Sat, 11am–5pm Sun & Mon • Admission charge • www.newvictory.org

6 F.A.O. Schwarz
Expect to be awed by this toy store selling giant stuffed animals to the last word in action toys. This wonderland of fun was founded by German immigrant Frederick August Otto Schwarz in 1862 and is now the flagship store for dozens of locations nationwide. Kids love looking,

but be prepared to be wheeled into a purchase. ✆ 767 5th Ave at 58th St • Map H3

F.A.O. Schwarz

7 Coney Island/ New York Aquarium

Although a bit frayed since its early 1900s heyday, Coney Island (undergoing some development) is still home to the landmark ferris wheel and roller-coaster rides, and the long sandy beach and beachside boardwalk. The excellent New York Aquarium, along the boardwalk, is an indoor /outdoor complex where whales, walruses, and dolphins play, and finny creatures range from sharks to seahorses. A great day's outing for the family (see p155).

8 Tall Ship Cruises

A boat ride in Manhattan harbor is always a thrill, and what better way to go to sea than aboard the 1885 Schooner Pioneer at South Street Seaport? Ninety-minute lunch sails are good for those with short attention spans; two-hour cruises depart afternoon and evening. ✆ South Street Seaport Museum: Pier 16 at South Street Seaport • Map Q4 • Thu–Sun May–Sep • Admission charge

9 The Circus

New York's own non-profit Big Apple Circus, with a delightful one-ring show, pitches its tent from October to December in Damrosch Park at Lincoln Center. Those who want the traditional three-ring extravaganza will find Ringling Bros. and Barnum & Bailey in town in March and April. ✆ Big Apple Circus, Lincoln Center Plaza; Ringling Bros./Barnum & Bailey, Madison Square Garden, 7th Ave at 32nd St • Map H2 & K3 • Admission charge

10 Children's Museum of the Arts

When little ones get fed up with sight-seeing, bring them to this SoHo stop where children can enjoy interactive exhibits. Those under the age of ten can create their own works of art using paint, collage, chalk, or you name it, and work off energy in the play areas. Under-fives have their own WEE (wondrous experimenting and exploring) Artists Drop-In section. Children's art from other nations is on show. ✆ 182 Lafayette St, between Broome & Grand Sts • Map P4 • Open noon–5pm Wed–Sun, noon–6pm Thu • Admission charge • www.cmany.org

Left **Four Seasons Spring Pool Room** Right **Nobu**

🔟 Restaurants

1 Union Square Café
Danny Meyer's first restaurant has been one of New York's most popular since 1985, loved for delicious fare served by friendly staff in comfortable surroundings. Chef Michael Romano's new

Union Square Café

takes on American standards include the freshest ingredients from the neighboring Union Square Greenmarket (see p115).

Gotham Bar

2 Gotham Bar and Grill
A perennial favorite. Alfred Portale was one of the first with "vertical food," deliciously stacked you can hardly bear to disturb them. The new American fare is elegant, and the lofty, columned space is sophisticated and casual. The $31 three-course lunch is a great buy. ◈ 12 East 12th St, between 5th Ave & University Pl • Map M3 • 212 620 4020 • $$$

3 Nobu
Reservations are hard to come by for Nobu Matsuhisa's Japanese/Peruvian fusion that produces inspired dishes. Say "Omakase" ("I leave it to you") and let the chef choose among the surprising and always sublime offerings. David Rockwell's whimsical setting adds to the experience. Casual Nobu Next Door

needs no reservations (see p103).

4 Jean Georges
Already a culinary star from his earlier Jo Jo and Vong restaurants, Jean-Georges Vongerichten in his namesake restaurant turns out food that is among the very best in New York, transformed by the French master's delicate sauces and creative combinations. Designer Adam Tihany has created a polished, almost austere, setting that does not upstage the four-star chef (see p143).

5 Daniel
Another luminary of the food world, Daniel Boulud now has a flower-filled, Venetian Renaissance-inspired dining room worthy of his extraordinary talents. Seasonal menus with choices such as roasted squab with spiced pineapple or black truffle-crusted cod are divine. Lunch is a less expensive opportunity to sample the master (see p137).

6 Momofuku Ssäm Bar
Wunderkind David Chang brings serious humor (and lots of pork products) to this extremely inventive restaurant. The steamed pork buns are legendary, and one can always count on some unusual seafood and market vegetables to appear as well (see p95).

For a table at a top New York restaurant, book up to two months in advance, or make a lunchtime reservation.

7 Per Se

You need to call two months in advance to get a seat in Thomas Keller's expensive restaurant. One of a handful of eateries to receive four stars from *The New York Times*, diners come for the food, service, and views of Central Park. Patrons can also visit the kitchen *(see p143)*.

8 Le Bernardin

Seafood doesn't come any better than at this quietly luxurious French restaurant lauded for revolutionizing the way fish is served in New York. Chef Eric Ripert seems to have no critics. Of course, perfection has its price and you'll pay dearly, but the meal will be memorable *(see p129)*.

Gramercy Tavern

9 Gramercy Tavern

Another Danny Meyer success, this rustic room is perhaps New York's most unpretentious fine dining. Chef Michael Anthony has maintained the high standard here. No reservations needed for the Tavern area *(see p115)*.

10 Four Seasons

This New York institution with landmark decor by Philip Johnson seems to go on forever, and it is always among the top-rated for Continental food. The Grill Room is still the prime place for power lunches, and the Pool Room is a perfect setting for special occasion dinners *(see p129)*.

Top 10 Cheap Eats

1 Lombardi's Pizza

On everybody's list of best-in-town for its thin-crust, coal-oven pizza *(see p89)*.

2 Salaam Bombay

A top-ranked Indian restaurant with bargain lunch and brunch. ⊗ *319 Greenwich St • Map Q3 • 212 226 9400*

3 Porchetta

Phenomenal slow-cooked pork sandwiches. ⊗ *110 East 7th St • Map M5 • 212 777 2151*

4 Nyonya

Good Malaysian fast food. ⊗ *194 Grand St • Map P4 • 212 334 3669*

5 Saigon Grill

Top Vietnamese fare in two convenient locations. ⊗ *91–3 University Place, Map P4 • 620 Amsterdam Ave at 90th St, Map E2 • 212 875 9072*

6 Flor de Mayo

A mix of Peruvian, Cuban, and Chinese cuisine; Peruvian-style rotisserie chicken is a specialty. ⊗ *2651 Broadway • Map D2 • 212 595 2525*

7 Republic

Lots of noodle dishes and noise at this Pan-Asian. ⊗ *37 Union Square West • Map M4 • 212 627 7168*

8 Il Bagatto

Even uptowners head for this East Village Italian with good food and prices. ⊗ *192 East 2nd St • Map N5 • 212 228 0977*

9 La Bonne Soupe

Midtown's best bet for onion soup, fondue, and other bistro specialties *(see p129)*.

10 Pomaire

This cheerful Chilean restaurant is the Theater District's best deal. ⊗ *371 West 46th St • Map J2 • 212 956 3056*

For more restaurants and a key to price categories **See pages 77, 83, 89, 95, 103, 109, 115, 121, 129, 137, 143, 149, and 157**

AROUND TOWN

NEW YORK'S TOP 10

Left **Federal Reserve Bank** Center **Federal Hall National Memorial** Right **Battery Park City**

Lower Manhattan

OLD AND NEW YORK *meet at the tip of the island. The city was born here under Dutch rule and became the nation's first capital after the Revolutionary War (1775–83). At the intersection of Broad and Wall streets are the Federal Hall National Memorial, marking the site where George Washington was sworn in as president in 1789, and the New York Stock Exchange, the financial giant founded in 1817, whose influence is felt worldwide. The 20th-century skyscraper era added drama to the skyline. The 2001 leveling of the World Trade Center towers damaged but certainly did not destroy lower Manhattan. The Tribute WTC Visitor Center offers visitors an opportunity to remember the events of September 2001 through photographic exhibitions, artifacts, personal stories, films, and a walking tour.*

Battery Park City esplanade

🔟 Sights

1. New York Stock Exchange
2. Trinity Church
3. Federal Hall National Memorial
4. U.S. Custom House
5. Battery Park City
6. World Financial Center
7. Museum of Jewish Heritage
8. Federal Reserve Bank
9. Charging Bull
10. Battery Park

Sign up for DK's email newsletter on traveldk.com

New York Stock Exchange

The present building opened in 1903, and behind its Neo-Classical facade is the financial heart of the U.S. The exchange has grown from a dealing with local businesses to a global enterprise. On the busiest days, billions of shares are traded for more than 8,500 listed issues, although the action is much calmer now that everything is computerized. On its most active days, between five and seven billion shares trade hands on the exchange.

Old stock ticker machine

◈ 20 Broad St at Wall St • Map R4 • www.nyse.com • Closed to public

Trinity Church

This much-admired Gothic building is the third church on this site for one of the U.S.'s oldest Anglican parishes, founded in 1697. The church has had notable additions since completion in 1846, including the sacristy, chapel, and Manhattan wing; the bronze doors were donated as a memorial to John Jacob Astor III. Trinity is known for its musical programs, with concerts each Monday and Thursday at 1pm and occasional Sunday concerts by the full choir. Trinity also oversees the programs at St. Paul's Chapel (see p80). ◈ Broadway at Wall St • Map Q4 • Open 7am–6pm daily (church), 7am–4pm (churchyard); tours 2pm daily and after 11:15am Sun service • Free

Federal Hall National Memorial

Although the bronze statue of George Washington on the steps marks the site where the nation's first president took his oath of office, the original building was replaced by this handsome, columned Greek Revival structure in 1842. It served as the U.S. Custom House and a branch of the Federal Reserve Bank before becoming a museum in 1955, with exhibits of the Constitution and the Bill of Rights. Ranger-led tours are offered several times daily. ◈ 26 Wall St at Nassau St • Map R4 • Open 9am–5pm Mon–Fri • www.nps.gov/feha • Free

Left **New York Stock Exchange** Right **Trinity Church**

4 U.S. Custom House

A renovation in 1994 installed gleaming galleries that circle the grand rotunda of this classic building. It is now the George Gustav Haye Center of the Smithsonian National Museum of the American Indian, with changing exhibits of Native American life, including costumes and fine crafts. Ceremonial objects, toys, and musical instruments in the research room can be examined and researched further on the computer installed there (see p47). ◈ 1 Bowling Green, between State & Whitehall Sts • Map R4 • Museum open 10am–5pm Fri–Wed, 10am–8pm Thu • Free

5 Battery Park City

Several prestigious architects were involved in this extension of Manhattan, a commercial and residential enclave built on a 92-acre landfill created with earth displaced by excavation for the World Trade Center. A 2-mile (3-km) esplanade offers grand Statue of Liberty views. Parts of the area were damaged by the Trade Center collapse but a brighter future is forecast. Enjoy the public works of art or visit the Skyscraper Museum. ◈ Off West St, Battery Place to Chambers St, bounded by the Hudson River • Map Q3–R3

George Washington in New York

A statue at the Federal Hall National Memorial (see p73) where George Washington was sworn into office is testament to the time the president spent in New York City. So too is the pew where he worshipped at St. Paul's Chapel (see p80), and the museum at Fraunces Tavern where he said farewell to his officers in 1789.

---

6 World Financial Center

Some of the top U.S. financial companies have headquarters in the World Financial Center, which was damaged in the September 11 attack. The center of the complex is the Winter Garden, with a 120-ft (37-m) atrium, palms and marble steps (see p45). ◈ Battery Park City at West St • Map Q3 • Open daily • www.worldfinancialcenter.com

7 Museum of Jewish Heritage

A memorable experience for all faiths is this chronicle of the 20th-century Jewish experience before, during, and after the Holocaust, told with over 2,000 photographs, hundreds of artifacts, and original documentary films. ◈ 36 Battery Place, Battery Park City • Map R3 • Open 10am–5:45pm Sun–Tue, Thu, 10am–8pm Wed, 10am–3pm Fri & Jewish holiday eves • Admission charge • www.mjhnyc.org

Left **Federal Hall interior** Center **Federal Reserve Bank** Right **U.S. Custom House**

Charging Bull

Federal Reserve Bank
8 Although gold is no longer transferred in payments between nations, much of the world's gold reserve remains stored in the five-story vault below this building. All bank notes from this branch have the letter B in the Federal Reserve seal. ◎ *33 Liberty St, between William & Nassau Sts • Map Q4 • Tours 9:30, 10:30, 11:30am, 1:30, 2:30pm, Mon–Fri • Free, reserve ahead (212 720 5000)*

Charging Bull
9 Sculptor Arturo di Modica unloaded this bronze statue in front of the New York Stock Exchange late at night in December 1989. It was removed, but was later given a "temporary" stomping ground on Broadway. The bull signifies the strength of the American people after the 1987 stockmarket crash. ◎ *Broadway at Bowling Green Park • Map R4*

Battery Park
10 Built largely on 18th- and 19th-century landfill, this park at New York harbor is usually visited for Castle Clinton, the 1811 fort and embarkation point for Ellis Island and Statue of Liberty ferries. This welcome swath of green is of interest for its many monuments and statues. ◎ *Broadway and Battery Place • Map R3 –4 • Open daily • Free*

A Day Exploring Lower Manhattan

Morning

Begin at **Battery Park** for a view of the waterfront, and look into **Castle Clinton** *(see p16)*, an 1807 fort, to see dioramas of a changing New York. Then visit the **Museum of the American Indian** at the **U.S. Custom House**. Cross to **Bowling Green**, the city's first park, then turn right on Whitehall, and left on Pearl Street for the **Fraunces Tavern Museum**, a restoration of the 1719 building where George Washington bade farewell to his troops.

Head up Broad Street to Wall Street to the **New York Stock Exchange**, where there is chaos on the trading floor. Close by is **Federal Hall** *(see p73)*, where the country's first president took his oath of office. Steak is a Financial District specialty, so stop for lunch at **Bobby Van's Steakhouse** *(see p77)*, on Broad Street and Exchange Place.

Afternoon

Continue uptown on Nassau Street (a continuation of Broad Street) to see **Chase Plaza** and its famous sculptures. At the end of the Plaza on Liberty Street is the ornate **Federal Reserve Bank** and then Louise Nevelson Square, featuring the artist's *Shadows and Flags*.

Go back on Liberty Street and take in the Tribute WTC Visitor Center at No. 120 (www.tributecenterwtc. org). End the day with dinner at the Ritz-Carlton's restaurant, **2 West @ Battery Park Place** *(see p77)*.

Left **The Immigrants** Center **The Four Continents** Right **Group of Four Trees**

Outdoor Sculptures

The Immigrants
1 Reflecting the diversity of newcomers to the U.S. from 1855–90, Luis Sanguino's 1973 work includes an African, a Jew, a family, a priest, and a worker.
◈ *Battery Park • Map R3*

Giovanni da Verrazzano
2 The first European to sail into New York Harbor in 1524 was honored by fellow Italians with this 1909 statue by Ettore Ximenes.
◈ *Battery Park • Map R3*

The Four Continents
3 Sculptor Daniel Chester French reflects 18th-century U.S. views – meditative Asia and exotic Africa to the sides, regal Europe and a dynamic U.S. in the center.
◈ *U.S. Custom House, 1 Bowling Green • Map R4*

Shadows and Flags
4 Louise Nevelson's 1977 figures enliven the traffic island they inhabit. The largest is rooted to the ground, others are on stilts.
◈ *Between Maiden Lane, William, & Liberty Sts • Map Q4*

Sunken Garden
5 The spray from a central fountain covers the floor of the recessed circular garden. Isamu Noguchi's 1960s work suggests rocks rising from the sea. ◈ *Chase Manhattan Bank Plaza, between Nassau & Liberty Sts • Map R4*

Group of Four Trees
6 Jean Dubuffet's 1972 mushroom-like sculptures hover over pedestrians nearby and bring a reason to smile in this busy area.
◈ *1 Chase Manhattan Plaza, between Nassau & Liberty Sts • Map R4*

George Washington
7 Designed and cast in 1883, a bronze Washington on a massive granite pedestal lifts his hand from the Bible after being sworn in.
◈ *Federal Hall National Memorial, 26 Wall St • Map R4*

Red Cube
8 Isamu Noguchi's 1967 red, 28-ft (9-m) high, metal cube balances on a corner defying gravity.
◈ *Marine Midland Plaza, 140 Broadway • Map Q4*

Double Check
9 The briefcase of J. Seward Johnson, Jr.'s 1982 seated bronze figure contains a stapler, calculator, and an occasional sandwich provided by a passerby. ◈ *Liberty Plaza, between Broadway & Church St • Map Q4*

Yu Yu Yang Sculpture
10 This untitled sculpture by artist Yu Yu Yang creates intriguing patterns with an L-shaped steel slab pierced by a circular disk. ◈ *Orient Overseas Building, 88 Pine St • Map R4*

Price Categories

For a three-course meal for one with a glass of house wine, and all unavoidable charges including tax.

$	under $25
$$	$25–$50
$$$	$50–$80
$$$$	over $80

Left **Fraunces Tavern** Right **Bobby Van's Steakhouse**

🔟 Restaurants

1 Battery Gardens
This restaurant offers a New American menu with Asian accents, and panoramic views of the harbor. ◈ *Battery Park, opposite 17 State St • Map R4 • 212 009 5508 • $$*

2 Gigino's at Wagner Park
Gigino's delivers excellent Italian food from the Amalfi coast and dazzling views from the sophisticated dining room and the waterfront terrace. ◈ *20 Battery Place, next to the Jewish Heritage Museum • Map R3 • 212 528 2220 • $$$*

3 Smorgas Chef
The Swedish meatballs are famous, and there's a range of lighter fare. Charming setting. ◈ *53 Stone St at William St • Map R4 • 212 422 3500 • $$$*

4 Bobby Van's Steakhouse
The excellent steaks, views of the Stock Exchange, and a setting within an 1898 Beaux Arts landmark are all highlights. ◈ *25 Broad St at Exchange Place • Map R4 • 212 344 8463 • $$$*

5 Fraunces Tavern
This unique 19th-century tavern is the former home of George Washington. The historic site features a restaurant as well as a museum. ◈ *54 Pearl St at Broad St • Map R4 • 212 968 1776 • $$*

6 Harry's Café
The historic India House is home to a downstairs café-steakhouse that draws Wall Street types in droves. ◈ *1 Hanover Square, between Pearl & Stone Sts • Map R4 • 212 785 9200 • $$–$$$$*

7 George's Café
For hearty American diner fare downtown. Burgers, wraps, sandwiches, and salads are on offer. ◈ *89 Greenwich St, at Rector St • Map R3 • 212 269 8026 • $*

8 Les Halles
Financial district meets Parisian bistro at this sister restaurant of the Park Avenue spot with celebrity chef Anthony Bourdain. ◈ *15 John St between Broadway and Nassau St • Map Q4 • 212 285 8585 • $$*

9 Joseph's
When Wall Streeters require Italian food, they often head for Joseph's. The menu includes linguine with clam sauce and fried calamari. ◈ *3 Hanover Square • Map R4 • 212 747 1300 • $$$*

10 2 West
A contemporary steakhouse with French influences. Located in the Ritz Carlton Hotel, with views across the Hudson and Battery Park. ◈ *2 West St, at Battery Park • Map R3 • 917 790 2525 • $$$*

Note: *Unless otherwise stated, all restaurants accept credit cards and serve vegetarian meals*

Left **Surrogate's Court** Center **Relief detail, the former AT&T Building** Right **Police Plaza**

Civic Center and South Street Seaport

SOME OF NEW YORK'S *finest architecture is found at its Civic Center, the headquarters for city government. Buildings here span the centuries, from the 18th-century St. Paul's Chapel to the pioneering 20th-century Woolworth Building. Nearby is the famous Brooklyn Bridge, and the old maritime center of the city, South Street Seaport, its piers and buildings now restored as a lively hub of cafés, restaurants, and museums.*

🔟 Sights

1. South Street Seaport
2. Brooklyn Bridge
3. Woolworth Building
4. Former AT&T Building
5. St. Paul's Chapel
6. City Hall
7. Municipal Building
8. New York County Courthouse
9. Surrogate's Court/ Hall of Records
10. Police Plaza

Woolworth Building

South Street Seaport

South Street Seaport

The cobbled streets, buildings, and piers that were the center of New York's 19th-century seafaring activity (known as "the street of sails") have been restored as a tourist center. There are shops, food stalls, restaurants, a museum with many seafaring exhibits, a fleet of tall ships for boarding, and plenty of outdoor entertainment.
⊗ Map Q4 • Museum open Jan–Mar: 10am–5pm Fri–Sun; Apr–Dec: 10am–6pm Tue–Sun • www.southstseaport.org

Brooklyn Bridge

When it was completed in 1883 linking Manhattan and Brooklyn, this was the largest suspension bridge in the world and the first to be built of steel. It took 600 workmen and 16 years to build, and claimed 20 lives, including that of the designing engineer, John A. Roebling. Now a symbol of New York, those who walk the 1-mile (1.8-km) span are rewarded with fabulous views of city towers seen through the artistic cablework.
⊗ (Manhattan side) Park Row near Municipal Building • Map Q4 • Free

Woolworth Building

Built in 1913, this has one of New York's great interiors; marble walls, bronze filigree, a mosaic ceiling, and stained glass combine to magical effect. Architect Cass Gilbert also had a sense of humor – sculptures include Five and Dime mogul Woolworth counting nickels and Gilbert himself cradling a model of the building. It set the standard for the skyscrapers that followed in the 1920s and 1930s (see p44).
⊗ Broadway, between Park Pl & Barclay St • Map Q4

Former AT&T Building

Built in 1922, this is a monument to excess but fun to see nevertheless. In its day, the façade was said to have more columns than any other building in the world; the vast lobby is a forest of marble pillars. Close by at 120 Broadway, the former Equitable Building, built in 1915, is of note for another excess: its immense bulk was responsible for the nation's first skyscraper zoning regulations. ⊗ 195 Broadway • Map Q4 • Open office hours • Free

Left **Brooklyn Bridge** Right **Bas-relief caricature of architect Cass Gilbert, the Woolworth Building**

5 St. Paul's Chapel

Manhattan's oldest church was built in 1766 as an "uptown" chapel for Trinity Church and took on added importance while Trinity was being rebuilt after the great fire of 1776. The chapel was modeled after London's St. Martin-in-the-Fields. One block from Ground Zero, the church has an interactive 9/11 exhibit. ◈ *209 Broadway, between Fulton & Vesey Sts • Map Q4 • Episcopal service 8am, 10am Sun, 12:30pm Wed • Concerts 1pm Mon, $2 donation • www.saintpaulschapel.org*

6 City Hall

The seat of city government since 1812, City Hall is considered one of the most beautiful early 19th-century public buildings in the U.S. The design, by architects Mangin and McComb, Jr., won a competition held in 1802. A statue of Justice crowns the structure. The rear of the building, facing north, was not clad in marble until 1954, since the architects never expected the city to develop further north. ◈ *Broadway and Park Row • Map Q4 • Open for pre-arranged tours only, call 212 788 2656 • Free*

City Hall

The "Boss Tweed" Courthouse

The first New York County Courthouse at 52 Chambers Street (completed in 1881) was built by Boss Tweed *(see p48)*, a corrupt politician who spent fortunes on this grand marble monument to himself. The elaborate interior and octagonal rotunda are being restored, though its future use is uncertain.

7 Municipal Building

This building dominating the Civic Center area, straddling Chambers Street, was the first "skyscraper" by McKim, Mead, and White, a 25-story structure completed in 1914. The top is a veritable wedding-cake fantasy of towers and spires topped by Adulph Wienman's famous statue, Civic Fame. The intricate terracotta vaulting above the street is modeled on the entrance of the Palazzo Farnese in Rome, and the subway entrance at the south end, an arcaded plaza, is a dramatic vault of Guastavino tiles. ◈ *1 Center St at Chambers St • Map Q4*

Left **Interior, St. Paul's Chapel** Right **Municipal Building**

New York County Courthouse

8 New York County Courthouse

Ascend the wide staircase of the 1926 New York County Courthouse (adjacent to the 31-story, pyramid-topped U.S. Courthouse dating from 1933), and enter to admire the marble-columned rotunda with Tiffany lighting fixtures. Note, too, the ceiling murals depicting Law and Justice. The hexagonal building has a courtroom in each of its six wings. ⌾ 60 Center St • Map P4 • Open 9am–5pm Mon–Fri; reserve tours in advance (646 386 3153) • Free

9 Surrogate's Court/ Hall of Records

With an interior inspired by the Paris Opéra, this 1907 Beaux Arts beauty boasts a magnificent central hall with marble stairways and ceiling mosaics. The façade features statues representing justice, the seasons, commerce, and notable New Yorkers, and figures depicting the stages of life. ⌾ 31 Chambers St • Map Q4 • Lobby open 9am–5pm Mon–Fri • Free

10 Police Plaza

Constructed in 1973, the city's police headquarters can be found on a spacious pedestrian plaza, a welcome area in a district with very few public spaces. The Tony Rosenthal abstract sculpture, Five in One, made of five sloping interlocked discs, symbolizes the city's five boroughs. ⌾ Park Row at Pearl St • Map Q4

A Walk Through Civic Center and South Street Seaport

Morning

🕐 Most subway routes lead to City Hall. When you come up to street level, walk down Broadway to see the lobbies of the **Woolworth** *(see p79)* and the former **AT&T Building** *(see p79)* and the Georgian interior of **St. Paul's Chapel**.

Return via Park Row, once known as Newspaper Row because it was lined with their offices. Printing House Square has a statue of Benjamin Franklin with his Pennsylvania Gazette. West of the Row lies small but beautiful City Hall Park, where the Declaration of Independence was read to George Washington's troops in July 1776. The park has a granite time wheel telling the city's history.

A walk along Center and Chambers streets takes you past the ornate **Municipal Building**.

Afternoon

At midday, head east for a seafood lunch at the **Bridge Café** *(see p83)*, housed in a 1794 wood-framed building. From here the East River is a short stroll away, offering excellent views of lower Manhattan.

Spend the afternoon at **South Street Seaport** *(see p79)*, visiting the museum and maritime crafts center, perhaps taking a cruise on one of the ships. Have dinner on Pier 17, enjoying Caribbean fare at the lively **Cabana** *(see p83)*, or New American fare at **Harbour Lights** *(see p83)*.

Left **Schermerhorn Row** Center **South Street Seaport Museum** Right **Pier 17**

TOP 10 Maritime Sights

1 South Street Seaport Museum
The city's maritime heritage is celebrated in art, photographs, workshops, and ships. ◈ *12 Fulton St • Map Q4 • Open Apr–Oct: 10am–6pm Tue–Sun; Nov–Mar: 10am–5pm Fri–Mon • Admission charge*

2 Schermerhorn Row
Federal-style houses built by Peter Schermerhorn in 1811–12 now house a permanent exhibition space, as well as shops and restaurants. ◈ *Fulton St, between Front & South Sts • Map Q4 • Free*

3 Historic Ships
Seven classic ships, several open for boarding, include the 1885 square-rigger *Wavertree*, and the landmark, four-masted *Peking*, built in 1911. ◈ *Piers 15, 16, South Street Seaport • Map Q4 • Open 10am–6pm daily • Admission charge*

4 Bowne & Company
Recreation of a 19th-century print shop with working printing presses. ◈ *211 Water St • Map Q4 • Open 10am–5pm Wed–Sun • Free*

5 Maritime Crafts Center
Marvel at the skill of woodcarvers at work, creating model ships and figureheads. ◈ *Pier 15, South Street Seaport • Map Q4 • Open 10am–6pm daily • Free*

6 Pilot House
The South Street Seaport ticket and information center is housed in this pilot house, taken from a steam tugboat built in 1923 by the New York Central Railroad. ◈ *South Street Seaport • Map Q4 • Open 10am–6pm daily*

7 Pier 17
A pier with three floors of restaurants, food stands and sweeping views of the East River and Brooklyn Bridge. ◈ *South Street Seaport • Map Q5*

8 Harbor Excursions
The 1885 schooner *Pioneer* offers 90-minute family sails and two-hour cruises in the afternoon and evening. ◈ *Pier 16, South Street Seaport • Map Q4 • Admission charge*

9 Titanic Memorial
This lighthouse was built to commemorate the sinking of the Titanic – the largest steamship ever made – in 1912. ◈ *Fulton St at Water St • Map Q4*

10 Seaman's Church Institute
Established in 1834, the institute is in a stunnning 1991 building with a gallery plus water views. ◈ *241 Water St, between Beekman St & Peck Slip • Map Q4 • Free*

For more historic buildings in New York **See pp46–7**

Price Categories

For a three-course meal for one with a glass of house wine, and all unavoidable charges including tax.

$	under $25
$$	$25–$50
$$$	$50–$80
$$$$	over $80

Left **Bridge Café** Right **Typical pizza menu**

🔟 Restaurants

1 Bridge Café
Opened in 1791, this is one of the oldest establishments in the city. Inside the quaint building, there are checked tablecloths, and a surprisingly sophisticated American menu. ◈ *279 Water St at Dover St • Map Q4 • 212 227 3344 • $$*

2 Harbour Lights
Incomparable views of the harbor and bridge account for the crowds, although the seafood-oriented fare is only average. The sirloin steak is a good alternative to fish. ◈ *Pier 17, 3rd level, South Street Seaport • Map Q5 • 212 227 2800 • $$$*

3 Sequoia
Nautical decor, a seafood menu, and breathtaking harbor views make this informal American restaurant a top choice. ◈ *Pier 17, South Street Seaport • Map Q5 • 212 732 9090 • $$*

4 Acqua
New American-influenced Italian food is served here, prepared with organic ingredients. A cozy ambience is provided by the vaulted ceilings and warm lighting. ◈ *21–23 Peck Slip • Map Q4 • 212 349 4433 • $$*

5 Cabana at the Seaport
A Latin flavor enlivens this Seaport favorite, serving a Cuban/Caribbean menu. Expect pitchers of sangria and spontaneous samba. ◈ *Pier 17, 3rd level, South Street Seaport • Map Q5 • 212 406 1155 • $$*

6 Heartland Brewery
Pub grub, with a menu that is strong on seafood. But the real attraction is the extensive selection of seasonal beers brewed at Heartland's own microbrewery. ◈ *93 South St • Map Q4 • 646 572 2337 • $*

7 Cosi Sandwich Bar
Pita bread warm from the oven laden with your choice of fillings, including ham, chicken, or roasted peppers. Part of a chain. ◈ *54 Pine St at William St • Map Q4 • 212 809 2674 • $*

8 Il Porto
Reviews are mixed, but pizza and pasta dishes and a good Sunday brunch menu make this restaurant a convenient choice around South Street seaport. ◈ *11 Fulton St, between Front & South Sts • Map Q4 • 212 791 2181 • $$*

9 Red
Wall Street suits and tourists alike can be found enjoying the famous blood orange margaritas at this colorful Tex-Mex spot. ◈ *19 Fulton St, between Front & Water Sts • Map Q4 • 212 571 5900 • $*

10 Pacific Grill
A Pan-Asian restaurant serving mostly seafood dishes, including tempura and coconut shrimp. The outside seating area boasts wonderful harbor views of Brooklyn Bridge. ◈ *Pier 17, South Street Seaport • Map Q5 • 212 964 0707 • $$*

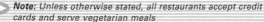

Note: Unless otherwise stated, all restaurants accept credit cards and serve vegetarian meals

Left **Police Headquarters Building** Center **Church of the Transfiguration** Right **Food shopping**

Chinatown and Little Italy

THESE TWO ETHNIC ENCLAVES *are among the most colorful parts of the city. Each was settled by early immigrants, who preserved their own language, customs, and food in the midst of the new and foreign land. Little Italy has dwindled to a few blocks, but it is still an atmospheric center of authentic Italian food and shops, especially on a warm night, when cafés set out sidewalk tables and the songs of Napoli fill the air. Chinatown, however, continues to grow. Up to 150,000 Chinese live there, in crowded quarters. The shops and sidewalk markets overflow with exotic foods and herbs, as well as gifts ranging from backscratchers to fine antiques; and it has been estimated that Chinatown contains an astounding 200 restaurants.*

Street scene, Chinatown

🔟 Sights

1. Mulberry Street
2. Police Headquarters Building
3. Museum of Chinese in America
4. Good Fortune Gifts
5. Mott Street Shopping
6. Pearl River Chinese Products Emporium
7. Eastern States Buddhist Temple
8. Church of the Transfiguration
9. Columbus Park
10. Bloody Angle

Sign up for DK's email newsletter on traveldk.com

Il Palazzo, Little Italy *(see p89)*

fits a wedge-shaped lot. Empty for more than a decade after the department relocated in 1973, the building has since been converted into luxury cooperatives, the Police Building Apartments.
🚫 *240 Centre St • Map P4*
• Closed to public

1 Mulberry Street

There are many trendy shops on Mulberry Street from Houston down to Spring Street and though Chinatown is overrunning much of Little Italy, the block between Broome and Canal remains strictly Italian. It is filled with restaurants, coffee shops with tempting Italian pastries, and stores selling pasta implements, statues of saints, and T-shirts saying "Kiss Me, I'm Italian." The Feast of San Gennaro packs the street each September *(see p62)*. 🚫 *Mulberry St, between Broome & Canal Sts • Map P4*

2 Police Headquarters Building

After the boroughs merged into Greater New York in 1898, the city's police department expanded rapidly. This 1905 headquarters near Little Italy was the result – a monumental, columned Baroque structure fit for "New York's Finest," with an ornate dome tall enough to be seen from City Hall. The strange shape of the building

3 Museum of Chinese in America

This fascinating museum, devoted to the Chinese experience in the West, features an exhibit called "Where is Home?," with personal stories, photographs, and poetry culled from the community. Among the topics explored are women's roles, religion, and the "bachelor society." Changing exhibits range from art to the experience of gay Chinese. Books, area guides, and free flyers on cultural events are available. 🚫 *211–215 Centre St • Map P4 • Open 11am–5pm Mon, Fri, 11am–9pm Thu, 10am–5pm Sat & Sun • Admission charge, free Fri • www.mocanyc.org*

4 Good Fortune Gifts

Originally known as Quong Yeun Shing & Company, this is the oldest store in Chinatown, established in 1891. The store was a social hub for Chinese men, who were not allowed to bring their wives to the U.S. under old immigration laws. 🚫 *32 Mott St • Map P4*

Left **Detail, Police Headquarters Building** Right **Museum of Chinese in America**

Mott Street Shopping

Clustered on this block are shops with a wonderful selection of Oriental goods. Iki Iki Gift Shop is a paradise for fans of Yu-Gi-Oh! and Hello Kitty. Lamps made from attractive Oriental vases are the specialty of Pearl of the Orient Gallery, while New Age Designer makes clothing to order in your choice of jewel-hued silks. Serious antiques collectors should head to the Sinotique Gallery. ⊗ *Iki Iki Gift Shop: 2 Mott St • Sinotique Gallery: 19A Mott St • Pearl of the Orient Gallery: 36 Mott St • New Age Designer: 38 Mott St • Map P4 for all*

Pearl River Chinese Products Emporium

The largest department store in Chinatown has a fascinating potpourri of goods for sale. There are Chinese musical instruments, paper lanterns, kites, dried herbs, embroidered silk tops, dresses and pajamas with mandarin collars, purses, dolls, pillows, and sandalwood and jasmine soaps. ⊗ *477 Broadway • Map P4*

Eastern States Buddhist Temple

Step into the incense-scented interior, where offerings of fresh fruit are piled high, and more than 100 gold Buddhas gleam in the candlelight. The temple takes advantage of Chinatown's

Chinatown's Early Days

The 1882 Chinese Exclusion Act prevented Chinese workers from bringing their families to New York, so the original Chinatown, bounded by Pell, Doyers, and Mott streets, was mostly male and dominated by *tongs*. These were sometimes social clubs and sometimes rival criminal fraternities, giving the old locale its dangerous reputation.

tourist traffic by offering $1 fortunes for sale near the front. ⊗ *64B Mott St • Map P4 • Open 8am–6pm daily • Free*

Church of the Transfiguration

Built by the English Lutheran Church in 1801 and sold to the Roman Catholic Church of the Transfiguration in 1853, this Georgian-style stone church with Gothic windows is typical of the influence of successive influxes of immigrants in New York. The church has changed with the nationalities of the community it serves, first Irish, then Italian, and now Chinese. As the focal point of today's Chinese Roman Catholic community, it offers classes and services to help newcomers and holds services in Cantonese and Mandarin. ⊗ *29 Mott St • Map P4 • Open 7:30–9am & 11:30am–1pm daily, 5:30–7pm Sat, 8am–2pm Sun • Free*

Left **Pearl River Chinese Products Emporium** Right **Eastern States Buddhist Temple**

Bloody Angle, Chinatown

Columbus Park

Chinatown's only park was created in the late 1890s as a result of the campaigning of newspaper reporter Jacob Riis and other social reformers. It filled a stretch of the city that at the time was New York's worst slum, where Riis reported a stabbing or shooting at least once a week. Though it features more concrete than greenery, the park is popular today, filled with Chinese kids at play, *mah jong* players, and people practicing *tai chi* and martial arts. On the weekends, Chinese fortune-tellers sometimes set up shop in the park. ◈ *Bayard and Mulberry Sts • Map P4*

Bloody Angle

The name for this sharp curve on Doyers Street was coined by a newspaper because this was the site of so many gangland ambushes during the 1920s. It was a period when the Hip Sing and On Leong *tongs*, groups similar to criminal gangs, were fighting for control of the opium trade and gambling rackets in Chinatown. The *tong* wars continued off and on until at least the 1940s, and their rivalries continue in the present-day youth gangs. ◈ *Doyers St near Pell St • Map P4*

A Stroll Around Chinatown and Little Italy

Morning

Take the No. 6 train to Spring Street, walk past Lafayette, and turn down Mulberry Street *(see p85)* for a stroll through Little Italy. Don't miss the old-fashioned food shops on Grand Street, such as cheese specialist Alleva Dairy (188 Mulberry Street at Grand) and Piemonte Co. (190 Grand Street), where two dozen shapes and varieties of pasta can be bought. At 206 Grand is DiPalo Dairy, where you can watch fresh mozzarella being made. Take a break at a classic Italian café, like Caffè Roma, 385 Broome Street, or Ferrara's, 195–201 Grand Street.

Take Grand Street west to Centre Street, then turn left and you'll find an introduction to what's ahead, the **Museum of Chinese in America** *(see p85)*. Walk east back to Mott Street, the center of Chinatown. Enjoy a dim sum lunch at **Jing Fong** or the **Golden Unicorn** *(see p89)*.

Afternoon

Remaining on Mott Street, spend some time browsing the many shops, exotic food stores, markets, and galleries that line the street. Step into Teariffic, 51 Mott Street, to sample a fad imported from Taiwan: tall glasses of flavored teas served with "pearls" of tapioca in the bottom and called "bubble tea".

End the afternoon with a visit to the golden Buddhas of the **Eastern States Buddhist Temple** and have your fortune read.

Left **Street market** Center **Ten Ren Tea & Ginseng Company** Right **Chinatown Ice Cream Factory**

Chinatown Food Shops

Street Markets
Canal Street and Hester Street are among the many blocks crowded with outdoor stands selling exotic Chinese vegetables, fruits, and dried foods. ✆ *Chinatown, including Canal & Hester Sts • Map P4*

Mark's Wine & Spirits
Authentic Chinese alcohol, such as *mei kuei lu chiew* with its rosewater scent, and Shaohsing wine, can be purchased here. ✆ *53 Mott St at Bayard St • Map P4*

Kamwo Herb and Tea
One of the better-known shops offering Chinese herbs said to cure anything from arthritis to impotence. Ginseng is available in teas or supplement form. ✆ *209–11 Grand St • Map P4*

Fay Da Bakery
Sample a delicious soft bun filled with roasted pork or beef for less than $1, then try almond cookies, red bean cakes, custard tarts, or cream buns for dessert. ✆ *83 Mott St at Canal St • Map P4*

Ten Ren Tea & Ginseng Company
An array of golden canisters holds many varieties of Chinese teas; knowledgeable clerks will explain the properties of each and how to brew them properly. ✆ *75 Mott St • Map P4*

Kam Man Food Products
One of the largest food emporiums in Chinatown stocks tonics, teas, jellies, ginseng, vegetables of every shape, and row upon row of sauces. ✆ *200 Canal St • Map P4*

Chinatown Food Market
This cramped store offers all manner of dried seafood, imported goods, noodles, watermelon seeds and counterfeit toothpaste. Try one of the inexpensive, wrapped hard candies. ✆ *225 Grand St at Elizabeth St • Map P4*

Deluxe Food Market
The Chinese come here for prepared foods, marinated meats and the fully stocked meat and fish counters. ✆ *79 Elizabeth St • Map P4*

May May Gourmet Chinese Bakery
On one of the streets of old Chinatown is this cheerful, modern shop best known for dim sum, to be enjoyed on the spot or to go. ✆ *35 Pell St • Map P4*

Chinatown Ice Cream Factory
Ginger, lychee, pumpkin, mango, and red bean are among the flavors that can be sampled at this popular dessert stop, a favorite with young visitors. ✆ *65 Bayard St at Mott St • Map P4*

For more on New York shopping See p165

Price Categories

For a three-course
meal for one with a   **$** under $25
glass of house wine,   **$$** $25–$50
and all unavoidable   **$$$** $50–$80
charges including tax. **$$$$** over $80

Left **Great N.Y. Noodletown** Right **Golden Unicorn**

🔟 Restaurants

Great N.Y. Noodletown
The decor is simple and so
is the menu, with wonderful
soups, noodles, meat dishes,
and creatively prepared seafood.
🛇 *28½ Bowery St at Bayard St • Map P4
• 212 349 0923 • No credit cards • $*

Joe's Shanghai
The Chinatown branch of
the Flushing (Queens) restaurant
famous for its soup dumplings
(look for steamed buns on the
menu) 🛇 *9 Pell St at Bowery • Map P4
• 212 233 8888 • No credit cards • $$*

Grand Sichuan
For the spicy flavors of
China's Sichuan province, this is
a no-frills bargain storefront with
authentic specialties. 🛇 *125 Canal St
at Broadway • Map P4 • 212 625 9212 •
No credit cards • $$*

Fuleen Seafood
Fresh, well-prepared seafood
dishes and bargain prices at this
Chinatown favorite. Dungeness
crab and lobster appetizers (four
ways) are a steal. 🛇 *11 Division St, off
Bowery • Map P4 • 212 941 6888 • $*

Golden Unicorn
Dim sum is the star
but all the dishes are
well prepared in this
crowded, third-floor
restaurant. Go in a large
group to enable more
sampling. 🛇 *18 East
Broadway at Catherine St •
Map P4 • 212 941 0911 • $*

Jing Fong
This glittery room is packed
daily for the vast selection of dim
sum. Just point at your choices
as the carts roll by. 🛇 *20 Elizabeth
St, between Bayard & Canal Sts • Map P4
• 212 964 5256 • $$*

New Green Bo
This busy Shanghai spot is
famous for its dumplings. Service
is perfunctory, but the lines move
quickly. 🛇 *66 Bayard St, between
Mott & Elizabeth Sts • Map P4 • 212
625 2359 • No credit cards • $*

Lombardi's
Pizza doesn't come much
better than at this unpretentious
old-timer that turns out delectable
thin-crust pies. 🛇 *32 Spring St,
between Mott & Mulberry Sts • Map P4
• 212 941 7994 • No credit cards • $*

Da Nico
A rustic setting and a wonder-
ful courtyard garden make this
family-run restaurant with a dozen
varieties of pizza a favorite.
🛇 *164 Mulberry St, between Broome &
Grand Sts • Map P4 • 212 343 1212 • $$*

Il Palazzo
One of the better
choices on Mulberry
Street; cozy, candlelit,
non-touristy. The menu
includes all the Italian
favorites, and the
garden is a summer
delight. 🛇 *151 Mulberry St
at Grand St • Map P4 • 212
343 7000 • $$*

Note: *Unless otherwise stated, all restaurants accept credit
cards and serve vegetarian meals*

Left **Orchard Street** Right **Street Scene**

Lower East Side and East Village

THE LOWER EAST SIDE IS ALIVE *with memories, a neighbor-hood still seeming to echo the calls of immigrants crowded into tenements, peddlers hawking wares from pushcarts, and children playing in the streets, the only open spaces to be found. Early churches became synagogues for the Jews who came in record numbers between 1880 and 1920. Some remain, but in recent decades, Latinos and Chinese have moved in, adding to the area's rich history. Meanwhile, Orchard Street* tempts with bargains, and a hip, young generation is rediscovering the old neighborhood. Nearby, the East Village has its own layers of history, an early Dutch enclave that changed from German to Jewish before becoming a 1960s haven for hippies and the place where punk rock was born. A Ukrainian community has remained through most of these changes, including recent gentrification.

Painting, Ukrainian Museum

🔟 Sights

1. Lower East Side Tenement Museum
2. Orchard Street
3. New Museum of Contemporary Art
4. Eldridge Street Synagogue
5. Beth Hamedrash Hagadol Synagogue
6. Guss' Pickles
7. St Mark's Place
8. St Mark's-in-the-Bowery Church
9. Renwick Triangle
10. Ukrainian Museum

Street vendor's pushcart, Tenement Museum

Lower East Side Tenement Museum

Guided tours inside a tenement building give an insight into the carefully researched lives of one of three families who lived here; a German-Jewish clan in 1874, an orthodox Jewish family from Lithuania in 1918, or a Sicilian Catholic family during the Depression in the 1930s.
⊗ 108 Orchard St • Map N5 • 212 431 0233 • Tours: run regularly 10:30am–5pm daily (call ahead) • www.tenement.org • Admission charge

Orchard Street

Orchard Street became a street of shops in 1940, when Mayor Fiorello La Guardia outlawed pushcarts in the city. Many merchants still put some of their wares on the sidewalk on Sundays and lure customers with 20 to 30 percent off brand names. The Lower East Side Visitor Center offers a free tour each Sunday between April and December.

⊗ Lower East Side Visitor Center, 261 Broome St • Map P4 • 212 226 9010 • Open 10am–4pm daily • www.lower-eastsideny.com

New Museum of Contemporary Art

Since its founding in 1977, this provocative museum has mounted shows featuring experimental work that other museums often overlook, particularly new multi-media forms, which sometimes extend into intriguing window displays. The museum opened in a new, cutting-edge building designed by Tokyo-based architects Sejima and Nishizawa in late 2007. It features a bookstore, theater, learning center, and café. ⊗ 235 Bowery St • Map N4 • Open noon–9pm Thu–Fri, noon–6pm Wed, Sat–Sun • Admission charge • www.newmuseum.org

Eldridge Street Synagogue

A National Historic Landmark. This 1887 Moorish-style synagogue was the first house of worship built in the U.S. by Jewish immigrants from Eastern Europe, the homeland of 80 percent of American Jews. As many as 1,000 people attended services here at the turn of the 20th century. As congregants left

Left **Art for sale, Orchard Street** Right **Stained glass, Eldridge Street Synagogue**

the neighborhood, attendance waned, and the temple closed in the 1950s. A 20-year restoration initiative was completed in 2007 and the synagogue has become a vibrant cultural center. ✎ *12 Eldridge St* • *Map P5* • *Open 10am–5pm Sun–Thu* • *Tours: half-hourly until 3pm* • *Admission charge* • *www.eldridgestreet.org*

5 Beth Hamedrash Hagadol Synagogue

Artists can often be seen sketching this small, picturesque building. It was constructed in 1850 as the Norfolk Street Baptist Church, but as the membership changed, the membership moved uptown, and in 1885 the structure was converted to a synagogue by America's oldest Russian, Orthodox Jewish congregation. Gothic woodwork and the iron fence from the original church remain. ✎ *60–64 Norfolk St* • *Map P5* • *Open by appointment* • *Free*

6 Guss' Pickles

One of the survivors from the old days of the Jewish Lower East Side, and a fixture for more than 80 years, Guss' was even featured in the movie *Crossing Delancey*. Fans stand in line on weekends for their fix from the barrels on the sidewalk filled with pickles – sour and half-sour. Guss' also does a thriving

The Changing Scene

Proving that change is the rule in New York, the Lower East Side has emerged as the newest trendy area for clubs, restaurants, and hip boutiques. Some residents are even moving into the tenement buildings their great-grandparents fought to escape from. Ludlow Street is one of the best streets to get a feel for the current scene.

business by mail, shipping all over the U.S. ✎ *85–87 Orchard St* • *Map P5* • *Open 9:30am–6pm Sun–Thu, 9:30am–5pm Fri*

7 St. Mark's Place

Once the heart of hippie-dom, this block still has a counterculture feel and is headquarters for the East Village youth scene. Sidewalks are crowded until late into the night with patrons of funky, punky bars and shops selling music, books, T-shirts, vintage clothing, beads, posters, and black leather everything. The place to get pierced or tattooed. ✎ *East 8th St, between 3rd Ave & Ave A* • *Map M4*

8 St. Mark's-in-the-Bowery Church

The second-oldest church in New York stands on land where Peter Stuyvesant, governor of Dutch New York in the 1600s, had his

Left **Beth Hamedrash Hagadol Synagogue** Center **Guss' Pickles** Right **Renwick Triangle**

Sign up for DK's email newsletter on traveldk.com

St. Mark's-in-the-Bowery Church

private chapel. Stuyvesant is also buried here. In the 1960s it served as one of the city's most politically committed congregations and continues to live on the avant-garde edge. ◈ *131 East 10th St • Map M4 • Open 8:30am–4pm Mon–Fri; service 10.30am Sun • Free*

9 Renwick Triangle
This handsome group of townhouses was created in 1861 by James Renwick, Jr., a prominent architect of the day. The houses are on land that was once Peter Stuyvesant's farm, developed by his descendants as stylish residences. ◈ *114–128 East 10th St, 23–25 Stuyvesant St, between 2nd & 3rd Aves • Map M4*

10 Ukrainian Museum
The museum showcases a beguiling collection of Ukrainian costumes, lavishly embroidered peasant blouses, colorful sashes, fancy sheepskin and fur vests, and wedding wreaths of yarn and ribbons. There are also ceramics, jewelry, and the intricately designed Ukrainian Easter eggs known as *pysanky*. ◈ *222 East 6th St, between 2nd and 3rd Aves • Map N4 • Open 11:30am–5pm Wed–Sun • www.ukranianmuseum.org • Admission charge*

East Side Exploration

Morning

🕐 From the Delancey Street subway walk south to Grand Street and Kossar's Bialys Bakery, 367 Grand, famous for chewy, onion-flavored rolls, or the Doughnut Plant, 379 Grand, where the oversize cakes achieve gourmet status. Walk east for two historic houses of worship, the **Beth Hamedrash Hagadol Synagogue** *(see p92)* and the Bialystoker Synagogue.

Return along East Broadway, passing the Henry Street Settlement at No. 281, in three restored Federal buildings. The gallery at the Educational Alliance, No. 197, has good art and photography exhibits. Walk to Orchard for **Guss' Pickles**, and pick up a bargain at the shops here. If you're hot, try one of the 50 flavors of ice cream at Il Laboratorio del Gelato at 95 Orchard, or continue to East Houston Street, and have lunch at **Katz's Delicatessen** *(p95)*, a New York institution.

Afternoon

🕐 After lunch, walk uptown on 2nd Avenue. Turn left on East 6th to visit the **Ukrainian Museum**, a small and hidden gem of costumes and culture. Walk to **St. Mark's Place**, browsing through the funky shops and bars on your way, and then walk east again on Stuyvesant Street, admiring the landmark townhouses of the **Renwick Triangle**. Lastly, stop at **St. Mark's-in-the-Bowery Church**, one of the oldest in the city, where you can pay your respects to Peter Stuyvesant's grave.

Left **Miss Lonelyhearts** Right **Zarin Fabric Home Furnishings**

Bargain Stores and Boutiques

Zarin Fabric Home Furnishings
Since 1936 this mammoth showroom and workshop has provided fabrics and upholstery to the public at wholesale prices. ✪ 314 Grand St • Map P5

Frock
Stylish women on a budget will find designer fashion including Dior and Valentino at this vintage boutique. ✪ 170 Elizabeth St • Map N4

The Dressing Room
More than just a boutique. It showcases the work of young designers, offers a clothing exchange, and also has a cocktail bar with live DJ sets. ✪ 75A Orchard St • Map P5

Hairy Mary's
As you may tell from the name, Hairy Mary's is a fun place. The shop carries both vintage and "reconstructed" outfits, coats and accessories, ranging from punk back to more modest eras. ✪ 149 Orchard St • Map N5

Coat of Arms
This unusual shop offers vintage hip-hop-styled pieces alongside contemporary streetwear. ✪ 43 Clinton St • Map N5

Giselle
Four floors of designer clothing by European names

such as Valentino, Escada, and Ungaro, promising 20 to 30 per cent off retail. ✪ 143 Orchard St • Map N5

A.W. Kaufman
Fine quality European lingerie is sold at an excellent price with personalised service. This third-generation store, established in 1924, offers a range of underwear for men and women, and some stunning bridal sets. ✪ 73 Orchard St • Map P5

Jodamo
An extensive range of European designer menswear can be found in this large store, including Versace, Valentino, and Missoni, as well as leather goods and shoes. ✪ 321 Grand St • Map N5

Altman Luggage
From computer cases to carry-ons, brand names like Lark, TravelPro, and American Tourister are sold for less at this well-stocked emporium. ✪ 135 Orchard St • Map N5

Miss Lonelyhearts
Inspired by vintage romance, this boutique is a fashionable playroom of clothing, accessories, and luxury handbags by local designer Jenny Yuen. ✪ 250 Broom St • Map N5

For more New York shops See pp64–5

Price Categories

For a three-course meal for one with a glass of house wine, and all unavoidable charges including tax.

$	under $25
$$	$25–$50
$$$	$50–$80
$$$$	over $80

Katz's Delicatessen

TOP 10 Restaurants

1 Schiller's Liquor Bar
An eclectic menu is served at this French-inspired restaurant, the latest by Keith McNally. Arrive early for dinner if you don't want to wait. Brunch is also very good. ◈ 131 Rivington St at Norfolk St • Map N5 • 212 260 4555 • $$

2 Katz's Delicatessen
Savor a pastrami sandwich on rye here, and you'll understand why New York delis are famous. ◈ 205 East Houston St at Ludlow St • Map N5 • 212 254 2246 • $

3 Sammy's Roumanian
It looks like a Jewish wedding every night. Chopped liver and shmaltz will freak your cholesterol level, but you'll enjoy every minute. ◈ 157 Chrystie St • Map N4 • 212 673 0330 • No vegetarian options • $$

4 WD-50
A hip, foodie café famous for the exciting creations of chef Wylie Dufresne. Be prepared to wait. ◈ 50 Clinton St, between Rivington & Stanton Sts • Map N5 • 212 477 2900 • $$$

5 Le Père Pinard
A fine place to relax with wine and French bistro fare in the heated garden out back. ◈ 175 Ludlow St, between Houston & Stanton Sts • Map N5 • 212 777 4917 • $$

6 Veselka
A funky Ukrainian diner serving borscht, blintzes, and pierogis for a pittance. Tables at the back are quieter. ◈ 144 2nd Ave at 9th St • Map M4 • 212 228 9682 • $

7 The Dumpling Man
The handmade pork, chicken, and vegetarian dumplings are a big draw. Save room for the shaved ice dessert. ◈ 100 St Mark's Place • Map M4 • 212 505 2121 • $

8 La Palapa
Authentic Mexican regional cuisine and great margaritas in a beautifully decorated dining room. ◈ 77 St Mark's Place, between 1st & 2nd Aves • Map M4 • 212 777 2537 • $$

9 Prune
Updated homestyle American is the game here, which translates to dishes like lamb chop with leeks and braised potatoes. Reliably crowded; brunch is also a hit. ◈ 54 East 1st St, between 1st & 2nd Aves • Map N4 • 212 677 6221 • $$$

10 Momofuku Ssäm Bar
This popular spot serves American food that usually veers through Korea or Asia on its way to the plate. Offal often figures in. Don't be scared, though – it's all delicious. ◈ 207 2nd Ave at 13th St • Map M4 • 212 254 3500 • $$$

Note: Unless otherwise stated, all restaurants accept credit cards and serve vegetarian meals

Left **Mural, Greene Street** Right **Haughwout Building**

SoHo and TriBeCa

THE AREA NAMED for its shape (TRIangle BElow CAnal) long consisted mostly of abandoned warehouses. Then Robert De Niro set up his Tribeca Film Center in 1988, stylish restaurants began to open, and the area started to draw celebrity residents. Now TriBeCa is one of New York's hottest neighborhoods, the center of the city's movie industry with the TriBeCa Film Festival and plenty of nightlife. SoHo (South of Houston) has also come full circle. The empty loft spaces first drew artists, then galleries, then crowds of browsers and the restaurants to serve them. The new chic image quickly drove up rents and drove out many galleries. Some remain, and the streets are lined with designer clothing and home furnishing boutiques, maintaining SoHo's lure as the city's favorite Sunday brunch-and-browse neighborhood. Both areas boast the cast-iron architecture that is a New York specialty.

Gallery, White Street

Sights

1 Greene Street
2 Children's Museum of the Arts
3 Prada
4 New York City Fire Museum
5 Haughwout Building
6 "Little" Singer Building
7 Canal Street
8 Harrison Street
9 White Street
10 TriBeCa Film Center

Preceding pages **New York skyline at night**

Greene Street

1 Cast-iron architecture flourished in New York in the late 19th century, as a way to produce decorative elements such as columns and arches and create impressive buildings inexpensively. Greene Street, between Canal and Grand streets, and between Broome and Spring streets, has 50 of these beauties, rows of columned façades creating a striking streetscape. ◉ *Map N4*

Children's Museum of the Arts

2 Founded in 1988, the CMA's mission is to enable children aged one to 12 to reach their full potential in the visual and performing arts. Children can work with paint, glue, paper, and recycled materials to paint, sculpt, build, and imagine.

They can also play in the ball pond and art house, design projects, explore exhibitions, and meet other children. ◉ *182 Lafayette St • Map N4 • 212 941 9198 • Open noon–5pm Wed & Fri–Sun, noon–6pm Thu • Admission charge*

Prada

3 The sign still reads "Guggenheim SoHo" but the current occupant of the building is an extraordinary $40 million flagship store for trend-setting Italian retailer Prada, a sign of SoHo's shift from art to fashion. Dutch architect Rem Koolhaas is responsible for the ultra-hip floating stairs, undulating walls, futuristic elevators, and hi-tech dressing rooms. ◉ *575 Broadway at Prince St • Map N4 • Open 11am–7pm Mon–Sat, 12–6pm Sun*

New York City Fire Museum

4 A nostalgic treasure housed in a 1904 firehouse, this splendid collection includes the city's fire fighting engines, equipment, garb and memorabilia from the 18th century to the present. A moving photo display depicts the World Trade Center attack of September 2001 and honors the hundreds of firefighters lost there. ◉ *278 Spring St • Map N3 • Open 10am–5pm Tue–Sat, 10am–4pm Sun • Admission charge • www. nycfiremuseum.org*

Around Town – SoHo & TriBeCa

Left **Children's Museum of the Arts** Right **Prada**

5 Haughwout Building

A cast-iron masterpiece, this structure was built in 1857 to house a fashionable china and glassware emporium. The design of colonnaded arches flanked by taller Corinthian columns was adapted from the façade of the Sansovino Library in Venice. This motif is repeated 92 times across the front of the building. A 1995 renovation removed grime and restored the elegant original pale color. This building boasted the first Otis safety elevator, an innovation that made the skyscraper possible. 🖎 488–492 Broadway at Broome St • Map P4

6 "Little" Singer Building

By the early 1900s, cast iron was giving way to steel-framed brick and terracotta. One notable example is Ernest Flagg's "Little" Singer Building (to distinguish it from a taller tower also built for Singer). Influenced by Parisian architecture of the period, it has a charming 12-story façade and graceful cast-iron balconies. 🖎 561–3 Broadway, between Prince & Spring Sts • Map N4

Haughwout Building

TriBeCa's Movie Business

TriBeCa is known as Hollywood East, and although much of its movie business is behind the scenes, many screenings take place. Big name stars have been sighted heading for the Grand Screen Room at the TriBeCa Grand Hotel (see p177). The TriBeCa Film Festival, begun in May 2002, is a further star-spotting event.

7 Canal Street

The end of SoHo, the beginning of TriBeCa, and a world of its own, no street better shows the contrasts of New York. Canal Street is crowded with peddlers selling fake Rolex watches and Gucci bags, electronics that may or may not be new, and bargain stores offering sneakers, jeans, and flea-market finds. Keep walking east into Chinatown, and the sidewalk goods shift to vegetables and displays of live and dried fish. 🖎 Map P3–4

8 Harrison Street

This rare group of Federal townhouses, built between 1796 and 1828, did not exist as a row until 1975, when the houses

Left **"Little" Singer Building** Right **Canal Street**

Harrison Street

were moved to this site to be saved from the urban renewal that razed much of the area. At the end of the block (No. 6) is the former New York Mercantile Exchange, a Queen Anne building dating from 1884 and in use until 1977 when the Exchange moved to the World Financial Center (see p45). ✎ Map P3

White Street

The best example of cast iron architecture in TriBeCa is a sampling of several styles. No. 2 has Federal features and a gambrel roof; Nos. 8–10, designed by Henry Fernbach in 1869, sport Tuscan columns and arches and use the Neo-Renaissance device of building shorter upper stories to give an illusion of height. There is a complete change of pace at No. 38, which houses neon artist Rudi Stern's gallery, Let There Be Neon. ✎ Map P3–4

TriBeCa Film Center

A turn-of-the-century coffee warehouse has been converted into office space for the film and entertainment industry. The guiding spirit was Robert De Niro, whose TriBeCa Productions was founded in 1988. Miramax has set up offices here and the building is also home to the TriBeCa Grill, owned by De Niro and restaurateur Drew Nieporent. The restaurant has managed to maintain its appeal for two decades. ✎ 375 Greenwich St • Map P3

A Stroll Around SoHo and TriBeCa

Morning

The Bleecker Street subway stop is a good starting point to explore Soho's shops and galleries. Galleries worth a visit are Peter Blum at 99 Wooster St; Spencer Brownstone at 39 Wooster St; David Beitzel at 102 Prince St; and Deitch Projects at 76 Grand St. **Greene Street** (see p99) has a number of interesting boutiques, such as Moss, Helmut Lang, Paul Smith, and Kirna Zabête.

The Drawing Center (see p43) exhibits work from emerging artists and has poetry readings. This is also a prime area for photography galleries. The most interesting are Janet Borden, David Nolan, and Staley Wise, all located at 560 Broadway. Afterwards, stop for Asian noodles at Keeley & Ping, 127 Greene St, between Houston and Prince Streets.

Afternoon

Drop in on designer boutiques Miu Miu, 100 Prince Street, and Anna Sui, 113 Greene Street, before proceeding to TriBeCa. Take a stroll along **White** and **Harrison** streets to view the historic architecture and stop for a drink at the **Church Lounge** (see p102).

Spend the rest of the afternoon taking in the varied exhibits at the Apex Art Gallery, 291 Church Street, which also hosts free public events. Afterwards make your way to **Dylan Prime** (see p102) for an early evening cocktail, then head to TriBeCa to a leading restaurant, such as Nobu, Bouley, or Chanterelle (see p103).

Left **Pravda** Center **Dylan Prime** Right **Temple Bar**

TOP 10 Nightlife

1 Pravda
Vodkas from across the world are served in this bar featuring Russian mementos, leather chairs, and a low gold ceiling. ◎ *281 Lafayette St, between Prince & Houston Sts • Map N4 • 212 226 4696*

2 Church Lounge
Almost the entire ground floor of the hotel is devoted to this popular bar with plush seats and a dramatic eight-story atrium. ◎ *TriBeCa Grand Hotel, 2 6th Ave • Map N3 • 212 519 6600*

3 Dylan Prime
An extensive cocktail menu, and an attractive space with lofty ceilings help make this a hotspot. ◎ *62 Laight St, between Greenwich & Collister Sts • Map P3 • 212 334 4783*

4 Thom Bar
A place to see and to be seen, this swanky bar draws beautiful people who sup cocktails while enjoying the low-key DJ sets nightly. ◎ *60 Thompson Hotel, 2nd floor, 60 Thompson St • Map P3 • 212 219 2000*

5 Ear Inn
This classy but cozy and casual spot is likely the oldest bar in the city (it dates to 1830). Fairly buzzy at night and at lunch, it's also good for a respectable cheap meal. ◎ *326 Spring St at Greenwich St • Map P3 • 212 226 9060*

6 Puck Fair
At this cosy multi-level pub you can settle in to enjoy a pint along with tasty Irish snacks. ◎ *298 Lafayette St, between Houston & Prince Sts • Map N4 • 212 431 1200*

7 Grand Bar
Like its sister TriBeCa Grand, the SoHo Grand is a neighborhood nightlife mecca, comfortable, softly lit, with food if you want it, and filled with beautiful people. ◎ *SoHo Grand Hotel, 310 West Broadway, between Canal & Grand Sts • Map P3 • 212 965 3588*

8 MercBar
This trendy SoHo meeting place attracts all manner of sophisticates who dig the mountain lodge decor. ◎ *151 Mercer St, between Houston & Prince Sts • Map N4 • 212 966 2727*

9 Temple Bar
Dark, swanky, sexy, and pricey, but the martinis are mammoth. A good place to bring a date – or find one. ◎ *332 Lafayette St, between Bleecker & East Houston Sts • Map N4 • 212 925 4242*

10 the room
This is a friendly, candle-lit place with no hard liquor, but offers over 120 types of beer and two dozen wine selections. ◎ *144 Sullivan St, between Prince & Houston Sts • Map N3 • 212 477 2102*

For more New York bars and lounges See pp54–5

Price Categories

For a three-course meal for one with a glass of house wine, and all unavoidable charges including tax.

$	under $25
$$	$25–$50
$$$	$50–$80
$$$$	over $80

Left **Chanterelle** Right **Balthazar**

🔟 Restaurants

The Harrison
With outside seating in the spring and summer, rustic, seasonally-inspired food is served here. ◈ 355 Greenwich St • Map P3 • 212 274 9310 • $$$

Nobu
Nobu Matsuhisa's sublime Japanese/Peruvian fusion fare in a whimsical setting (see p68). An outpost, Nobu 57, is also open at 40 West 57th Street (212 757 3000). ◈ 105 Hudson St • Map P3 • 212 219 0500 • $$$$

Nobu Next Door
The no-reservations policy here means you might get to taste the famous Nobu black cod with miso. ◈ 106 Hudson St at Franklin St • Map P3 • 212 334 4445 • $$$

Bouley
David Bouley demonstrates his legendary culinary skills in a vaulted dining room. Another floor holds a bakery, café, and market. Upstairs has an open kitchen and sushi bar. ◈ 163 Duane St • Map P3 • 212 964 2525 • $$$$

Chanterelle
Art Nouveau decor and divine French food have made Chanterelle a winner. The tasting menu dinners are expensive but worth it. ◈ 2 Harrison St at Hudson St • Map P3 • 212 966 6960 • $$$$

Aquagrill
Ultra-fresh seafood is the draw at this popular SoHo restaurant. Save some room for choices from the raw bar and the chocolate tasting plate. ◈ 210 Spring St at 6th Ave • Map N3 • 212 274 0505 • $$

Balthazar
As close to a Parisian bistro as you're likely to find in SoHo, Balthazar's only problem is its popularity. A buzzing scene. ◈ 80 Spring St at Broadway • Map N3 • 212 965 1414 • $$$

Raoul's
Another bit of the Left Bank in SoHo, with an updated French menu and a great garden. ◈ 180 Prince St, between Sullivan & Thompson Sts • Map N4 • 212 966 3518 • $$$

The Odeon
Art Deco decor, consistently good French-American food, and a star-studded crowd keeps the vibe right, even after 30 years. ◈ 145 West Broadway at Thomas St • Map P3 • 212 233 0507 • $$

Hampton Chutney Co.
Perfect for an inexpensive snack of dosas: Indian rice crêpes stuffed with creative combinations. ◈ 68 Prince St • Map N4 • 212 226 9996 • $

Left **Washington Square Park** Center **Jefferson Market Courthouse** Right **Bar on Bleecker Street**

Greenwich Village

IT WAS DIFFERENT FROM THE START, *a crazy pattern of streets that broke from the city's grid plan, reflecting the boundaries of a rural village. As a bohemian haven, the leafy lanes of the Village have been home to artists and writers. Jazz musicians, beat poets, and performers like the young Bob Dylan found their places here. Later it became popular with gays, and today cafés and funky shops attract young people from all over the city. The village really comes to life at night, when cafés, theaters, and clubs beckon at every turn.*

🔟 Sights

1. Washington Square Park
2. MacDougal Alley
3. Washington Mews
4. Grove Court
5. Jefferson Market Courthouse
6. Cherry Lane Theatre
7. Bleecker Street
8. New York University
9. Judson Memorial Church
10. 75½ Bedford Street

Balconies, Greenwich Village

Sign up for DK's email newsletter on traveldk.com

Street performers in Washington Square Park

Washington Square Park
In 1826, a marshy area was filled to form this popular park. The restored marble arch by Stanford White went up in 1892, replacing a wooden version that marked the centenary of George Washington's inauguration. Mothers with strollers, chess players, and young lovers now occupy benches where drug dealers once reigned. The fountain in the center is where Bob Dylan sang his first folk songs. ⊗ *5th Ave, between Waverly Pl & 4th St • Map N3*

MacDougal Alley
These 19th-century stables for the fine homes on Washington Square North were converted into studios by artists early in the 20th century, causing the street to be known as "Art Alley de Luxe."

Among the residents were painter Guy Pene du Bois and sculptor Gertrude Vanderbilt Whitney, who established the first Whitney Museum in 1914 at 8 West 8th Street, adjoining her studio. ⊗ *East of MacDougal St, between 8th St & Waverly Pl • Map M3*

Washington Mews
Another group of stables turned into houses around 1900, the Mews attracted both writers and artists. No. 14A housed, at various times, author John Dos Passos and artists Edward Hopper, William Glackens, and Rockwell Kent. Writer Sherwood Anderson often stayed at No. 54 with his friend and patron, Mary Emmett. In contrast to the modern buildings in much of Manhattan, this type of quaint enclave is the reason many find the Village so appealing. ⊗ *University Place to 5th Ave • Map M3*

Grove Court
This group of six townhouses in a bend in the street was developed by grocer Samuel Cocks, who thought that having residents nearby would help his business at No. 18. But while such private courts are prized today, they were not considered respectable in the 1850s, and the disreputable types who moved in earned it the nickname "Mixed Ale Alley." O. Henry used the block as the setting for *The Last Leaf*. ⊗ *Grove St near Bedford St • Map N3*

Left **MacDougal Street** Right **Grove Court**

5 Jefferson Market Courthouse

The site was a market in 1833, named after the former president, Thomas Jefferson. The fire lookout tower had a giant bell that alerted volunteer firefighters. When the courthouse was built in 1877, the bell was installed in its clock tower. The building became a treasured Village landmark, and, after the market had moved and court sessions were discontinued, it was eventually saved from demolition after a spirited local campaign and converted into a branch of the New York Public Library *(see p124)* in the 1950s.
◈ *425 6th Ave, between 9th & 10th Sts • Map M3 • Open 9am–8pm Mon, Wed, 10am–6pm Tue, Thu, 10am–5pm Fri, Sat • Free*

6 Cherry Lane Theatre

In 1924, a warehouse was converted into one of the first Off-Broadway theaters and showcased plays by the likes of Edward Albee, Eugene Ionesco, David Mamet, and Harold Pinter. Today, the "Cherry Lane Alternative" uses established playwrights to mentor talented newcomers.
◈ *38 Commerce St, between Bedford & Barrow Sts • Map N3 • 212 989 2020 • www.cherrylanetheatre.org*

7 Bleecker Street

The present line-up of ordinary shops and restaurants belies the history of this street. James

---

The Halloween Parade

Anything goes in this wildly gaudy annual parade of cross-dressers and amazing costumes. It draws 25,000 marchers and reportedly two million spectators. The parade route goes up 6th Avenue, from the Village to 23rd Street, starting at 7pm.

Fenimore Cooper lived at No. 145 in 1833, Theodore Dreiser stayed at No. 160 when he came to New York in 1895, and James Agee lived at No. 172 from 1941 to 1951. The café at No. 189, on the corner of Bleecker and MacDougal, was the San Remo bar, the favorite gathering place for William Burroughs, Allen Ginsberg, Gregory Corso, and Jack Kerouac, leading lights of the beat generation. ◈ *Between 6th Ave & West Broadway • Map N3*

8 New York University

Founded in 1831, N.Y.U. enlarged the scope of early 19th-century study from its previous concentration on Greek and Latin to contemporary subjects: a "rational and practical education" for those aspiring to careers in business, industry, science, and the arts, as well as in law, medicine, and the ministry. It has grown into the largest private university in America and now occupies many blocks around Washington Square. ◈ *Washington Square • Map N4*

Left **Cherry Lane Theatre** Right **Bleecker Street**

Judson Memorial Church

9 Judson Memorial Church

An elegant work in Romanesque style by Stanford White, with stained glass by John La Farge, the church was built in 1888–93 as a memorial to Adoniram Judson, the first American Baptist missionary in Asia. John D. Rockefeller, Jr. *(see p48)* contributed to the construction. White's use of mottled yellow brick and white terracotta trim introduced light coloration into American church architecture. ⊗ *55 Washington Square South • Map N3 • Open for services 11am Sun • Free*

10 75½ Bedford Street

New York's narrowest home, just 9.5 ft (3 m) wide, was built in 1873 in a passageway in the Village. Poet Edna St. Vincent Millay lived here, as did actors John Barrymore and, later, Cary Grant. No. 77 is the oldest house in the Village, dating from around 1799, and at No. 103 is "Twin Peaks," an 1830 structure remodeled in 1925 by Clifford Reed Daily to house artists and writers, who would presumably be inspired by the architecture. ⊗ *Between Morton & Barrow Sts • Map N3*

A Village Stroll

Morning

Begin at **Washington Square** *(p108)* and the elegant townhouse row where Edith Wharton and Henry James once lived. Find the charming houses of **Washington Mews** and **MacDougal Alley** *(p105)*, then follow 6th Avenue, past the **Jefferson Market Courthouse**, to West 10th Street.

Stroll down the passageway at the front of the Alexander Onassis Center for Hellenic Studies. This walkway once led up to the Tile Club, a gathering place for the artists of the Tenth Street Studio, where Augustus Saint-Gaudens, John La Farge, and Winslow Homer lived and worked. Continue along Waverly Place, Grove Steet, and Bedford Street, each with its share of prize townhouse architecture. Have lunch at a typical Village bistro like **Café Loup** *(see p109)*.

Afternoon

After lunch, why not while away a few hours browsing in the local shops? Vintage clothing can be admired at specialty shops such as Andy's Chee-pees at No. 18 West 8th Street, while at No. 840 Broadway you'll find Forbidden Planet, a nirvana for comic book fanatics.

West 8th Street and West 4th Street are also crammed with shops, and there are several coffeehouses, which are great for people-watching. Try Caffe Reggio, 119 MacDougal Street, where the literary lights of the beat generation used to read their poetry.

Left **Washington Mews** Center **Patchin Place** Right **White Horse Tavern**

TOP 10 Literary Landmarks

1 Washington Square
Prominent figures who lived here include Edith Wharton, at No. 7 in 1882. Henry James was born at No. 21 in 1843. ⊗ *Map N3*

2 St. Luke's Place
Poet Marianne Moore lived here, and Theodore Dreiser wrote *An American Tragedy* at No. 16. ⊗ *Between Hudson St & 7th Ave South • Map N3*

3 Patchin Place
A charming pocket of 19th-century houses that later attracted E. E. Cummings, John Masefield, and Eugene O'Neill, among others. ⊗ *West 10th St • Map N3*

4 Café Wha?
Beat poet Allen Ginsburg was a regular here, a venue that also saw early appearances from Bob Dylan and Jimi Hendrix. ⊗ *115 Macdougal St, between Bleecker and West 3rd Sts • Map N3*

5 White Horse Tavern
Favorite hangout of Norman Mailer and Dylan Thomas, who announced one night in 1953, "I've had 18 straight whiskeys," and passed out. He died the next day. ⊗ *567 Hudson St at 11th St • Map N3*

6 Willa Cather Residence
Willa Cather wrote six novels here and her Friday "at homes" were attended by the likes of D. H. Lawrence. ⊗ *5 Bank St, between West & Greenwich Sts • Map N3 • Closed to public*

7 Mark Twain Residence
A plaque marks the home (1904–08) of Mark Twain, designed by James Renwick, Jr., architect of St. Patrick's Cathedral. Twain received guests while propped up in a huge carved bed. ⊗ *21 5th Ave at 9th St • Map M3 • Closed to public*

8 William Styron Residence
This was Styron's first "tiny but rather nice" apartment after writing *Lie Down in Darkness* at age 23. ⊗ *43 Greenwich Ave • Map M3 • Closed to public*

9 Edward Albee Residence
Albee wrote *The Zoo Story* here. He first saw the words "Who's Afraid of Virginia Woolf?" written in soap on a saloon mirror nearby. ⊗ *238 West 4th St • Map N3 • Closed to public*

10 West 10th Street
Mark Twain lived at No. 14 in 1900–1, Hart Crane at No. 54 in 1917, and Edward Albee lived in the carriage house at No. 50 during the 1960s. ⊗ *Map M3 • Closed to public*

For more on figures in New York history See pp48–9

Price Categories

For a three-course
meal for one with a | **$** under $25
glass of house wine, | **$$** $25–$50
and all unavoidable | **$$$** $50–$80
charges including tax. | **$$$$** over $80

Left **Babbo** Right **Blue Ribbon Bakery**

🔟 Restaurants

Babbo
An attractive setting and the inventive Italian fare created by TV chef Mario Batali make this a very popular spot. Reserve in advance to ensure a table. ◈ *110 Waverly Place • Map N3 • 212 777 0303 • $$$*

Il Mulino
Another top Italian. Quality is consistent, portions are large, and the brick-walled room is inviting. Try the homemade capellini with mushrooms, peas, and pancetta in a black truffle vodka cream sauce. ◈ *86 West 3rd St, between Sullivan & Thompson Sts • Map N3 • 212 673 3783 • $$$*

Blue Hill
Highly praised New American fare that uses local, seasonal ingredients, served in intimate, elegant surroundings. ◈ *75 Washington Place at MacDougal St • Map N3 • 212 539 1776 • $$$*

Blue Ribbon Bakery
A casual Village favorite with an enormous, eclectic menu that includes everything from croissants and caviar to the signature fried chicken. ◈ *33 Downing St at Bedford St • Map N3 • 212 337 0404 • $$*

Café de Bruxelles
Mussels and frites can't be beat at this comfortable restaurant. Don't miss the impressive selection of Belgian beers either. ◈ *118 Greenwich Ave at West 13th St • Map M3 • 212 206 1830 • $$*

Café Loup
An agreeable French bistro, where favorite dishes include tuna carpaccio, steak, and pan-roasted tarragon chicken. The setting is romantic, but there's also a funky bar. ◈ *105 West 13th St • Map M3 • 212 255 4746 • $$*

Da Silvano
Watch the celebrities come and go from a table outside. The northern Italian fare here is consistent, and the buzz even better. ◈ *260 6th Ave, between Bleecker & West Houston Sts • Map N3 • 212 982 2343 • $$$*

Home
Food like Mom used to make (provided she was a terrific cook) keeps this narrow café crowded. The patio provides a breath of fresh air. ◈ *20 Cornelia St, between Bleeker St & 6th Ave • Map N3 • 212 243 9579 • $$*

Pastis
Hot, hot, hot is this straight-out-of-Paris café; order steak frites or escargots, and get into the spirit. ◈ *9 9th Ave at Little West 12th St • Map M2 • 212 929 4844 • $$$*

Sushi Samba
The Japanese/Brazilian fusion cuisine and cocktails are inspired, but the trendy crowd comes here for the rooftop deck and live music on sunny days. ◈ *87 Seventh Ave South at Bleecker St • Map N3 • 212 691 7885 • $$$*

Note: *Unless otherwise stated, all restaurants accept credit cards and serve vegetarian meals*

Left **Gramercy Park** Center foreground **Metropolitan Life Tower** Right **Rooftops on Broadway**

Union Square, Gramercy Park, and Flatiron

CHANGE IS IN THE AIR *in this flourishing section of Manhattan. Union Square, once a hangout for drug dealers and scene of protest rallies, has been renovated and transformed. A Greenmarket fills the square with fresh produce four times a week, drawing patrons from all over the city, and the neighborhood around the square is attracting an increasing number of new apartments, shops, and restaurants. The shops and lively eating places now extend up Fifth Avenue into the once-neglected Flatiron District, named for the building at the intersection of Fifth Avenue and Broadway at 23rd Street. Quiet Madison Square, opposite the Flatiron Building, is the site of two of the city's hottest restaurants and home to the public square, Madison Square Park. No change was needed in Gramercy Park, the most European of the city's neighborhoods.*

Fantasy Fountain, Greg Wyatt, Gramercy Park

🔟 Sights

1. Union Square Greenmarket
2. ABC Carpet & Home
3. Madison Square
4. Theodore Roosevelt Birthplace
5. Metropolitan Life Tower
6. Flatiron Building
7. Gramercy Park
8. National Arts Club
9. 69th Regiment Armory
10. "Curry Hill"

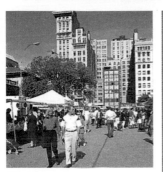

A Manhattan market scene

Union Square Greenmarket

Herbs and berries, miniature vegetables, fresh flowers, homebaked pastries, newly woven yarns, hams, honey – all of these and more can be found at the bountiful Greenmarket that fills Union Square each Monday, Wednesday, Friday, and Saturday. Over 200 regional farmers take part in the market, each offering only goods that they have grown or made. Not to be missed. ✆ *At Broadway & 14th St • Map M4 • Open 8am–6pm Mon, Wed, Fri, Sat*

ABC Carpet & Home

The city's most eclectic emporium, two landmark buildings that are part flea market, part antiques fair, and part Middle Eastern bazaar. Offerings include fancy French or rugged Mexican furniture, antiques, fabrics and accessories, linens, bedding, flowers, and rugs. There are two dining places: Dessert Studio and Pipa. ✆ *881 & 888 Broadway at East 19th St • Map L4*

Madison Square

The square opened in 1847 at the center of a residential area where politician Theodore Roosevelt and writer Edith Wharton were born. The original Madison Square Garden was here, at Madison Avenue and 26th Street. Development brought distinguished sites such as the Flatiron and Metropolitan Life buildings. Today the statue-filled park and the area are being rediscovered. ✆ *23rd to 26th Sts, between Broadway & Madison Ave • Map L3*

Theodore Roosevelt Birthplace

The boyhood home where the colorful 26th President was born in 1858 has been reconstructed. Exhibits trace his political career as well as his explorations, displaying everything from toys to campaign buttons, and emblems of the trademark "Rough Rider" hat Roosevelt wore in the Spanish-American war. The house offers a rare glimpse of a privileged 19th-century New York lifestyle. ✆ *28 East 20th St, between Broadway & Park Ave South • Map L4 • Open 9am–5pm Tue–Sat • Admission charge • Visits are by guided tour only • www.nps.gov/thrb*

Left **Madison Square** Right **Theodore Roosevelt Birthplace**

5 Metropolitan Life Tower

This 54-story tower, built along the east side of Madison Square in 1909, was the world's tallest building at that time, an appropriate corporate symbol for the world's largest insurance company. Designed by Napoleon Le Brun and Sons, the tower follows the form of the campanile in the Piazza San Marco in Venice. Although it was altered in the 1960s, when the entire structure was renovated, the ornate four-faced clock and crowning cupola remain a familiar landmark on the New York skyline. ✆ 1 Madison Ave, near 24th St • Map L4 • Open during office hours • Free

6 Flatiron Building

Though dwarfed by countless taller structures today, this unusual building – its shape conforming to a triangular plot of land – remains striking, a symbol of the beginning of the skyscraper era. Its slim, rounded façade is as proud as a ship's prow sailing up the avenue. Completed in 1902, it anchored the north end of the prestigious Ladies' Mile shopping district, located between Union and Madison squares. The designer, famous Chicago architect Daniel Burnham, included detailed Italian Renaissance decoration on the building from top to bottom, much of it in terracotta. ✆ 175 5th Ave at Broadway & 23rd St • Map L3 • Open office hours • Free

The City's Squares

Manhattan has only four London-style squares: Union, Madison, Stuyvesant, and Gramercy Park, all formed in the 1800s by real estate speculators hoping to profit by selling surrounding lots to the wealthy. The squares provide welcome breaks among the city's dense, tall buildings, but only Gramercy Park has remained residential.

7 Gramercy Park

Samuel Ruggles laid out this neighborhood around a private park in the 1830s. It remains the city's only private park and a desirable place to live. Stanford White remodeled No. 16 in 1888 for Edwin Booth, who founded the Players Club here. His statue stands in the park (see pp114). ✆ Lexington Ave, between 20th & 21st Sts • Map L4 • Closed to public

8 National Arts Club

Originally the home of Samuel Tilden, a governor of New York and opponent of the notorious Boss Tweed (see pp48–9). The Gothic Revival brownstone was designed by Calvert Vaux, of Central Park fame. The National Arts Club, whose members have included leading American artists since the 1800s, bought the building in 1906. Each member is asked to donate a work to the club. Its galleries are open to the public. ✆ 15 Gramercy Park South • Map L4

Flatiron Building

Writers' faces, National Arts Club

9 69th Regiment Armory

This Beaux Arts building was used as the drill hall and offices of a military unit privately formed in 1848. In 1913, the controversial exhibition of modern art known as the Armory Show was held here, including works by Van Gogh, Duchamp, and Brancusi. The show was widely panned in the press, but it brought modern art to New York on a large scale and had a profound and lasting effect on American art. ◈ *Lexington Ave, between 25th & 26th Sts • Map L4 • Closed to public*

10 "Curry Hill"

Despite changes around it, this three-block corridor just south of Murray Hill remains filled with Indian shops selling saris and gifts, and is lined with restaurants that are a boon for diners (particularly vegetarians) in search of interesting food at reasonable prices. Kalustyan's, 123 Lexington Avenue, is a treasure trove of fragrant spices and grains and features some 31 different kinds of rice.
◈ *Lexington Ave, between 26th & 29th Sts • Map L4*

Exploring Gramercy Park and Flatiron

Morning

Book-lovers should start on 12th Street, where the city's biggest used bookstore, the Strand, is located at No. 828. From here, head north up Broadway to Union Square, visiting the **Greenmarket** *(see p111)*. Continuing up Broadway brings you to the Paragon Sports superstore, 867 Broadway at 18th Street, and Fishs Eddy, 889 Broadway at 19th, selling all but indestructible vintage and new china. The fascinating **ABC Carpet & Home** awaits at No. 888 *(see p111)*.

At the **Flatiron Building**, turn east to **Madison Square** *(p111)*, then have lunch at **Tabla** or the gourmet **11 Madison Park** *(p115)*. Several restaurants on **"Curry Hill"** also offer inexpensive lunches, including Pongal, No. 110, and Saravanaas at 81 Lexington Ave.

Afternoon

While you are in the neighborhood, check out the intriguing spices at Kalustyan's, 123 Lexington Avenue.

More shops can be found on Fifth Avenue between 14th and 23rd streets, including Anthropologie, No. 85, Zara, No. 101, Juicy Couture, No. 103, and H&M, No. 111.

End your day in the civilized oasis of the **Gramercy Park** neighborhood. Be sure to stroll up East 19th Street, known as the "Block Beautiful," for its handsome 1920s houses.

Left **Farragut Monument** Center **George Washington** Right **Marquis de Lafayette**

Statues and Monuments

George Washington
The city's first major outdoor statue was created in 1856 by Henry Kirke Brown. The statue is a 14-foot (4.26-metre) equestrian figure on a granite pedestal. ◉ *Union Square facing 14th St • Map M4*

Abraham Lincoln
This pensive figure by Henry Kirke Brown was commissioned shortly after the president's assassination in 1865. ◉ *North end of Union Square near 16th St • Map M4*

Marquis de Lafayette
A larger-than-life 1873 statue of Lafayette pledging his heart to the American Revolution by Frédéric-Auguste Bartholdi, creator of the Statue of Liberty. ◉ *Madison Square • Map L3–4*

Mohandas K (Mahatma) Gandhi
The site for this 1986 statue of the hero of Indian independence was chosen because the park was frequently the site of protest gatherings. ◉ *Union Square • Map M4*

Edwin Booth as Hamlet
The founder of the Players Club is shown in his most famous role, about to give Hamlet's soliloquy. The 1917 statue faces his former house. ◉ *Gramercy Park • Map L4*

Fantasy Fountain
Greg Wyatt's 1983 smiling sun and moon flanked by dancing giraffes, from whose mouths water flows in warm weather. ◉ *Southeast corner of Gramercy Park • Map L4*

Worth Monument
An 1850s obelisk marks the grave of the only public figure buried under the streets of Manhattan, General Worth, hero of the Mexican Wars. ◉ *Traffic Island, 23rd St & Broadway • Map L3*

Farragut Monument
This 1880 memorial to a naval hero established Augustus Saint-Gaudens as the nation's foremost sculptor; Stanford White designed the base. ◉ *Madison Square • Map L3–4*

Chester Alan Arthur
Arthur became the 21st President when James Garfield was assassinated. George Edwin Bissell sculpted him in 1898, standing in front of an elaborate chair. ◉ *Madison Square • Map L3–4*

William Seward
In 1876 Randolph Rogers immortalized the secretary of state under Lincoln, best remembered for his much-criticized purchase of Alaska in 1867. ◉ *Madison Square • Map L3–4*

For more on figures in New York's history See pp48–9

Price Categories

For a three-course meal for one with a glass of house wine, and all unavoidable charges including tax.		
	$	under $25
	$$	$25–$50
	$$$	$50–$80
	$$$$	over $80

Tabla Bread Bar

🔟 Restaurants

Union Square Café
One of New York's most popular restaurants uses ingredients from the neighboring Union Square Greenmarket *(see p68)*. ❧ *21 East 16th St at Union Square West • Map M4 • 212 243 4020 • $$$*

Gramercy Tavern
Unpretentious fine dining where the inventive American cuisine is universally praised. Great desserts *(see p69)*. ❧ *42 East 20th St at Broadway • Map L4 • 212 477 0777 • $$$*

11 Madison Park
Danny Meyer has made 11 Madison Square chic with his imaginative New American cuisine in an elegant Art Deco setting. ❧ *Madison Ave at East 24th St • Map L4 • 212 889 0905 • $$$*

Tocqueville
French cuisine is prepared with Japanese touches in this hidden gem. ❧ *15 East 15th St, between Union Square West & 5th Ave • Map M4 • 212 647 1515 • $$$*

Tabla and Tabla Bread Bar
Another Danny Meyer success on Madison Square; New American with Indian seasonings, served in colorful surroundings. ❧ *11 Madison Ave at East 25th St • Map L4 • 212 889 0667 • Tabla $$$; Bread Bar $$*

Blue Water Grill
The ultra fresh seafood (plus sashimi and sushi rolls) isn't the only draw; there's also the bustling sidewalk café, and downstairs jazz bar. ❧ *31 Union Square West at 16th St • Map M4 • 212 675 9500 • $$$*

Olives
This restaurant for the beautiful set is in the W Hotel. The menu features modern Mediterranean dishes, and they serve afternoon tea. ❧ *201 Park Ave South at East 17th St • Map M4 • 212 353 8345 • $$$*

Veritas
An amazing wine list is the big draw, but the New American cuisine is also outstanding. Reserve ahead. ❧ *43 East 20th St, between Broadway & Park Ave South • Map L4 • 212 353 3700 • $$$$*

Novitá
This chef-owned Northern Italian restaurant is warm and intimate. Try the pan-roasted sea bass with artichokes. ❧ *102 East 22nd St, between Lexington & Park Ave South • Map L4 • 212 677 2222 • $$*

Craftbar
Tom Collichio's scaled-down version of Craft next door gives diners the chance to experience the chef's take on flavor, but at cheaper prices. ❧ *900 Broadway, at East 20th St • Map M4 • 212 461 4300 • $$*

Around Town – Union Square, Gramercy Park, & Flatiron

Note: Unless otherwise stated, all restaurants accept credit cards and serve vegetarian meals

Left **Macy's façade** Center **Ornamental clock, Herald Square** Right **Chelsea Piers**

Chelsea and Herald Square

A NEIGHBORHOOD *that has seen a great deal of change, Chelsea was a quiet enclave of 19th-century brownstones that never made it as a fashionable address. Now it is a hub for gay New Yorkers and center for the city's avant-garde art galleries and nightclubs. Buildings along 6th Avenue are now occupied by superstores and discount outlets, and to the west, Chelsea Piers has transformed the waterfront. Uptown, the Garment District begins around 27th Street, with Herald Square and Macy's at the heart of the city's busiest shopping area.*

🔟 Sights

1. 6th Avenue Shopping
2. West 25th Street Market and Antiques Garage
3. Flower District
4. Chelsea Hotel
5. Chelsea Historic District
6. General Theological Seminary
7. Chelsea Piers
8. Fashion Institute of Technology (F.I.T.)
9. Herald Square
10. Macy's

Cheerleaders at Macy's

1 6th Avenue Shopping

This was once a popular district known as "Fashion Row". The 1876 cast-iron façade of the Hugh O'Neill Dry Goods Store at Nos. 655–71 exemplifies the era, when the arrival of the 6th Avenue elevated line provided easy access to the area. As Manhattan's commercial center moved northward, these cast-iron palaces were left deserted until the 1990s, when they found new life as bargain fashion outlets and superstores. ◎ 6th Ave, West 18th to 23rd Sts • Map L3

2 West 25th Street Market and Antiques Garage

On weekends, year-round, an empty parking lot becomes one of the city's most popular outdoor markets. A tradition for more than 30 years, some 100 vendors, from Maine to Maryland, set up booths selling clothing, silver, jewelry, furniture, art, and "junktiques" from old tools to vintage eyeglasses. Many prize antiques can be discovered at The Antiques Garage, an indoor market just around the corner at 112 West 25th Street, and at The Showplace, 40 West 25th Street, with over 60 dealers on three floors. ◎ West 25th St between Broadway and 7th Ave • Map L3 • Open sunrise to sunset • Admission charge

Façade, Chelsea Hotel

3 Flower District

Here, at the heart of the city's wholesale flower district, you can hardly see the sidewalk for the masses of greenery, shrubs, and flowers. Manhattan's largest concentration of shops selling house plants, trees, blooming plants, and all manner of flowers, fresh, dried, and artificial can be found here; if you can't find what you want, it probably doesn't exist. The district extends along 6th Avenue roughly from 25th to 30th streets. ◎ 6th Ave at 27th St • Map L3

4 Chelsea Hotel

Seedy it is, yet there's a definite mystique to this 1884 building bedecked with wrought-iron balconies. Once a fancy apartment, it became a hotel favored by musicians, artists, and writers. Former guests, commemorated on brass plaques outside, include Tennessee Williams, Mark Twain, Jack Kerouac, and Brendan Behan. Dylan Thomas spent his last years here. Notoriously, it was also the place where punk rocker Sid Vicious killed his girlfriend Nancy Spungen in 1978. Step into the lobby and take a look at the wild artwork. The bar downstairs is now called the Star Lounge. ◎ 222 West 23rd St, between 7th & 8th Aves • Map L3

Left **The Flower District** Right **Chelsea Hotel, cast-iron stairwell**

Chelsea Historic District

Clement Moore, author of *A Visit from St. Nicholas*, developed this land in the 1830s. The finest of the town houses built here are the seven known as "Cushman Row," Nos. 406–18 West 20th Street, which are among the city's best examples of Greek Revival architecture. Houses at Nos. 446–50 West 20th are in the Italianate style, for which Chelsea is also known. ◈ *Between 9th & 10th Aves, 20th & 21st Sts • Map L2*

General Theological Seminary

America's oldest Episcopal seminary was founded in 1819. This campus was built around two quadrangles in the 1830s, on a site donated by Clement Moore, who taught at the seminary. The main building, added in 1960, includes a library with the largest collection of Latin Bibles in the world. There are lovely inner gardens (9th Avenue entrance). ◈ *20th to 21st Sts • Map L2 • Open 10am–3pm Mon–Sat • Free*

Chelsea Piers

Four neglected piers have been turned into a 30-acre sports and recreation complex, and Manhattan's largest venue for

The World's Largest Store

Macy's is more than a store to most New Yorkers. It is a major part of the city, sponsoring the famous Thanksgiving Day Parade, the city's Fourth of July fireworks and everything from an annual spring flower show filling the main floor, to Tap-O-Mania, when thousands of tap dancers converge on Herald Square.

film and TV production. Sports facilities include ice skating, inline skating and skateboarding, batting cages, playing fields, a basketball court, bowling alley, golf driving ranges, and a marina offering harbor cruises and sailing instruction. Pier Park is a place to relax with a water view. ◈ *23rd St at the Hudson River • Map L2 • Open 6:30am– 11pm Oct–Mar (to midnight Apr–Sep) • Admission charge • www.chelseapiers.com*

Fashion Institute of Technology (F.I.T.)

Founded in 1944 and now a branch of the State University of New York, the Fashion Institute of Technology is a prestigious school teaching art, fashion design, and marketing, and boasts famous alumni, including Calvin Klein, Norma Kamali, and David Chu. Students benefit from internships with New York's

Left **Chelsea Piers** Center **"Cushman Row", Chelsea Historic District** Right **6th Avenue shops**

34th Street entrance, Macy's

leading stores and designers. Of greatest interest to the public is the gallery, which has changing exhibits, often from their clothing and textile collections. ⊛ *7th Ave at West 27th St • Map L3 • Museum open noon–8pm Tue–Fri, 10am–5pm Sat • Free*

Herald Square

The center of a rowdy theater district known as the Tenderloin in the 1870s and 80s, until it was reformed. The Manhattan Opera House was razed in 1901 to make way for Macy's, and other stores soon followed. The clock on the island where Broadway meets 6th Avenue is all that is left of the building that was occupied by the *New York Herald* until 1921. ⊛ *Broadway at 6th Ave • Map K3*

Macy's

Former whaler R. H. Macy founded the store in 1858 on 6th Avenue and 14th Street; the red star logo was from his tattoo, a souvenir of sailing days. Innovations included pricing goods a few cents below a full dollar and offering a money-back guarantee. The store was sold in 1888 and moved to the present building *(see p64)*. ⊛ *151 West 34th St, between Broadway & 7th Ave • Map K3 • www.macys.com*

A Day Around Chelsea

Morning

🕐 Wind your way through Chelsea, starting with the megastores now occupying former "Fashion Row," on **6th Avenue** *(p117)* between 18th and 23rd streets. Walk west on 16th Street to 9th Avenue and Chelsea Market, a one-time Nabisco factory where the first Oreo cookies were made, now a block-long line of stalls offering all manner of food. The Food Network tapes its TV shows in a street-level studio here.

Continue up 9th Avenue to 20th Street for the **Chelsea Historic District** and **General Theological Seminary**. Then head for the ever-expanding "Gallery Row," from 21st to 24th streets, 10th to 11th avenues. A good lunch bet in the neighborhood is **The Red Cat**, offering Mediterranean fare *(see p121)*.

Afternoon

Walk east on 23rd Street to the **Chelsea Hotel** *(see p117)*, and when you get to 6th Avenue, turn uptown for the big antiques market and the colorful **Flower District** *(see p117)*. A stroll for one block further west on 27th brings you to the **Fashion Institute of Technology**, where the gallery usually has interesting displays.

Head for one of the great hidden treasures in this area, St. John the Baptist Church, at 210 East 31st Street, whose dingy façade belies a glowing Gothic interior. Continue to 34th Street for **Herald Square** and **Macy's**.

Left **Barbara Gladstone** Right **Andrea Rosen**

TOP 10 Chelsea Galleries

Gagosian Gallery
Gagosian is one of the premier names in the gallery scene *(see p42)*. ✪ *555 West 24th St & 522 West 21st St • Map L2 • Open 10am–6pm Tue–Sat*

Matthew Marks
Of the two galleries, the original shows large-scale works, while the second specializes in new work *(see p43)*. ✪ *522 West 22nd St at 10th Ave • Open 11am–6pm Tue–Sat; 523 West 24th St at 10th Ave • Map L2 • Open 11am–6pm Tue–Sat • Free*

Paula Cooper
The lofty setting itself is worth a visit. Many of Cooper's shows are controversial *(see p43)*. ✪ *534 West 21st St at 10th Ave • Map L2 • Open 10am–6pm Tue–Sat • Free*

Paul Kasmin
Son of a British art dealer, Kasmin has nurtured many newcomers *(see p43)*. Previous exhibitions have featured Kenny Scharf, Robert Indiana, Deborah Kass, and Barry Flanagan. ✪ *293 10th Ave at 27th St • Map M2 • Open 10am–6pm Tue–Sat • Free*

Barbara Gladstone
A dramatic backdrop for large-scale pieces, video pioneers, and photography. ✪ *515 West 24th St at 10th Ave • Map L2 • Open 10am–6pm Tue–Sat • Free*

Andrea Rosen
Since moving from SoHo to Chelsea, Rosen's eclectic exhibitions have made this one of the most visited galleries in the area. ✪ *525 West 24th St at 10th Ave • Map L2 • Open 10am–6pm Tue–Sat • Free*

Marlborough, Chelsea
The 57th Street gallery shows established luminaries, while this downtown satellite has new sculpture and painting *(see p42)*. ✪ *545 West 25th St at 7th Ave • Map L3 • Open 10am–5:30pm Tue–Sat • Free*

Robert Miller
This gallery shows big names like Diane Arbus, Walker Evans, Andy Warhol, and Jacob Epstein. ✪ *526 West 26th St at 10th Ave • Map L2 • Open 10am–6pm Tue–Sat • Free*

Sonnabend
A power in the art world, representing early pop artists, and still on the lookout for new trends. ✪ *536 West 22nd St at 10th Ave • Map L2 • Open 10am–6pm Tue–Sat • Free*

303 Gallery
Featuring artists of critical acclaim in several media. ✪ *525 West 22nd St at 10th Ave • Map L2 • Open 10am–6pm Tue–Sat • Free*

For more on New York galleries **See pp42–3**

Price Categories

For a three-course meal for one with a glass of house wine, and all unavoidable charges including tax.

$	under $25
$$	$25–$50
$$$	$50–$80
$$$$	over $80

Left **Rocking Horse Café Mexicano** Right **Empire Diner**

🔟 Places to Eat

Da Umberto
Popular over the years for sophisticated Tuscan fare and a long list of daily specials. ◎ *107 West 17th St, between 6th & 7th Aves • Map M3 • 212 989 0303 • $$$*

Periyali
A billowing canopy and white walls set the scene for classy Greek dining; creative dishes put the food in gourmet territory. ◎ *35 West 20th St, between 5th & 6th Aves • Map L3 • 212 463 7890 • $$$*

The Red Cat
This warm neighborhood place serves first-rate American fare; don't miss the Parmesan frites with mustard aioli. ◎ *227 10th Ave, between 23rd & 24th Sts • Map L2 • 212 242 1122 • $$*

East of Eighth
Many locals frequent this spot, which has an eclectic international menu. The prix-fixe brunch is particularly good value. ◎ *254 West 23rd St, between 7th & 8th Aves • Map L3 • 212 352 0075 • $$*

Buddakan
The star here is not the good Asian fusion food, but the decor. For such a trendy spot, the staff are quite friendly. ◎ *75 9th Ave at 16th St • Map M2 • 212 989 6699 • $$$*

Rocking Horse Café Mexicano
Always packed with diners who come for the great margaritas and Mexican food at reasonable prices. ◎ *182 8th Ave, between 19th & 20th Sts • Map L2 • 212 463 9511 • $$*

Hill Country
This addition to the barbecue scene is known for its brisket and sausages (shipped from the name-sake Texas region). Live music Thu–Sat evenings. ◎ *30 West 26th St • Map L3 • 212 255 4544 • $$*

Monster Sushi
As the name implies, massive rolls of sushi are provided at very reasonable prices. ◎ *158 West 23rd St • Map L3 • 212 620 9131 • $$*

Bottino
Thanks to the booming gallery scene, this attracts a stylish crowd for good northern Italian fare and a lovely garden. ◎ *246 10th Ave, between 24th & 25th Sts • Map L2 • 212 206 6766 • $$*

Empire Diner
The door is always open at this rail car converted to a 24-hour Art Deco diner. The best people-watching comes after midnight. ◎ *210 10th Ave at 22nd St • Map L2 • 212 243 2736 • $*

Note: *Unless otherwise stated, all restaurants accept credit cards and serve vegetarian meals*

Left **Prometheus, Rockefeller Center** Center **Grand Central Terminal** Right **Chrysler Building**

Midtown

THE LIGHTS OF TIMES SQUARE, THE SPIRES *of the Empire State and Chrysler buildings, Rockefeller Center, the United Nations Headquarters, stores on 5th Avenue, museums, theaters, and grand buildings galore – all are found in the midtown area between 34th and 59th streets, extending from the East River as far as Broadway. The concentration of attractions makes this the most important area of the city for* visitors, and many a day can be spent taking in the sights. Fifth Avenue, the dividing line between the East and West sides, is in many ways the Main Street of Manhattan, and in itself offers a generous sampling of the city's riches, from architecture to commerce. Midtown also reflects the city's characteristic diversity, with attractions that range from the bustling retail of the Diamond District, to the stately halls of the New York Public Library.

St. Patrick's Cathedral

Sights

1. Times Square
2. Empire State Building
3. Rockefeller Center
4. Chrysler Building
5. Grand Central Terminal
6. New York Public Library
7. St. Patrick's Cathedral
8. United Nations Headquarters
9. Diamond District
10. Carnegie Hall

Times Square

Times Square
The city's most famous intersection, and symbol of the lively theater district *(see pp22–5)*.

Empire State Building
New York's most famous, and tallest, skyscraper is a classic. Since the structure was completed in 1931 more than 120 million visitors have looked down on the city from its observatories *(see pp8–9)*.

Rockefeller Center
Rockefeller Center is the hub of midtown New York, alive with activity day and night, integrating shops, gardens, dining and office space, and its own aerial vantage point *(see pp12–15)*.

Chrysler Building
The unmistakable shimmering spire of the Chrysler Building is one of New York's great landmarks. The grand Art Deco lobby, once used as a showroom for Chrysler cars, has been restored to show off its lavish marble and granite, and a vast painted ceiling depicts transportation scenes of the late 1920s *(see p44)*. ◐ *405 Lexington Ave at 42nd St • Map K4 • Open (lobby only) 7am–6pm Mon–Fri • Free*

Grand Central Terminal
One of the world's great rail terminals, the outstanding Beaux Arts building *(see p47)* is New York's most visited, with 500,000 people passing through it daily. Since restoration work was completed, its admirers are no longer limited to travelers. Grand Central has become an attraction in its own right, with shops, close to 50 restaurants and food purveyors, and the New York City Transit Museum. ◐ *42nd St, between Park & Lexington Aves • Map J–K4 • Open 5:30am–1:30am daily • Free • www.grandcentralterminal.com*

Left **Empire State Building** Center **Rockefeller Center** Right **Chrysler Building**

New York Public Library

6 Carrère and Hastings won a competition for the design of this great Beaux Arts building. Their genius reached its height in the Main Reading Room, a paneled space as majestic as a cathedral, extending almost two city blocks, with enormous arched windows, 18 grand chandeliers, and an elaborately decorated, vaulted ceiling (see p47). ⌕ 5th Ave at 42nd St • Map K3 • Open 10am–6pm Mon, Thu–Sat, 10am–9pm Tue & Wed, 1–5pm Sun • Free • www.nypl.org

St. Patrick's Cathedral

7 America's largest Catholic cathedral is a place where more than 5,000 people worship every Sunday. When Archbishop John Hughes decided to build a cathedral here in 1850, many criticized the choice of a site so far from the city's center at the time. Today his foresight has given the church one of the best locations in Manhattan (see p46). ⌕ 5th Ave, between 50th & 51st Sts • Map J3 • Open 6:30am–8:45pm daily • Free

William O. Partridge's Pieta, St. Patrick's Cathedral

Time for Tea

Taking tea is an increasingly popular custom in New York. Among the top places are the elegant Four Seasons Hotel, 57 East 57th Street near Madison, the Tea Box Café at Takashimaya (see p126), the tea room at the St. Regis Hotel (see p172), and the salon de thé at Fauchon, 442 Park Avenue at 56th.

United Nations Headquarters

8 John D. Rockefeller, Jr. donated $8.5 million to purchase the 18-acre East River site, and American Wallace Harrison worked with international consultants to create this striking headquarters. The United Nations was formed in 1945, to work for peace and economic and social well-being around the globe. Currently, 192 members meet in the General Assembly, the closest thing to a world parliament. Guided tours allow visitors to see the various council chambers, the General

Left **New York Public Library** Right **St. Patrick's Cathedral**

Assembly Hall, and many of the works by prominent artists, including Marc Chagall and Henry Moore. ✪ 1st Ave at 46th St • Map J5 • Open (for tours) 9:45am–4:45pm daily (Jan–Feb: Mon–Fri only) • Admission charge • www.un.org

9 Diamond District
Jewels glisten in every window of this block, the center of the city's retail and wholesale trade. It handles 80 percent of the diamonds coming into the U.S. Developed largely by Orthodox Jews, the district grew in importance during the World War II when thousands fled the diamond centers of Antwerp and Amsterdam to settle in New York. Above the shops are offices and workshops where the stones are cut and set.
✪ 47th St, between 5th & 6th Aves • Map J3

10 Carnegie Hall
New York almost lost its most famous concert hall when the New York Philharmonic moved to the newly built Lincoln Center in the 1950s. However, a coalition, led by violinist Isaac Stern, successfully fought to save the building from demolition. It was bought by the city in 1960 and became a National Historic Landmark in 1964. A major 1986 renovation restored much of the original appearance while updating technical facilities and preserving the hall's famous acoustics. Musical memorabilia fills the halls and the Rose Museum (see p46). Tours are available for a fee. ✪ West 57th St at 7th Ave • Map H3 • Museum open 11am–4:30pm daily • Free • www.carnegiehall.org

A Day Exploring Midtown

Morning

🕙 Start at the **Morgan Library & Museum** (see p41), and see Morgan's opulent study, then proceed to 42nd Street and turn east for a tour through **Grand Central Terminal** (see p123). Continue east on 42nd Street, stopping to look at the outstanding lobbies of the **Chrysler Building** (see p123), the **Daily News Building**, and the **Ford Foundation**, and climbing the stairs to see the **Tudor City** complex (see p127).

End the morning with a tour of the **United Nations HQ**. If you reserve ahead, you can have lunch in the very special U.N. delegate's dining room (212 963 7625).

Afternoon

Take the 42nd Street crosstown bus back to Fifth Avenue and visit the **New York Public Library**. Walk uptown to 47th Street and turn west for the **Diamond District**, then pay a quick visit to the **Paley Center For Media** (see p128) on 52nd Street between Fifth and Sixth avenues. Pop in to the new home of the **American Folk Art Museum** (see p128) and stop for a coffee in the museum's café before taking in the exhibits of traditional art.

Return to 5th Avenue where the uptown shops include **Tiffany and Company**'s (see p10) windows of jewels, **Bergdorf Goodman**'s (see p10) stylish displays, and F.A.O. Schwarz. Round the day off at **Salon de Ning** in the Peninsula Hotel (see p55), with views over Central Park.

Left **H&M** Center **Henri Bendel** Right **Niketown**

TOP 10 Places to Shop

1 Department Stores
Bountiful stocks of beautiful clothing await at Bergdorf Goodman, Saks Fifth Avenue, Lord & Taylor, and Bloomingdales. ✪ *5th Ave, between 38th & 58th Sts • Map K3–H3*

2 H&M
Flagship store of the Swedish retailer known for great young fashion with small price tags *(see p65)*. ✪ *5th Ave at 51st St • Map J3*

3 Henri Bendel
This is one of the most attractive stores in the city, featuring designer fashions and a notable selection of cosmetics *(see p64)*. ✪ *712 5th Ave at 55th St • Map H3*

4 Takashimaya
Tasteful New York home of a leading Japanese department store, filled with the finest clothing, home accessories, and art *(see p64)*. ✪ *693 5th Ave, between 54th & 55th Sts • Map H3*

5 F.A.O. Schwarz
Anyone who is a kid at heart will love this toy store. From ride-on Ferraris to cuddly versions of American Kennel Club purebreds, the displays here never fail to delight *(see pp66–7)*. ✪ *767 5th Ave at 58th St • Map H3*

6 Museum of Modern Art Design Shop
Lamps, furniture, toys, jewelry, posters – whatever the item here, you can be sure it will be the epitome of good design. ✪ *44 West 53rd St, between 5th & 6th Aves • Map J3*

7 Designer Boutiques
Many designers have moved north, but 57th Street between 5th and Madison remains impressive, with Burberry, Hermes, Chanel, Tiffany & Co., and Dior. Prada is at No. 724 5th Avenue. ✪ *57th St, between 5th & Madison Aves • Map H4*

8 Harry Winston
You'll likely only be window shopping here; the diamonds and gems, many of which Harry Winston supplies to celebrities, are very expensive. ✪ *718 5th Ave • Map H4*

9 Niketown
Commercial, high-tech shopping fun, all to entice you to buy sneakers and sportswear. ✪ *6 East 57th St, between 5th & Madison Aves • Map H4*

10 Louis Vuitton
Perhaps the flashiest of the high-end shops from the outside, LV's windows are imprinted with the same multi-colored pattern as on the handbags for sale here. ✪ *1 East 57th St • Map H4*

For more on shopping See p165

Left **Ford Foundation Building** Center **Lever House** Right **Tudor City**

🔟 Midtown Architecture

1 Lever House
This 24-story building of glass and steel by Gordon Bunshaft was the first "glass box" in New York *(see p44)*. ⓢ *390 Park Ave • Map H4 • Lobby open during office hours*

2 General Electric Building
This 1931 Art Deco building has a clock whose arms grasp at lightning bolts. ⓢ *570 Lexington Ave • Map H4 • Closed to public*

3 Chanin Building
One of the great early Art Deco skyscrapers (c.1929) notable for its terracotta frieze and bronze band illustrating the theory of evolution. ⓢ *122 East 42nd St • Map K4 • Lobby open during office hours*

4 Daily News Building
The *Daily News* has moved on, but this fine 1930 building is still an Art Deco classic. Step inside and marvel at the revolving globe. ⓢ *220 East 42nd St at 2nd Ave • Map K4 • Lobby open during office hours*

5 Ford Foundation
Considered one of the city's best modern designs (1967). Every office opens onto a skylit, 12-story atrium with lush landscaping and a pond. ⓢ *320 East 43rd St at 1st Ave • Map J4 • Lobby open during office hours*

6 Fred F. French Building
Built for the best-known real estate firm of its day, this 1927 building is opulent inside and out. Don't miss the lobby. ⓢ *551 5th Ave • Map J3 • Lobby open during office hours*

7 Tudor City
Fred F. French created this mock Tudor enclave, designed to prove that middle-class housing could succeed in Midtown. ⓢ *1st to 2nd Aves, 40th to 43rd Sts • Map J4–K4 • Lobby open during office hours*

8 NY Yacht Club
The window bays of this 1899 private club are the carved sterns of ships, sailing on a sea of sculpted waves. ⓢ *37 West 44th St at 5th Ave • Map J3 • Closed to public*

9 American Standard Building
Raymond Hood's first New York skyscraper is an ornate black tower built in 1924, now a hotel. ⓢ *40 West 40th St • Map K3 • Lobby open during office hours*

10 Condé Nast Building

The 48-story tower, built in 1999, is striking and environmentally friendly, with photovoltaic cells on the façade and integrated recycling chutes. ⓢ *4 Times Square • Map J3 • Lobby open during office hours*

For more on architecture **See pp46–7**

127

Left **Morgan Library** Center **Paley Center for Media** Right **New York Public Library**

📖10 Midtown Museums & Art

1 Morgan Library & Museum
The library holds a private collection of rare books, prints, and manuscripts *(see p41)*. The steel-and-glass pavilion houses an impressive performance hall. ⊛ *225 Madison Ave at 36th St • Map K4 • Open 10:30am–5pm Tue–Thu (to 9pm Fri), 10am–6pm Sat & Sun • Admission charge*

2 Museum of Modern Art
Reopened in 2005 following a massive renovation program, the new building is worthy of this outstanding collection *(see p40)*. ⊛ *11 West 53rd St at 5th Ave • Map H3*

3 American Folk Art Museum
This extensive collection of folk art is now housed in an elegant eight-story building. ⊛ *45 West 53rd St • Map H3 • Open 10:30am–5:30pm Tue–Sun (to 7:30pm Fri) • Admission charge*

4 Museum of Arts and Design
The permanent collection, which dates from 1900, includes 2000 craft exhibits. ⊛ *2 Columbus Circle • Map H3 • Open 11am–8pm Tue–Sun (11am–9pm Thu) • Admission charge*

5 International Center of Photography
Two floors of retrospectives and changing exhibits. ⊛ *1133 6th Ave • Map J3 • Open 10am–6pm Tue–Sun (to 8pm Fri) • Adm*

6 Paley Center for Media
Watch your favorites from over 60,000 radio and TV programs, plus special exhibits and classic screenings. ⊛ *25 West 52nd St, between 5th & 6th Aves • Map J3 • Open noon–6pm Wed–Sun (to 8pm Thu) • www.mtr. org • Admission charge*

7 Transit Museum Gallery Annex
Images and objects from the Brooklyn Museum are on display here. ⊛ *Shuttle Passage, Grand Central Terminal • Map K3 • Open 8am–8pm Mon–Fri, 10am–6pm Sat–Sun • Free*

8 New York Public Library Galleries
Rare prints, paintings, and changing exhibitions. ⊛ *5th Ave at 42nd St • Map K3 • Open 11am–6pm Tue–Wed, 10am–6pm Thu–Sat • Free*

9 Sculpture Garden at 590 Madison
The zen-like atrium of the IBM building houses a rotating cast of sculptures in glass walls. ⊛ *590 Madison Ave at 57th St • Map J3 • Free*

10 Municipal Art Society Galleries
Changing exhibits covering the city's architecture and neighborhoods. ⊛ *457 Madison Ave • Map J4 • Open 10am–6pm Mon, Tue, Wed, Fri, Sat • Free*

For more New York museums See pp40–41

Price Categories

For a three-course meal for one with a glass of house wine, and all unavoidable charges including tax.

$	under $25
$$	$25–$50
$$$	$50–$80
$$$$	over $80

Left **Grand Central Oyster Bar and Restaurant** Right **Le Colonial**

TOP10 Restaurants

Four Seasons
An award-winning New York institution with landmark decor and great celebrity spotting opportunities *(see p69)*. ⊗ *99 East 52nd St at Park Ave • Map J4 • 212 754 9494 • $$$*

Le Bernardin
Acclaimed chef Eric Ripert does wonders with every kind of fish and seafood – the dining experience here is sheer perfection *(see p69)*. ⊗ *155 West 51st St at 6th Ave • Map J3 • 212 554 1515 • $$$$*

Blue Fin
One of the coolest places in the area, this restaurant is dedicated to serving seafood dishes including sushi and raw bar selections. ⊗ *1567 Broadway at 47th St • Map J3 • 212 918 1400 • $$$*

Whole Foods Café
A self-service cafeteria where you can choose from a range of freshly prepared meals at the buffet. Proceed through the check-out and find a table. ⊗ *Time Warner Center, downstairs, 10 Columbus Circle, 60th St at Broadway • Map H2 • 212 823 9600 • $*

Le Colonial
Sultry decor straight out of 1930s Saigon sets the scene for a Vietnamese/French menu full of delicate contrasts and combinations. Relax with an after-dinner drink in the lounge upstairs. ⊗ *149 East 57th St at Lexington Ave • Map H4 • 212 752 0808 • $$$*

Osteria del Circo
The sons of Le Cirque's owner have created their own whimsical circus, serving traditional Tuscan fare. ⊗ *120 West 55th St at 6th Ave • Map H3 • 212 265 3636 • $$$*

Grand Central Oyster Bar and Restaurant
A New York classic, this bustling and ever-popular restaurant serves only the freshest seafood. ⊗ *Grand Central Terminal, lower level, 42nd St at Lexington Ave • Map K4 • 212 490 6650 • $$*

Brasserie
Remodeled with sleek, high-tech decor, the updated bistro menu features modern French/American Pacific dishes but still includes a few classics. ⊗ *100 East 53rd St at Lexington Ave • Map J4 • 212 751 4840 • $$*

Convivio
High-end Italian food served in a cozy dining room tucked away in Tudor City. Excellent menu, crowd-pleasing desserts, and outstanding service. ⊗ *45 Tudor City Place • Map J5 • 212 599 5045 • $$$*

La Bonne Soupe
A midtown haven for the thrifty, with comfortable, old-fashioned, French bistro charm. This theater district favorite is a great place to eat after a show. Most of the entrées are under $15. ⊗ *48 West 55th St, between 5th & 6th Aves • Map H3 • 212 586 7650 • $$*

Note: Unless otherwise stated, all restaurants accept credit cards and serve vegetarian meals

Left **Toward Roosevelt Island** *(see p134)* Right **River promenade, Carl Schurz Park** *(see p135)*

Upper East Side

WHEN NEW YORK'S UPPER CRUST *moved uptown a century ago, their destination was the Upper East Side, and it is still the address of choice for many wealthy families. Most of the older Beaux Arts mansions around 5th Avenue are now occupied by embassies or museums; today's elite live in the solid apartment buildings that went up on 5th and Park Avenues, convenient for patronizing the boutiques on Madison, the city's most exclusive shopping street. Only churches and a few restaurants remain of German Yorkville or the Hungarian and Czech neighborhoods that used to fill the blocks east of Lexington. Young families now occupy the newer buildings in this area. For visitors, the Upper East Side is home to many of the city's best museums.*

Mount Vernon *(see p135)*

🔟 Sights

1. Central Park
2. Metropolitan Museum of Art
3. Solomon R. Guggenheim Museum
4. Museum Mile
5. Bridgemarket
6. Roosevelt Island
7. Park Avenue Armory
8. Henderson Place Historic District
9. Gracie Mansion and Carl Schurz Park
10. Mount Vernon Hotel Museum and Gardens

Preceding pages **Central Park skaters**

Central Park

Central Park
The 843-acre swathe of green provides recreation and beauty for more than two million visitors each year *(see pp26–7)*.

Metropolitan Museum of Art
More a collection of museums, with more than two million pieces spanning 5,000 years of global culture *(see pp28–31)*.

Solomon R. Guggenheim Museum
A notable collection of modern art is located in Frank Lloyd Wright's spiral-design building, which is the only one in New York he designed *(see pp32–3)*.

Museum Mile
Nine museums are situated within one convenient mile. They unite for a free open house day one Tuesday in June. Participants include the Metropolitan Museum of Art, National Academy of Fine Arts, Cooper-Hewitt National Design Museum, Soloman R. Guggenheim Museum, Jewish Museum, Neue Gallery for German and Austrian Art, Museum of the City of New York *(see p41)*, and El Museo del Barrio. Street entertainers and musicians provide entertainment, and Fifth Avenue closes to traffic. ✪ *5th Ave from 82nd to 104th Sts • Map F4–D • Opening times vary*

Bridgemarket
Britain's Sir Terence Conran was a major player in the development of this cathedral-like space beneath the 59th Street bridge. The vaults are among the most dramatic works by Rafael Guastavino, a Spanish architect noted for his use of Catalan-style tiling. Beneath the grand ceilings are a restaurant and a Food Emporium market. The complex, which is responsible for the rapid revitalization of the neighborhood, also includes the Conran Shop for high-end home decor, and a public plaza. ✪ *59th St, between 1st & York Aves • Map H5*

Left **Museum of the City of New York** Right **Bridgemarket**

For New York's Top 10 museums **See pp40–41**

6 Roosevelt Island

A four-minute tram ride is the route to this East River enclave. Once known as "Welfare Island," when it was home to a prison, poor house, and hospital for the insane, the 147-acre island was renamed and redeveloped in the 1970s according to a master plan drawn up by Philip Johnson and John Burgee, intended to create a quiet, almost traffic-free residential community. The plan was not fully developed, although more than 3,000 apartments were built, and while there is a subway stop from Manhattan, the only auto access is via a bridge in Queens.
🔊 *Trams every 15 mins from TramPlaza, 2nd Ave at 59th St • Map H5*

7 Park Avenue Armory

The socially prominent members of the Seventh Regiment, formed in 1806, constructed a remarkable armory in 1877–89, with a drill room 200 by 300 feet (60 by 90 m) and 100 feet (30 m) high, and an administration building in the form of a medieval fortress. Interior decoration was by Louis Comfort Tiffany, Stanford White, and others, and the result is opulent rooms with lavish Victorian furnishings. The drill room is used for the prestigious Winter Antiques Show every January. Following a $150-million renovation project, the space now

---

St. Nicholas Russian Orthodox Cathedral

An unexpected bit of Russia, this building was constructed in 1902 in Muscovite Baroque style with a façade of red brick, white stone, and blue and yellow tiles. The incense-filled interior has marble columns and an altar enclosed by wooden screens trimmed with gold. Mass is still said in Russian. It is located at 15 East 97th Street.

---

allows for the development of unconventional performing and visual art. 🔊 *643 Park Ave at 66th St • Map G4 • 212 616 3930 • Open noon–8pm Tue–Fri, noon–6pm Mon, Sat, Sun*

8 Henderson Place Historic District

Built in 1881 by the developer John C. Henderson for "persons of moderate means," these winning Queen Anne houses made of brick and stone are embellished with towers, bays, gables, dormers, and slate roofs. They were an investment and remained in Henderson's family until the 20th century. Today they are unique in the city and rank among the most desirable places to live. Each block front was composed as a unit, with small towers at the end. Twenty-four of the original 32 units remain.
🔊 *East End Ave, between 86th & 87th Sts • Map F5*

Left **Park Avenue Armory** Right **Henderson Place Historic District**

Sign up for DK's email newsletter on traveldk.com

Official residence of the Mayor
of New York

9 Gracie Mansion and Carl Schurz Park

The wooden country home built by merchant Archibald Gracie in 1799 was the original home of the Museum of the City of New York and became the official residence of Mayor under Fiorello LaGuardia in 1942. It is located at the northern end of a park laid out in 1891, with a wide promenade that stretches along the East River. The park was named for a statesman and newspaper editor who lived in the neighborhood. *East End Ave at 88th St • Map E5 • 212 639 9675 • Open Apr–mid Nov, tours at 10am, 11am, 1pm, 2pm; Wed for pre-booked tours • Admission charge*

10 Mount Vernon Hotel Museum and Gardens

This was the stone carriage house of a 1799 estate. When the house burned in 1826, the carriage house was converted into an inn and became a fashionable resort for New Yorkers who wanted to escape to what was then still countryside. The building and garden were restored by the Colonial Dames of America in 1939, and furnished with historic objects. Guides explain the unique history of the attraction. *421 East 61st St, between 1st & York Aves • Map H5 • Open 11am–4pm Tue–Sun, closed August, public holidays • Admission charge • www.mvhm.org*

A Day Exploring the Upper East Side

Morning

🕐 Start at the **Guggenheim** *(see pp32–3)* and admire Frank Lloyd Wright's great architectural achievement before seeing the fine modern art collection. "Must sees" include Chagall's *Paris Through the Window*, Modigliani's *Nude*, and Picasso's *Woman Ironing*. Stop for coffee at the café on the main floor of the museum before leaving.

Head east along 92nd Street to see two rare remaining wooden houses, No. 120, built in 1859, and No. 122, in 1871. Continue east for **Gracie Mansion** and **Henderson Place** and rest on a bench with a river view in **Carl Schurz Park**. One block west on York Avenue, a No. 31 bus will take you to the spectacular **Bridgemarket** *(see p133)*. Recharge your batteries at **Daniel** *(see p137)*, an elegant French restaurant.

Afternoon

Take the 57th Street crosstown bus back to Madison Avenue and head uptown, browsing the designer boutiques. Detour on any of the side streets in the upper 60s and 70s to see the townhouses of affluent New Yorkers. Pay a quick visit to the **Frick Collection** *(see p40)* then stop for coffee at one of the cafés on Madison Avenue.

Spend the rest of the afternoon at the **Metropolitan Museum of Art** *(see pp28–31)*, a New York "must," and see Rembrandt's *Self-portrait*, *Cypresses* by Van Gogh, and Michelangelo's Sistine Chapel studies. End the day with a candlelit meal at **Erminia** *(see p137)*.

Left **Giorgio Armani** Right **Yves Saint Laurent**

TOP 10 Madison Avenue Boutiques

1 Bottega Veneta
The first in the uptown Madison Avenue boutique line-up, known for luxury leather goods, shoes, and fashion.
⬥ 635 Madison Ave, between 59th & 60th Sts • Map H4

2 Shanghai Tang
The colorful townhouse home of a well-known Hong Kong retailer, selling luxury fashions and home furnishings.
⬥ 600 Madison Ave, between 63rd & 64th Sts • Map H4

3 Valentino
If you can afford it, join the rich and famous; many of his gowns are worn at the Oscars.
⬥ 747 Madison Ave at 65th St • Map G4

4 Giorgio Armani
The New York flagship of the Italian master, known for his superb tailoring, offers a good range from his collection.
⬥ 760 Madison Ave at 65th St • Map G4

5 BCBG Max Azria
"Bon chic, bon genre," (good style, good attitude), is the motto of this hot designer. Fans of his sexy fashions include many young Hollywood stars. ⬥ 770 Madison Ave at 66th St • Map G4

6 Tom Ford
Off-the-rack options at this dual-level store include three-piece suits, dressing gowns, and dress shirts in 350 colors. The store also offers customized suits and private shopping appointments. ⬥ 845 Madison Ave • Map B1

7 Dolce & Gabbana
Spot the celebrities at this chic Italian outpost, with its striking all-black decor. ⬥ 825 Madison Ave, between 67th & 68th Sts • Map G4

8 DKNY
Donna Karan designs wearable fashions for every lifestyle and occasion. ⬥ 655 Madison Ave at 60th St • Map H4

9 Yves Saint Laurent
The legacy of the legendary French couturier lingers, with a particular appeal to the young.
⬥ 855-59 Madison Ave, between 70th & 71st Sts • Map G4

10 Ralph Lauren
The 1898 Rhinelander Mansion is the backdrop for the king of preppy fashion, who spent $14 million renovating the old mansion. Sportswear is in a separate shop across the street.
⬥ 867 Madison Ave at 72nd St • Map G4

Price Categories

For a three-course
meal for one with a   **$** under $25
glass of house wine,   **$$** $25–$50
and all unavoidable   **$$$** $50–$80
charges including tax.   **$$$$** over $80

Left **Daniel** Right **Orsay**

🔟 Restaurants

1 Daniel
A flower-filled dining room provides the setting for Daniel Boulud's award-winning seasonal French menus *(see p68)*. ✆ 60 East 65th St at Park Ave • Map G4 • 212 288 0033 • $$$$

2 Ottomanelli New York Grill
This Italian restaurant-cum-steakhouse serves delicious food at bargain prices. The cons? The place is small and a little low on ambience. ✆ 1424 Lexington Ave at East 93rd St • Map F4 • 212 426 6886 • $$

3 Café d'Alsace
A cheerful and charming bistro that blends French regional and contemporary New York cuisines. Highlights include a great lunchtime prix-fixe menu and a huge beer selection. ✆ 1695 2nd Ave at 88th St • Map F4 • 212 722 5133 • $$–$$$

4 Café Boulud
Since Daniel *(above)* opened, Boulud's original restaurant here has become more casual, but the menu and tab are serious. In summer, the terrace tables are a fine dining spot convenient for Museum Mile. ✆ 20 East 76th St at 5th Ave • Map G4 • 212 772 2600 • $$$

5 davidburke townhouse
Creative New American cuisine, inventively presented, is served in a stunning modern space. ✆ 133 East 61st St, between Lexington & Park Aves • Map H4 • 212 813 2121 • $$$

6 Erminia
They don't come more romantic than this tiny, candlelit Italian with beamed ceilings and a menu of well-prepared classics. A popular choice on Valentine's Day. ✆ 250 East 83rd St, between 2nd & 3rd Aves • Map F4 • 212 879 4284 • $$$

7 Uva
An intimate, cozy winebar serving genuine Italian cuisine at reasonable prices, Uva is *the* go-to spot for wine connoisseurs. ✆ 1486 2nd Ave, between 77th & 78th Sts • Map F4 • 212 472 4552 • $$

8 Orsay
This chic French café is busy and cozy, serving authentic bistro fare. It also has a Gallic vibe. ✆ 1057–59 Lexington Ave at 75th St • Map G4 • 212 517 6400 • $$$

9 Taste
Self-serve commissary by day, sophisticated ambience by night. The simple style allows the flavors to speak for themselves. The wine list provides some bargains to accompany the new American cuisine. ✆ 1413 3rd Ave at 80th St • Map F4 • 212 717 9798 • $$

10 E.J.'s Luncheonette
A family-friendly diner that serves large portions of well-prepared American breakfasts. Great pancakes are served all day, along with granola and fresh fruit. ✆ 1271 3rd Ave at 73rd St • Map G4 • 212 472 0600 • No credit cards • $

Note: *Unless otherwise stated, all restaurants accept credit cards and serve vegetarian meals*

Left **Riverside Park Gardens** Right **Apartment buildings**

Upper West Side

THIS AREA DID NOT BEGIN TO DEVELOP *until the 1870s, when the 9th Avenue El went up, making it possible to commute to midtown. When the Dakota, New York's first luxury apartment building, was completed in 1884, it was followed by others on Central Park West and Broadway, while side streets were filled with handsome brownstones. The West Side remains a desirable neighborhood with a reputation for attracting intellectuals, and much of the city's best residential architecture.* The creation of Lincoln Center in the 1950s was a great boost, and the American Museum of Natural History is also a draw.

Mask, Natural History Museum

🔟 Sights

1. **American Museum of Natural History**
2. **Lincoln Center for the Performing Arts**
3. **New York Historical Society**
4. **Columbus Circle**
5. **Pomander Walk**
6. **Riverside Park**
7. **Riverside Drive/West End Historic District**
8. **Children's Museum of Manhattan**
9. **Zabar's**
10. **Green Flea Market/ 77th Street Flea Market**

Share your travel recommendations on traveldk.com

Natural History Museum seen from gardens

1 American Museum of Natural History

The mammoth museum's holdings include 32 million artifacts (see pp34–7).

2 Lincoln Center for the Performing Arts

Built on 15 acres during the 1950s, transforming slums into a giant cultural complex, the Lincoln Center houses an array of venues: the Metropolitan Opera; the New York City Opera and Ballet; the New York Philharmonic; the Lincoln Center and Walter Reade theaters; Avery Fisher and Alice Tully halls; and the Julliard School (see p50). In the summer, popular Mostly Mozart concerts take place, and free concerts are held in the adjacent park. In October 2004, Jazz at Lincoln Center moved into a new headquarters in the Time Warner building at Columbus Circle. ⚲ Columbus to Amsterdam Aves, between 62nd & 66th Sts • Map G2 • Tours twice daily • Admission charge

3 New York Historical Society

New York's oldest museum, founded in 1804, has organized much of its vast collection into the 4th floor Henry Luce III Center, which displays 40,000 objects divided into areas such as paintings, sculpture, furniture, silver, tools, and, notably, Tiffany lamps. Other galleries are used for changing exhibits. The society also maintains a research library. ⚲ 2 West 77th St at Central Park West • Map G2 • Open 10am–6pm Tue–Sat (to 8pm Fri), 11am–5:45pm Sun; Library 10am–5pm Tue–Sat (Tue–Fri in summer) • www.nyhistory.org • Admission charge

4 Columbus Circle

One of the largest building projects in New York's history has transformed this neglected urban plaza into an important public site. The redevelopment has attracted national and international businesses, such as giant media company Time Warner, which has its headquarters in an 80-story skyscraper. The building contains shops, entertainment, restaurants, and the Mandarin Oriental hotel. It is also home to Jazz at Lincoln Center, the world's first performing arts facility dedicated to jazz. Other structures around Columbus Circle include Hearst House, Trump International Hotel, and the Maine Monument. ⚲ Columbus Circle • Map H2

Lincoln Center for the Performing Arts

Pomander Walk

This double row of small brick and stucco, timbered, Tudoresque townhouses, hidden on a private street, is one of the many delightful surprises to be discovered in Manhattan. The developer, a restaurateur named Thomas Healy, took his inspiration in 1921 from the sets used for a popular play by Lewis Parker called *Pomander Walk*, hoping to recreate the village atmosphere depicted in the play. Gloria Swanson, Rosalind Russell, and Humphrey Bogart are among the players who have lived here.
Ⓢ *261–7 West 94th St, between Broadway & West End Ave • Map E2*

Riverside Park

Another example of the landscape genius of Frederick Law Olmsted, a woodsy, hilly band of green planned in 1873, following curving Riverside Drive for 70 blocks and hiding the abandoned railroad tracks below. Playgrounds, sports fields, a promenade, and monuments were added later. The impressive 1902 marble Soldiers' and Sailors' Monument at 89th Street, a memorial to those who died in the Civil War, was modeled after the Monument of Lysicrates in Athens.
Ⓢ *Riverside Drive, 72nd to 155th Sts • Map C1 • Open 6am–1am daily • Free*

Soldiers' and Sailors' Monument

Riverside Drive/West End Historic District

A walk through this historic area showcases the late 19th-century townhouses that characterize the Upper West Side. West 88th Street is a good example. The earliest houses, Nos. 267–71, were built in 1884. Nos. 302–38, dating from the early 1890s, have stepped gables and Roman brick, while Nos. 315–23, built around 1896, have bow fronts in brown or white stone. The Yeshiva Ketana School, at 346 West 89th Street, begun in 1901 by Herts and Tallant, occupies one of the few surviving mansions that once lined Riverside Drive. Ⓢ *Between Riverside Drive & West End Ave, 85th & 95th Sts • Map E1*

Children's Museum of Manhattan

Founded in 1973, in a former school building, this is a museum dedicated to the principle that

Left **House façade, Pomander Walk**

Upper West Side Architecture

The Upper West Side's side streets are lined with fine rows of the brownstones favored by New York's 19th-century middle classes. Built of inexpensive, local, brown sandstone, the narrow buildings are typically three or four stories high, and have a flight of steps called a "stoop" leading to the living floors.

children learn best through self-discovery. It uses a variety of participatory activities and fantasy world environments to engage its young visitors in learning that is fun. The museum's many activities include exhibits to intrigue older children, while Playworks and Adventures with Dora and Diego provide distraction for newborns to four year olds *(see p66).* ❧ *212 West 83rd St at Broadway • Map F2 • Open 10am–5pm Tue–Sun • www.cmom.org • Admission charge*

Zabar's

A monument to New York's mania for finding the best foods and a landmark since 1934, this always-crowded market sells smoked salmon, sturgeon, and other Jewish delicacies, wonderful bread, desserts, coffee, and cheeses, and big selections of oils, vinegars, olives, and gourmet gift baskets. The second floor is filled with cooking equipment, and the adjacent coffee counter at the 80th Street corner offers delicious baked goods, sandwiches, coffees, and smoothie drinks. ❧ *2245 Broadway at 80th St • Map F2*

Green Flea Market/77th Street Flea Market

Flea market junkies throng this school yard every Sunday, hoping for finds from among the piles of vintage clothing, crafts, books, jewelry, prints, and all manner of memorabilia. Less glamorous, new merchandise, from socks to T-shirts, is also sold here. On a good day as many as 300 booths crowd the premises. A weekly green market shares the same space. ❧ *I.S.44, 77th St at Columbus*

Walk on the West Side

Morning

Begin at **Lincoln Center** *(see p139)* and admire the plaza, the Chagall windows at the Metropolitan Opera, and the Henry Moore statue in front of Lincoln Center Theater. The New York Public Library for the Performing Arts on Amsterdam Avenue, behind the theater, is notable for its enormous collection of books on the performing arts.

Make your way up Broadway, window shopping and noting some of the landmark buildings such as the **Apthorp Apartments** *(see p142)* and the **Ansonia Hotel** *(p142)*, and the West Side's gastronomic palaces, such as Fairway, at 75th Street, and **Zabar's**. Almost any of the side streets will reveal examples of the area's great line-up of brownstone townhouses. Finally, head east to Columbus Avenue and **Calle Ocho** *(p143)* for a Cuban lunch.

Afternoon

The **American Museum of Natural History** *(see pp34–7)* can easily fill an entire afternoon, and the **New York Historical Society** *(p139)* has an amazing collection on show.

Stroll down Central Park West and admire the landmark **apartment buildings** *(p142)* that can be seen here, and then head for **Central Park** *(pp26-7)*, the city's vast "backyard". Take a boat out on the lake, or enjoy a gondola ride around it, followed by refreshments at the Loeb Boathouse, the perfect end to an afternoon.

Left **Detail, Dakota** Center left **Balcony, Dorilton** Center right **San Remo** Right **Hotel des Artistes**

TOP 10 Apartment Buildings

1 Dakota
Famous as the site where John Lennon was shot, the block was thought so far west in 1884, it might as well be in Dakota. ✆ 1 West 72nd St at Central Park West • Map G2 • Closed to public

2 Dorilton
One of the most flamboyant examples of the Beaux Arts era, this 1902 apartment house has an iron gate fit for a palace. ✆ 171 West 71st St at Broadway • Map G2 • Closed to public

3 Ansonia Hotel
This 1908 apartment-hotel included soundproof partitions, a feature that has attracted many distinguished musicians. ✆ 2109 Broadway, between 73rd & 74th Sts • Map G2 • Closed to public

4 Apthorp Apartments
Modeled after an Italian Renaissance palazzo, this 1908 building includes a huge interior courtyard. ✆ Broadway, between 78th & 79th Sts • Map F2 • Closed to public

5 Belnord
Even larger than the Apthorp, this 1908 Renaissance Revival structure is where Nobel Prize-winning author Isaac Bashevis Singer lived and wrote. ✆ 225 West 86th St, at Amsterdam Ave • Map F2 • Closed to public

6 Majestic
The first of Irwin Chanin's two 1931 landmarks, one of the original four twin towers that dominate the West Side skyline. ✆ 115 Central Park West, between 71st & 72nd Sts • Map G2 • Closed to public

7 Century
Irwin Chanin's second twin tower, the tallest on the block, and an Art Deco icon. ✆ 25 Central Park West, between 62nd & 63rd Sts • Map H2 • Closed to public

8 San Remo
Emery Roth's 1930 Art Deco masterpiece is a sophisticated adaptation of Renaissance forms. The twin towers hide water tanks. ✆ 145–6 Central Park West, between 74th & 75th Sts • Map G2 • Closed to public

9 Eldorado
Another Art Deco Roth design. Groucho Marx and Marilyn Monroe were once tenants. ✆ 300 Central Park West, between 90th & 91st Sts • Map E2 • Closed to public

10 Hotel des Artistes
Built in 1918 as artists' studios and apartments, the spaces are much coveted. Residents have included Noel Coward, Isadora Duncan, and Joel Grey. ✆ West 67th St, between Central Park West & Columbus Ave • Map G2 • Closed to public

For more historic New York buildings **See pp46–7**

Price Categories

For a three-course meal for one with a glass of house wine, and all unavoidable charges including tax.

$	under $25
$$	$25–$50
$$$	$50–$80
$$$$	over $80

Left **Shun Lee Café** Right **Rosa Mexicano**

🔟 Restaurants

1 Jean Georges
Jean-Georges Vongerichten's namesake restaurant is among the best in New York *(see p68)*. ⚲ *1 Central Park West, Trump International Hotel • Map H2 • 212 299 3900 • $$$$*

2 Per Se
Book well in advance for this critically acclaimed restaurant owned by Thomas Keller. ⚲ *Time Warner Center, Columbus Circle • Map H2 • 212 823 9335 • $$$$*

3 Shun Lee Café
This clean-lined, black-and-white dim sum café is arguably the best north of Chinatown. ⚲ *43 West 65th St at Columbus Ave • Map G2 • 212 769 3888 • $$*

4 Café Fiorello
The bountiful antipasto bar is good enough reason to visit, but the thin-crust pizzas and Italian menu are equally tempting. ⚲ *1900 Broadway, between 63rd & 64th Sts • Map H2 • 212 595 5330 • $$*

5 Tavern On The Green
Eclectic contemporary American cuisine is served at this grand restaurant on the edge of Central Park. Dine al fresco in the private garden in summer. ⚲ *Central Park West at 67th St • Map G2 • 212 873 4111 • $$$*

6 Gabriel's
Sophisticated Tuscan food keeps this stylish room filled with Lincoln Center-goers at night. ⚲ *11 West 60th St at Columbus Ave • Map H2 • 212 956 4600 • $$$*

7 Rosa Mexicano
A branch of New York's top Mexican restaurant, famous for its guacamole made to order and power packed margaritas ⚲ *61 Columbus Ave at 62nd St • Map H2 • 212 977 7700 • $$*

8 Café Luxembourg
A classic Parisian bistro with a zinc-topped bar and a hip clientele. The steak frites can't be beat. ⚲ *200 West 70th St at Amsterdam Ave • Map G2 • 212 873 7411 • $$$*

9 Calle Ocho
Every night feels like a Latin party here; modern dishes from the Cuban chef are inspired by cuisine from Peru to Puerto Rico. ⚲ *446 Columbus Ave, between 81st & 82nd Sts • Map F2 • 212 873 5025 • $$$*

10 Gennaro
Fans say this tiny café serves the best Italian food on the Upper West Side, at the most reasonable prices, which explains the constant lines. ⚲ *665 Amsterdam Ave, between 92nd & 93rd Sts • Map E2 • 212 665 5348 • No credit cards • $$*

Note: *Unless otherwise stated, all restaurants accept credit cards and serve vegetarian meals*

Left **Columbia University** Center **Rose Window, St. John the Divine** Right **Streetside musicians**

Morningside Heights and Harlem

THE AREA BETWEEN MORNINGSIDE PARK and the Hudson River, from 110th–125th streets, is dominated by Columbia University and two important churches. Further west and extending north is Harlem, America's best-known African-American community. In the 1880s, when rail connected the neighborhood to Midtown, the large townhouses were occupied by Irish, Italian, and Jewish families, but by the 1920s black families predominated. The Harlem Renaissance, when nightclubs with black entertainers were frequented by whites, ended with the Depression. Nevertheless, development is reviving the area, causing some to declare a second Renaissance.

TOP 10 Sights

1. Columbia University
2. Cathedral Church of St. John the Divine
3. Riverside Church
4. Hamilton Heights Historic District
5. St. Nicholas Historic District (Strivers' Row)
6. Abyssinian Baptist Church
7. Marcus Garvey Park
8. Studio Museum in Harlem
9. Schomburg Center for Research in Black Culture
10. Malcolm Shabazz Mosque/Harlem Market

144

Front of Columbia University Library

Columbia University

One of America's oldest universities, noted for its law, medicine, and journalism schools, Columbia was founded in 1754 as King's College. It moved in 1897 to its present campus, designed by Charles McKim. Notable buildings include McKim's 1898 Low Memorial Library, and St. Paul's Chapel with three windows by La Farge. ✆ West 116th St at Broadway • Map C3 • www.columbia.edu

Cathedral Church of St. John the Divine

The mother church of the Episcopal Diocese of New York, begun in 1892 and still incomplete, is the largest cathedral in the world. Over 600 feet (180m) long and 320 feet (96m) wide, the church is a mix of Romanesque and Gothic styles. Features include the west entrance, the rose window, bay altars, and the Peace Fountain on the south lawn. The medieval stone carving techniques used on the building are taught in workshops for disadvantaged youths *(see p46)*.

✆ 1047 Amsterdam Ave at 112th St • Map C3 • Open 7am–6pm Mon–Sat, 7am–7pm Sun (to 6pm Jul–Aug) • Free • www.stjohndivine.org

Riverside Church

This skyscraper Gothic church modeled on Chartres cathedral and financed by John D. Rockefeller Jr. in 1930, has a 21-story tower with wonderful Hudson River views. Inside the tower is the world's largest carillon, dedicated to Rockefeller's mother. The brilliant stained-glass windows are copies of those at Chartres with four notable exceptions – the early 16th-century Flemish windows on the east wall. The congregation has long been active in liberal social causes. ✆ 490 Riverside Drive, between 120th and 122nd Sts • Map C1 • Open 7am–midnight daily • www.theriversidechurchny.org

Hamilton Heights Historic District

Once part of the country estates of the wealthy, like Alexander Hamilton whose 1802 home, Hamilton Grange, is here, this location on a hill above Harlem became desirable in the 1880s when an elevated rail line was built. Fine residences went up between 1886 and 1906, and in the 1920s and 30s they attracted Harlem's elite, when the area was dubbed Sugar Hill. Chief Justice Thurgood Marshall and musicians Count Basie, Duke Ellington, and Cab Calloway were among those who lived here. ✆ West 141 St to West 145th St • Map A2

Riverside Church

St. Nicholas Historic District

5 St. Nicholas Historic District (Strivers' Row)

These fine houses, originally known as the King Model Houses, went up in 1891 when Harlem was a neighborhood for the gentry. Three architects, including McKim, Mead, and White, managed to blend Renaissance, Georgian, and Victorian styles and create a harmonious whole. Successful African-Americans moved here in the 1920s and 30s, giving rise to the nickname Strivers' Row. ⊗ *202–250 West 138th St, between Powell and Frederick Douglass Blvds • Map A3*

6 Abyssinian Baptist Church

One of the oldest and most influential African-American churches in the U.S. was organized in 1808 by a group protesting segregation within the Baptist church. The congregation became politically active (starting in 1908) under such leaders as congressman Adam Clayton Powell, Jr. Today the church is widely attended on Sundays by many who come to hear the wonderful gospel choir. ⊗ *132 West 138th St, at Powell Blvd • Map A3 • Sunday services 9am & 11am • www.abyssinian.org*

7 Marcus Garvey Park

A black nationalist who encouraged emigration to Africa, Garvey became a hero of the Black Pride movement, and the park's name was changed from Mount Morris in 1973 to honor him. It adjoins the Mount Morris Historical District of handsome houses and churches from an earlier, affluent, German-Jewish era. In the 1920s, as Harlem became mostly African-American, the synagogues became churches, and the houses were divided up. ⊗ *West 120th to West 124th Sts, between Lenox & 5th Aves • Map B3*

8 Studio Museum in Harlem

Opened in 1967 as an artists' studio, the organization expanded to become an important center for work by black artists. A local bank donated space for the present building, which opened in 1982 and has undergone a major expansion to add more gallery space, an enlarged sculpture garden, an auditorium, and a café. ⊗ *144 West 125th St, at Lenox Ave • Map B3 • Open noon–6pm Wed–Fri, Sun, 10am–6pm Sat • Donations • www.studiomuseum.org*

Studio Museum, Harlem

Harlem Market

9 Schomburg Center for Research in Black Culture

This complex, opened in 1991, houses the largest research center for African and African-American culture in the U.S. The immense collection was assembled by the late Arthur Schomburg, who became curator when the collection was given to the New York Public Library. The original building was the unofficial meeting place for writers in the black literary renaissance of the 1920s, and the present building includes a theater and two art galleries. ◈ 515 Lenox Ave at 135th St • Map A3 • Open noon–8pm Mon–Wed, 11am–6pm Thu–Fri, 10am–5pm Sat • Free

10 Malcolm Shabazz Mosque/Harlem Market

The mosque, Masjid Malcolm Shabazz, was the ministry of the late Malcolm X, and the area around it has become the center of an active Muslim community. Local shops sell books, tapes, and Muslim clothing, and restaurants serve Senegalese cuisine. Street vendors who used to crowd the sidewalks of 125th Street have been moved into an organized complex of market stalls selling African art, dolls, drums, masks, dashiki shirts, and fabrics in African prints. ◈ Mosque, 102 West 116th St at Lenox Ave • Map C3 • Open 9am–5pm daily • Free • Harlem Market, 52–60 West 116th St, between 5th & Lenox Aves • Map C3 • Open 10am–8pm daily • Free

A Day in Harlem and Morningside Heights

Morning

🕑 Begin late Sunday morning and take the No. 2 or No. 3 subway uptown to 135th Street and Lenox Avenue. Walk to Odell Clark Place and turn west to hear the fabulous choir at the **Abyssinian Baptist Church**.

Continue west along the street to see the fine 1890s homes of the **St. Nicholas Historic District** and stop on 8th Avenue to enjoy a gospel brunch at **Londel's Supper Club** (see p148).

Afternoon

Retrace your steps to Lenox Avenue and head downtown to 125th Street to peruse the shops. Turn west for the famous **Apollo Theater** (see p148) and excellent displays of African-American art at the **Studio Museum in Harlem**. Afterwards, stop for coffee at the Starbucks on Lenox Avenue at 125th Street.

Take the M60 bus to West 120th Street and Broadway. Walk down to **Riverside Church** (see p145) for fine views over the Hudson River from the bell tower. Across the street is the monument honoring the 18th U.S. president, Ulysses S. Grant. At 116th Street, head east two blocks to Broadway and the entrance to **Columbia University** (see p145). One block east on Amsterdam Avenue is the **Cathedral Church of St. John the Divine** (see p145) with its immense interior. End the day with some good southern cooking at **Miss Mamie's** (see p149) and return to Broadway for the No. 1 or No. 9 subway back downtown.

Left **Gospel at Sylvia's** Right **Apollo Theater**

Places for Music

1 Lenox Lounge
A mainstay for over 50 years, the lounge has been restored to its original decor. It features the latest jazz as well as traditional numbers. ✆ *288 Malcolm X Blvd, between West 124th & 125th Sts • Map B3*

2 Showman's
Live jazz is the lure on Wednesday and Saturday nights at this club, where the vibes and people are as cool as the music. ✆ *375 West 125th St, between St. Nicholas & Morningside Dr • Map B2*

3 Londel's Supper Club
Part of the new Harlem, with upscale ambience, waiters in tuxedos, delicious Southern fare, and live jazz on weekends. ✆ *2620 Frederick Douglass Blvd, between West 139th & 140th Sts • Map A3*

4 St. Nick's Pub
Savion Glover and Ray Charles have been known to drop by at this popular venue. Live jazz can be heard six nights a week. ✆ *773 St. Nicholas Ave at West 149th St • Subway line A, B, C, or to 145th Street*

5 Sylvia's
The place is jammed for Saturday and Sunday gospel brunches, and always fun despite the tour groups. ✆ *328 Lenox Ave, between West 126th & 127th Sts • Map B3*

6 Cotton Club
Duke Ellington and Cab Calloway are long gone, and the location has changed, but the famous club of the 1920s is currently making a comeback. ✆ *656 West 125th St nr West 125th and Dr Martin Luther King Jr Blvd • Map B2*

7 Apollo Theater
This theater is Harlem's famous showcase, where Ella Fitzgerald and James Brown launched their careers. ✆ *253 West 125th St, between 7th & 8th Aves • Map B3*

8 Harlem Stage
Home to jazz series, as well as ballet, opera, and the Harlem Film Festival. ✆ *City College campus, West 135th St & Convent Ave • Map A2*

9 Miller Theatre
Columbia's main performance venue runs the musical gamut, with jazz an important part. ✆ *Columbia University, 2960 Broadway at West 116th St • Map C2*

10 Smoke
Columbia students and music lovers congregate at this intimate club to hear top notch jazz groups every weekend. ✆ *2751 Broadway at West 106th St • Map D2*

For more entertainment venues See pp50–51

Price Categories

For a three-course meal for one with a glass of house wine, and all unavoidable charges including tax.

$	under $25
$$	$25–$50
$$$	$50–$80
$$$$	over $80

Left **Miss Maude's/Miss Mamie's** Right **Terrace in the Sky**

Restaurants

1 Frizzante Italian Bistro & Bar
Opened in 2010, and fast becoming Harlem's favorite cozy Italian spot, Frizzante offers great cured meat platters and pastas at reasonable prices. ⊗ 2168 Frederick Douglass Blvd, at 117th St • 212 866 0526 • Map C2 • $

2 Acapulco Caliente
Authentic Mexican food at easy-on-the-wallet prices. ⊗ 3508 Broadway, between West 143rd & 144th Sts • Map A2 • 212 926 5558 • $

3 Miss Maude's/Miss Mamie's
Cheerful cafés run by Norma Jean Darden, who knows her Southern cooking. ⊗ Miss Maude's, 547 Lenox Ave at West 137th St • 212 690 3100 • Miss Mamie's, 366 Cathedral Pkwy, between Manhattan Ave and Columbus Ave • 212 865 6744 • Map A3, D2 • Both $

4 Dinosaur Bar-B-Que
The generous portions live up to the name of this roadhouse-style BBQ joint. A wide selection of microbrews along with pit-smoked meats. ⊗ 646 West 131st St at 12th Ave • Map B1 • 212 694 1777 • $

5 River Room
Southern soul food and weekend jazz performances in a spectacular setting overlooking the Hudson. Service can be slow. ⊗ Riverbank State Park, 750 West 145th St • Map A1 • 212 491 1500 • $$

6 Mo Bay
A lively Jamaican restaurant serving ribs, catfish, and jerk chicken with nightly jazz. ⊗ 17 West 125th St, between Lenox & 5th Aves • 212 876 9300 • Map B3 • $$

7 Amy Ruth's
A cheerful café with an up-dated slant on Southern classics. Waffles are a house specialty. ⊗ 113 West 116th St, between Powell & Lenox Aves • Map C3 • 212 280 8779 • $$

8 Le Baobab
The Senegalese cooking and the tab are both agreeable here. ⊗ 120 West 116th St at Lenox Ave • Map C3 • 212 864 4700 • No credit cards • $$

9 Toast
Sandwiches are the forte of this informal café, and the home-fries unmissable. ⊗ 3157 Broadway, between Tiemann Pl & LaSalle St • Map B2 • 212 662 1144 • $

10 Terrace in the Sky
This elegant, rooftop restaurant is so romantic, weddings are held here. The continental fare lives up to the setting. ⊗ 400 West 119th St at Amsterdam Ave • Map C2 • 212 666 9490 • $$$

Left **New York Botanical Garden** Center **Bronx Zoo** Right **Park Slope Historic District**

The Outer Boroughs

MANHATTAN IS JUST ONE of New York's five boroughs, each of which has its own unique attractions. Brooklyn alone, with its fine brownstone neighborhoods and numerous top-class sights, would be one of the largest cities in the U.S. The Bronx, to the north, boasts one of New York's finest zoos, plus the New York Botanical Garden and Yankee Stadium, while Queens, a veritable melting pot of nationalities, is famous for its museums, ethnic dining, and numerous sports events. The ferry to Staten Island leads to New York's only restored historic village.

TOP 10 Sights

1. Bronx Zoo
2. New York Botanical Garden
3. Brooklyn Botanic Garden
4. Brooklyn Heights Historic District
5. Prospect Park
6. Park Slope Historic District
7. Flushing Meadow-Corona Park
8. Yankee Stadium
9. Historic Richmond Town
10. Williamsburg

Brooklyn Bridge

Bronx Zoo

Bronx Zoo

1 Well past its 100th birthday, this sprawling zoo on 265 acres gets better all the time. The newest exhibit is Madagascar!, while Tiger Mountain and the 6.5-acre Congo Gorilla Forest, an African rainforest habitat, bring visitors nose to nose with the inhabitants. The unusual World of Darkness shows nocturnal animals like bats in action *(see p64)*. ⊗ *Bronx River Parkway & Boston Rd, Bronx • Subway (2, 5) West Farms Sq/East Tremont Ave • Open Apr–Oct: 10am–5pm Mon–Fri, 10am–5:30pm Sat, Sun, & hols; Nov–Mar: 10am–4:30pm daily • Admission charge • www.bronxzoo.com*

New York Botanical Garden

2 One of the oldest and largest botanical gardens in the world, this National Historic Landmark covers 250 acres and includes 50 gardens and plant collections and 50 acres of forest, the only remains of woods that once covered New York. The Enid A. Haupt Conservatory, a restored Victorian glass house, is home to tropical rain forest and arid desert plants. A tram makes it easy to see the highlights; guided tours are offered. The Leon Levy Visitor Center has a shop, a visitor orientation area, and a café. ⊗ *Bronx River Parkway & Kazimiroff Blvd, Bronx • Subway (B, D, 4) Bedford Park Blvd • Open 10am–6pm Tue–Sun • Admission charge • www.nybg.org*

Brooklyn Botanic Garden

3 This 52-acre garden designed by the Olmsted brothers in 1910 is home to more than 12,000 plantings. It is best known for the Cranford Rose Gardens where thousands of roses cascade down arches and climb lattices, and the authentic Japanese Hill-and-Pond Garden, planted in 1915. It is also known for its Cherry Esplanade and Cherry Walk, one of the foremost cherry-blossom sites outside Japan. The Steinhardt Conservatory houses tropical and desert plants, and a large bonsai collection. ⊗ *900 Washington Ave, Brooklyn • Subway (2, 3) Eastern Pkwy • Open Mar–Oct: 8am–6pm Tue–Fri, 10am–6pm Sat, Sun, & hols; Nov–Feb: 8am–4:30pm Tue–Fri, 10am–4:30pm Sat, Sun, & hols • Admission charge (free Tue & Sat am) • www.bbg.org*

Brooklyn Botanic Garden

4 Brooklyn Heights Historic District

Overlooking the East River and lower Manhattan skyline, this district is an enclave of old-world charm. Along its quaint streets are preserved, Federal, wooden and brick townhouses of the 1820s and even grander Greek Revival homes of the following decades. ❧ *Court St to Furman St, between Fulton & State Sts • Subway (2, 3) Clark St*

5 Prospect Park

Frederic Olmsted and Calvert Vaux considered this park, opened in 1867, to be their masterpiece. The 90-acre Long Meadow is the longest unbroken green space in the city. The pools and weeping willows of the Vale of Cashmere are particularly fine, along with Vaux's Oriental Pavilion and Concert Grove. ❧ *Between Eastern Pkwy & Parkside Ave, Brooklyn • Subway (2, 3) Grand Army Plaza*

Carousel horse, Prospect Park

6 Park Slope Historic District

These blocks on the western edge of Prospect Park became desirable places to live after the opening of the Brooklyn Bridge in 1883. The Victorian brownstones from the late 19th and early 20th centuries are outstanding U.S. Romanesque Revival and Queen Anne residences. ❧ *Prospect Park West to 8th Ave, between 14th St & St. John's Pl, Brooklyn • Subway (F) 7th Ave*

The No. 7 Train to Queens

This subway route, dubbed the International Express, serves New York's most varied ethnic communities. Take 61st Street, Woodside for Irish pubs, 46th Street for the Middle East, 69th Street for the Philippines. A $1 guide is available from Queens Council on the Arts, 79-01 Park Lane South, Woodhaven, NY 11421 (www.queenscouncilarts.org).

7 Flushing Meadow-Corona Park

The site of two World Fairs, this is now a spacious park with picnic areas, fields for cricket and soccer, paths for bikers and skaters, boating lakes, and many other attractions. The New York Mets' Citi Field, the U.S. Tennis Center, the New York Hall of Science, and the Queens Museum of Art are also here. The Unisphere, the symbol of the 1964 World Fair, still stands. ❧ *Queens • Subway (7) 111th St, Willets Pt–Shea Stadium*

8 Yankee Stadium

A sports shrine, completed in 1923 and known as "The House that Ruth Built" for the legions of fans who came to see superhero Babe Ruth, was retired in 2008. Other legendary heroes of America's most winning baseball

Left **World's Fair Unisphere, Flushing Meadow-Corona Park** Right **A Yankees game**

Historic Richmond Town

team include Joe DiMaggio and Mickey Mantle. The new Yankee stadium incorporates Monument Park, consisting of retired number plaques and statues of the greatest players. 🅢 *East 161st St and River Ave, Bronx • Subway (B, D, 4) 161st St Yankee Stadium • Opening times vary • Admission charge*

9 Historic Richmond Town
This restored village has 29 buildings from the town of Richmond, Staten Island's seat of government from 1729. Other historic buildings were moved here from other sites. The Dutch-style Voorlezer's House (1695) is the island's oldest home on its original site. 🅢 *441 Clarke Ave, Staten Island • Bus S74 from ferry • Open Sep–Jun: 1–5pm Wed–Sun; Jul–Aug: 11am–5pm Wed–Sat, 1–5pm Sun • Admission charge • www.historicrichmondtown.org*

10 Williamsburg
This was mostly a community of Hasidic Jews, Puerto Ricans, and Italians until the 1990s when artists from Manhattan began to move here. The heart of Williamsburg is Bedford Avenue, which is only a short journey from Manhattan on the L subway line. Here you'll find stores promoting local designers, as well as bars and restaurants, where prices are often lower than in Manhattan. 🅢 *Bedford Ave, Brooklyn • Subway L to Bedford Ave; Bus B39 or B61*

A Day Out in Brooklyn

Morning

🕐 Take the No. 2 or 3 subway train to Eastern Parkway – Brooklyn Museum, for the world-class **Brooklyn Museum** *(see p41)*. The museum is part of a civic complex that includes the stately Grand Army Plaza, the **Brooklyn Botanic Garden** *(see p151)*, with its well-known Japanese garden, and neighboring **Prospect Park**.

Along the western edge of Prospect Park is the beautiful **Park Slope Historic District**. Stop for coffee at Ozzie's, 57 7th Avenue, before taking in the area's historic residences. Browse the hip line-up of small shops along 7th Avenue, and stop for lunch at one of the many cafés here.

Afternoon

Return by train to Borough Hall and head for the **Brooklyn Heights Historic District** Walk along Pierre-pont, Willow, and Cranberry streets to see some 19th century houses; Truman Capote wrote *Breakfast at Tiffany's* in the basement of No. 70 Willow, and Arthur Miller once owned the property at No. 155.

A short walk east brings you to **Atlantic Avenue** *(see p156)*. Look in on the spice shops here, and stop for refreshments at the Waterfront Ale House, 155 Atlantic Avenue. Head back to the Brooklyn Bridge, stopping at the Brooklyn Heights Prom-enade for dramatic vistas of Lower Manhattan's towers. End the day with dinner at the romantic **River Café** *(see p157)*.

Left **Brooklyn Museum** Center **Hall of Science** Right **Museum of the Moving Image**

TOP 10 Museums

1 Brooklyn Museum
The permanent collection has objects from ancient Egyptian to contemporary art *(see p41)*. ⊗ *200 Eastern Parkway, Brooklyn • Subway (2, 3) Eastern Pkwy • Open 10am–5pm Wed– Fri, 11am–6pm Sat & Sun; 11am–11pm first Sat of month • Admission charge*

2 Isamu Noguchi Garden Museum
Thirteen galleries and a serene Japanese sculpture garden. ⊗ *9–101 33rd Rd at Vernon Blvd, Queens • Bus 103 to Vernon Blvd • Open 10am–5pm Wed–Fri, 11am–6pm Sat & Sun • Admission charge*

3 Museum of the Moving Image
Artifacts and screenings show the history and techniques of film and TV. ⊗ *35th Ave at 36th St, Queens • Subway Steinway St • Open 10am–3pm Tue–Fri during renovation; subject to change • Admission charge*

4 New York Hall of Science
A science and technology museum with hands-on exhibits and outdoor play area. ⊗ *4701 111th St, Queens • Subway (7) 111th St • Open Sep–Mar: 9:30am–2pm Tue–Thu, 9:30am–5pm Fri, 10am–6pm Sat & Sun; Apr–Jun: also open 9:30am–2pm Mon • Admission charge*

5 Queens Museum of Art
The New York Panorama scale model has 800,000 buildings. ⊗ *New York City Building, Queens • Subway 111th St • Open Sep–Jun: noon–6pm Wed–Sun; Jul–Aug: noon–6pm Wed–Sun (to 8pm Fri) • Admission charge*

6 P.S. 1 MoMA
Since 1976 this center has displayed contemporary art and provided studio space for artists. ⊗ *22–25 Jackson Ave at 46th Ave, Queens • Subway (E, V) 23rd St-Ely Ave • Open noon–6pm Thu–Mon • Admission charge*

7 Van Cortlandt House Museum
This restored 1748 Georgian house is the Bronx's oldest building. ⊗ *Van Cortlandt Park, Broadway and West 246th St, Bronx • Subway (1) 242nd St • Open 10am–3pm Tue–Fri, 11am–4pm Sat & Sun; last tickets 30 mins before closing • Admission charge • www.vancortlandthouse.org*

8 Jacques Marchais Museum of Tibetan Art
A collection of Tibetan art in a Himalayan-style building with a garden. ⊗ *338 Lighthouse Ave, Staten Island • Bus S74 from ferry • Open 1–5pm Thu–Sun • Admission charge*

9 Historic Richmondtown
The museum housed in the County Clerk's office, built in 1848, is just one of the 27 buildings in the museum village. ⊗ *441 Clarke St, Staten Island • Bus S74 from ferry • Opening times vary • Admission charge*

10 Snug Harbor Cultural Center
Chinese garden, performance spaces, art center, children's museum, and a maritime collection. ⊗ *1000 Richmond Terrace, Staten Island • Bus S40 from ferry • Opening times vary • Admission charge*

Left **New York Aquarium** Center **Staten Island Ferry** Right **Staten Island Children's Museum**

🔟 Family Adventures

1 New York Aquarium
Walk through a swamp; stay dry beneath a waterfall *(see p67)*. ⟨ Surf Ave and West 8th St, Brooklyn • Subway (F, Q) W 8th St • Open Apr–May, Sep Oct: 10am–5pm Mon–Fri (5:30pm Sat, Sun & hols); Jun–Aug: 10am–6pm Mon–Fri (7pm Sat, Sun & hols); Nov–Mar: 10am–4:30pm daily • Admission charge

2 Brooklyn Children's Museum
Permanent collections and changing exhibits. ⟨ 145 Brooklyn Ave at St. Marks Pl, Brooklyn • Subway (3) Kingston • Open noon–5pm Wed–Fri, 10am–5pm Sat & Sun; Jul–Aug: noon–6pm Tue–Thu, noon–6:30pm Fri • Admission charge

3 Prospect Park Zoo
Tunnel through a prairie dog town, master baboon language, leapfrog across lily pads. ⟨ 450 Flatbush Ave, Brooklyn • Subway (B, Q) Prospect Park • Open 10am–4:30pm daily; Apr–Oct: 10am–5:30pm Mon–Fri, 10am–5:30pm Sat, Sun & hols • Admission charge

4 Prospect Park Carousel
This 1912 carousel with hand-carved animals was moved here from Coney Island in 1950. ⟨ Prospect Park, Brooklyn • Subway (B, Q) Prospect Park • Open Apr–Oct: noon–5pm Sat, Sun, hols (6pm Jul–Aug) • Rides $1.50

5 Lefferts Homestead Children's House Museum
A rare 18th-century Dutch Colonial farmhouse shows early farm life. ⟨ Prospect Park, Brooklyn • Subway (B, Q) Prospect Park • Open Apr–Nov: noon–5pm Thu–Sun & hols • Free

6 Puppetworks
Hand-carved marionettes are used to present children's classics. ⟨ 338 6th Ave at 4th St, Brooklyn • Subway (F) 7th Ave (Brooklyn) • Performances 12:30pm, 2:30pm Sat & Sun • Admission charge, reservations required

7 Sheepshead Bay Fishing Boats
A fishing fleet takes passengers for day and evening trips. ⟨ Emmons Ave, Brooklyn • Subway (B, Q) to Sheepshead Bay • Boats leave 6:30–9am, 1pm, & 7pm, or can be chartered • Charge

8 Staten Island Children's Museum
A 6-ft (2-m) kinetic porpoise welcomes you to this interactive playground exploring water, insects, and visual and performing arts. ⟨ 1000 Richmond Terrace, Staten Island • Bus S40 from ferry • Open summer: 10am–5pm Tue–Sun; winter: noon–5pm Tue–Sun • Admission charge

9 Staten Island Zoo
The African Savannah at Twilight is a highlight. Other top sights include the Tropical Forest and Serpentarium. ⟨ 614 Broadway, Staten Island • Bus S48 from ferry • Open 10am–4:45pm daily • Admission charge

10 Staten Island Ferry
A free ride with fabulous views of Manhattan. St. George Terminal buses go to Staten Island's sights *(see p59)*. ⟨ Bus to St. George Terminal, Staten Island • Boats every 15 mins–1 hr, 24 hours daily from Whitehall and South Sts • Free

For more family days out in New York **See pp66–7**

Left **Designer shoes, Madison Avenue** Right **Household goods on display**

TOP 10 Ethnic Shopping

1 Broadway, Astoria
Astoria has the largest Greek community outside Greece, with restaurants, coffee shops, and bakeries on Broadway. ⊗ *Broadway, Astoria, Queens • Subway (N, W) Broadway*

2 Main Street, Flushing
Flushing's Chinatown offers bakeries, food, gifts, restaurants, herbal remedies, and acupuncture. Queensborough Library has material in 40 languages. ⊗ *Main St, Flushing, Queens • Subway (7) Main St*

3 74th Street, Jackson Heights
New York's Indian community's shop windows are filled with ornate gold jewelry and rich saris. Food stores are redolent with spices. ⊗ *74th St, Jackson Heights, Queens • Subway (E, F, R, V) Roosevelt Av*

4 Roosevelt Avenue, Jackson Heights
Around the corner from Indian 74th Street, loudspeakers play Latin American rhythms, street vendors sell hot *churros* (fried dough), and shops offer music, foods, gaucho boots, hats, and piñatas. ⊗ *Roosevelt Ave, Jackson Heights, Queens • Subway (E, F, R, V) Roosevelt Ave*

5 Arthur Avenue, Bronx
In this Italian neighborhood, dozens of small, family-run stores sell everything from Italian wines, handmade pastas, and sausages to rosaries and votive candles. ⊗ *Arthur Ave, Bronx • Subway (4) Fordham Rd*

6 Nassau Avenue, Greenpoint
Shops in America's largest Polish community are laden with home made *kielbasas* and *babkas*, statues of saints, Polish books, music, and cosmetics. ⊗ *Nassau Ave, Greenpoint, Brooklyn*

7 Brighton Beach Avenue, Brooklyn
Known as "Little Odessa," Russian is the first language on this busy street selling everything from smoked fish to Russian dolls.
⊗ *Brighton Beach Ave, Brooklyn*
• Subway (B, Q) Brighton Beach

8 13th Avenue, Borough Park
The main street of Borough Park, home to America's largest Orthodox Jewish community, bustles with shops filled with religious articles, tempting baked goods, children's clothing, and linens. ⊗ *13th Ave, Borough Park, Brooklyn • Subway (D) 55th St*

9 18th Avenue, Bensonhurst
Though the old-world Italian community is slowly giving way to other nationalities, the street still offers generous samplings of authentic Italian foods and coffee shops. ⊗ *18th Ave, Bensonhurst, Brooklyn • Subway (D) 18th Ave*

10 Atlantic Avenue, Brooklyn
This Middle-Eastern shopping center offers baklava and many varieties of olives, dried fruits, and spices. ⊗ *Atlantic Ave, Brooklyn • Subway (R) Court St*

Price Categories

For a three-course meal
for one with a glass of
house wine, and all
unavoidable charges
including tax.

$	under $25
$$	$25–$50
$$$	$50–$80
$$$$	over $80

River Café

🔟 Restaurants

1 River Café
Lobster, duck, and seafood are among many specialties. The Chocolate Duo dessert includes a mini chocolate Brooklyn Bridge *(see p58).* ⌖ 1 Water St, Brooklyn • Subway (A, C) High St • 718 522 5200 • *Men require jackets after 5pm* • $$$$

2 The Grocery
With its New American menu and fresh produce, The Grocery has been drawing Manhattanites to Brooklyn since 1999. The restaurant boasts a lovely garden. ⌖ 288 Smith St, Brooklyn • Subway (F) Carroll St • 718 596 3335 • $$

3 Peter Luger Steak House
Beef lovers flock to Peter Luger's gritty, beer hall-style location for what has long been considered New York's best steaks. Reservations are necessary. ⌖ 178 Broadway, Brooklyn • Subway (J, M, Z) Marcy Ave • 718 387 7400 • $$$

4 Al Di La Trattoria
This cozy, northern Italian trattoria serves regional dishes like hanger steak, mussels in tomato sauce, and wonderful pastas. ⌖ 248 5th Ave, Brooklyn • Subway (R) Union St • 718 636 8888 • $$

5 Dominick's Restaurant
Stand in line, join a table, and feast on homemade Southern Italian food at its best. There's no menu; order your favorite or trust the waiter's choice. ⌖ 2335 Arthur Ave, Bronx • Subway (D) Fordham Road • 718 733 2807 • *No credit cards* • $$

6 S'Agapo
Greek for "I love you," the name is apt for this cheerful, unpretentious spot with wonderful Greek food, weekend music, and a summer terrace. ⌖ 3421 34th Ave, Queens • Subway (N, W) Broadway • 718 626 0303 • $$

7 Kum Gang San
The place to sample Korean stews, noodle dishes, or do-it-yourself Korean barbecue cooked at the table. Meals begin with *Panchan*, small dishes of hot and cold, sweet and sour foods. ⌖ 138–28 Northern Blvd, Queens • Subway (7) Main St • 718 461 0909 • $$

8 Joe's Shanghai
The original of this Chinese café chain is popular for its pork or crab soup dumplings, or "steamed buns." There's also a menu of Shanghai specialties. ⌖ 136–21 37th Ave, Queens • Subway (7) Main St • 718 539 3838 • *No credit cards* • $

9 Jackson Diner
No ambience, but one of New York's best Indian restaurants, with an all-you-can eat buffet lunch. ⌖ 37–47 74th St, Queens • Subway (E, F, G, R, V) Roosevelt Ave • 718 672 1232 • *No credit cards* • $

10 Denino's
A family pizzeria with all the favorites and some adventurous alternatives at the right price. ⌖ 524 Port Richmond Ave, Staten Island • Bus 44 from ferry • 718 442 9401 • *No credit cards* • $

Note: Unless otherwise stated, all restaurants accept credit cards and serve vegetarian meals

STREETSMART

NEW YORK'S TOP 10

Left **Umbrella** Center left **Comfortable shoes** Center Right **Sunglasses** Right **Seasonal clothing**

Planning Your Trip

Streetsmart

1 Seasonal Clothing

New York has distinct seasons with average temperatures ranging from 26–38° F (-3–3° C) in the winter to 67–84° F (19–29° C) in the summer. Despite the averages New York weather is predictably unpredictable. Layers are the solution – a short-sleeved knitted shirt, long-sleeved cotton shirt, and sweater will see you through most changes, plus a warm coat for winter.

2 Umbrella and a Raincoat

The months of March and August have the heaviest rainfall, but an umbrella and raincoat are useful all year round.

3 Walking Shoes

Midtown streets are often clogged with traffic, meaning that walking is not only the most pleasant, but often the fastest, way to get around. Invest in a pair of sturdy walking shoes, and break them in before you leave home to avoid developing blisters.

4 Dark Colors

Dry cleaning is expensive in New York, and laundromats are scarce in midtown where most visitors stay. The practical solution is to pack dark clothing, preferably in fast-drying, drip-dry fabrics that can be rinsed out overnight.

5 Hat and Sun-Glasses

Most visitors are more than likely to undertake a lot of walking in New York. Don't make the mistake of thinking that those tall buildings shut out the sun; if anything, it seems intensified in the city. So come prepared with a hat and sunglasses, and don't forget to pack the suntan lotion.

6 Electric Current Adapter

The U.S. uses a 115–120V current, rather than the 220V current used in Europe and elsewhere. Some hair dryers are equipped with an automatic conversion switch, but most 220V appliances will need an adapter, available in airport shops and some department stores. The U.S. also uses two-prong plugs, and travelers will need a two-prong plug adapter.

7 Metric Conversion Chart

Unlike most of the world, the U.S. does not use the metric system. A conversion chart or electronic pocket converter makes it simple to convert miles into kilometers for distances, ounces into litres for capacity measurements, kilograms to pounds for weight, and celcius into fahrenheit for the weather.

8 Student or Senior ID

Subways and buses, movie houses, most major attractions, and many hotels offer discounted rates for seniors over the age of 65. But proof of age is sometimes requested, so bring along a valid photo identification to take advantage of the discounts. Most museums and sightseeing attractions also offer discounted rates for students, again on presentation of the relevant ID. The minimum age for entry into bars and clubs in the U.S. is 21 and proof of age will be required.

9 Pocket Calculator

To save having to do laborious calculations in your head to convert the price of goods from dollars into pounds or euros when out shopping, bring a pocket calculator with you. Some are almost as small as a credit card, and fit easily into a wallet or pocket.

10 Driving Licence

If you plan on any out-of-New York trips with a rented car, be sure to bring a valid driving licence with you. You will also need to show official identification with a photograph and signature, such as a passport. A credit card will also be required when renting a car.

160

Left **Arriving by air** Center **Arriving by ship** Right **Arriving by bus**

Streetsmart

1 Arriving by Air
International flights land at John F. Kennedy Airport and Newark. La Guardia Airport serves mostly domestic flights. Cab fares to the city are a fixed $45 from Kennedy Airport, $34–$50 from Newark, and $20–$30 from LaGuardia, plus $3.50 toll and tips.

2 Limousine Service
Several limousine companies offer private door-to-door services by appointment, to or from the airports, rail, or ship terminals, at pre-arranged rates averaging $10–$20 more than taxi fares. Reputable services include Carmel and Dial 7. 🅢 *Carmel: 212 666 6666 • Dial 7: 212 777 7777*

3 Supershuttle
Supershuttle vans operate door-to-door and are less than limousines or taxis. They pick up several passengers so allow plenty of time. Prices are $16–$21 according to zip code. 🅢 *Supershuttle: 212-BLUEVAN*

4 Coach Companies
Coaches from the airports to central midtown points cost $8–$13. Shared minibuses with hotel drop-offs cost $13–$19. Transportation information is available at the baggage checkout areas in all airports. 🅢 *Advance information: 800 247 7433 • NY–NJ Port Authority: www.panynj.gov*

5 Arriving by Train
Amtrak trains from all parts of the U.S. arrive at Penn Station, 7th Avenue and 33rd Street. Long Island Railroad and New Jersey Transit commuter trains also use Penn station; MetroNorth regional trains use Grand Central Terminal, at Lexington Avenue and 42nd Street. Cabs are available at all terminal entrances. 🅢 *Amtrak trains: 800 872 7245 • Long Island Railroad: 718 217 5477 • New Jersey Transit: 973 275 5555 • MetroNorth: 212 532 4900*

6 Arriving by Bus
Intercity bus and commuter lines arrive at the Port Authority Bus Terminal. Cabs wait at the 8th Avenue entrance. 🅢 *Port Authority Bus Terminal: 8th Ave at 42nd St • 212 564 8484*

7 Arriving by Ship
Cruise ships arrive in New York at the NYC Passenger Ship Terminal. Customs and immigration officials are on duty to process passengers on overseas cruises. Cabs are found outside the terminal. 🅢 *NYC Passenger Ship Terminal: 711 12th Ave • 212 246 5450*

8 Arriving by Car
Parking expenses in Midtown can cost around $40 a day. Check in advance with your hotel over the availability and cost of parking, and, if necessary, consider using a suburban motel located near convenient transportation into Manhattan.

9 Customs Allowances
$100 worth of gifts ($400 for U.S. citizens), one carton of 200 cigarettes, 100 cigars, and one litre of liquor may be brought into the U.S. without incurring customs fees. No meat, seeds, growing plants, or fresh fruit may be brought in. Prescription drugs should be clearly marked. People flying within the U.S. can only carry liquids in 100 ml bottles. This means you can carry duty-free alcohol only to your first port of call within the U.S. If you have a connecting flight, the liquids will be confiscated unless you can move them to your checked luggage. 🅢 *U.S. Customs Service: 800 697 3662. For general information: 877 CUSTOMS*

10 Immigration
Landing cards and customs declaration forms are usually distributed on the plane. Most UK and Canadian passport holders do not need visas if staying in the U.S. for 90 days or less; however, those planning to visit under the Visa Waiver Scheme must register in advance online and pay a charge. Visit *https://esta.cbp.dhs.gov* for further details.

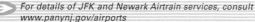
For details of JFK and Newark Airtrain services, consult www.panynj.gov/airports

Left **The Visitors Bureau** Center **New York taxi** Right **Big Onion Walking Tours**

Useful Information

1 Tourist Information

NYC & Company, the New York Convention & Visitors Bureau, operates a Visitor Information Center with multilingual counselors and free information.
⊗ Visitor Information Center: 810 7th Ave at 53rd St • Map J3
• www.nycgo.com
• 8am–8pm daily

2 New York Newspapers

The New York Times is read nationally and internationally for its extensive foreign coverage. The city's tabloids, the New York Post and New York Daily News, are known for their attention-grabbing headlines and a number of pages of sports coverage. Many young New Yorkers read the free weekly Village Voice and rival New York Press.

3 Out-of-Town Newspapers

Foreign and out-of-town newspapers may be found at branches of Barnes & Noble bookstore, and many Sunday papers are carried at the Universal News Stand. If you can't find what you want, Hotalings News Agency, a wholesaler, may be able to help.
⊗ Universal News Stand: 234 West 42nd St • Map K3 • Hotalings News Agency: 212 974 9419

4 Entertainment Listings

The Friday New York Times arts section, Time Out New York, the New Yorker, and New York Magazine are all comprehensive weekly sources of current happenings in the city, readily available at any newsstand.

5 Museum/ Gallery Guides

Besides listings in the entertainment magazines, Museums New York is a quarterly publication ($4.95) available at most newsstands, with writeups of current museum and gallery exhibitions. The Art Now Gallery Guide, free in most galleries, details current offerings around the city.

6 Opening Hours

Most stores and sightseeing attractions are open daily (see p165); some banks open on weekends, but ATMs are always available (see p169); post offices close on Sundays with the exception of the General Post Office (see p169). Many museums close on Mondays and major holidays – check with individual venues for their specific times.

7 Tipping

A tip of at least 15–20 per cent is the norm for meals, taxis, and personal services such as haircuts or massages. Bellboys at

hotels usually receive $1 per bag, and bartenders $1 per drink. Many diners find it easiest to calculate a tip by simply doubling the tax (8.375 percent) on a restaurant bill.

8 Taxes

Be sure to factor in taxes when you calculate costs. Sales tax is an extra 8.375 percent on every purchase greater than $110. Hotel taxes add 14.25 percent to the bill, plus an extra $3.50 per night occupancy tax.

9 Resident tours

Visitors might like to try an afternoon with a Big Apple Greeter. A volunteer guide from this not-for-profit organization will take small groups or couples on a 2–4 hour tour of any New York neighborhood or give you an insider's view of the city free of charge. Big Onion Walking Tours (see p164) offer similar tours, but for a fee.
⊗ Big Apple Greeter: 212 669 8159 • www. bigapplegreeter.org

10 Restrooms

Hotels (see pp172–9) and department stores (see p64) are the best places for restrooms. Most fast-food restaurants, such as McDonald's, and coffee shops such as Starbucks, also have restrooms and although intended for patrons, these are usually available if you ask for the key.

Left **Traffic control** Center **Staten Island Ferry** Right **Traffic and street signs**

Getting Around

The Street Plan
Above Greenwich Village, Manhattan is laid out on a straight grid plan, with the avenues running to the north and south, and the streets crossing east to west. Most avenues are one-way, alternating the direction with each block, except for Park Avenue, which runs both ways. 5th Avenue is the dividing line between the East and West sides.

Finding an Address
To locate the nearest cross street for avenue addresses in Manhattan, drop the last digit of the street number, divide by 2 and add these key numbers:

3rd Avenue	10
6th Avenue	12
7th Avenue	20
8th Avenue	9
Lexington Avenue	22
Madison Avenue	27

This is only if the street number is below 1800.

Traffic Signs
Traffic lights show red for stop, yellow for caution, and green for go for vehicles. At crosswalks, the red hand means "wait", the white walking figure means it's okay to cross. The red hand sign blinks when the lights are about to change; given the aggressive traffic, it's wise not to attempt to beat the light.

Subway Routes
Subways run north and south, uptown and downtown on Lexington Avenue, 6th Avenue, 7th Avenue, Broadway, and 8th Avenue. The Q, N, R, W, E, F, V and 7 trains to Queens run east to west, crossing Manhattan. A, C, B, D, J, M, Z, L, N, Q, R, 2, 3, 4 and 5 lines all run to Brooklyn. Passenger information: 718 330 1234 • www.mta.info

Bus Routes
Manhattan buses run on every north-south artery except on Park and West End avenues. The most useful crosstown buses run on 96th, 86th, 79th, 67th, 57th, 49/50th, 42nd, 34th, 23rd, and 14th streets. Route numbers are posted on a lighted strip above the front windshield. Free maps are available on most buses.

The Metrocard
Metrocards are sold in subways and in shops displaying the sign and are good for subways and buses. Each ride deducts one $2.25 fare from the card; transfers are free between buses, and between subway and bus, but not between two subways. Weekly passes for unlimited travel cost $27.

Taxi Know-how
Manhattan yellow taxis can be hailed anywhere you spy one. Lights atop the cab go on when the car is available, or to show that the driver is off-duty. Hotel cab stands are good places to look for a cab. For taxi complaints: 311

Car Rentals
Rentals offices are found throughout the city; drivers must be over 25, and have a valid license and major credit card. Weekends are heavily booked, so phone in advance. Hertz: 800 654 3131 • Avis: 800 331 1212 • National: 800 227 7368 • Budget: 800 527 0700

Parking Rules and Penalties
Street parking is not available midtown and is scarce elsewhere. Some avenues have curb meters allowing 15- to 60-minute stays; overstaying means an extremely expensive ticket or towing fee. Side streets have "alternate side" regulations banning cars, during certain hours and on alternate days, from parking on alternate sides of the street.

Ferries and Water Taxis
New York Waterways ferries connect Manhattan with New Jersey and provide transportation to New York Yankee and Mets baseball games. Water taxis run from East 90th Street Pier to Pier 84. For ferry schedules: 800 533 3779 • Staten Island ferry information: see p59 • Water taxi information: www.nywatertaxi.com

Left **Circle Line boat** Center **Touring by bus** Right **Carriage in Central Park**

Guided Tours

1 Neighborhood Walking Tours

The best way to see New York is on foot with a knowledgeable guide. Top leaders include: Big Onion Walking Tours (history oriented), Joyce Gold History Tours, and the 92nd Street Y (Jewish oriented). ✆ *Big Onion Walking Tours: 212 439 1090 • Joyce Gold History Tours: 212 242 5762 • 92nd St Y: 212 415 5500*

2 Architectural Tours

The Municipal Art Society, which is dedicated to preservation and excellence in urban design, offers enlightening "Discover New York" tours highlighting the city's buildings and neighborhoods. The tours are led by architectural historians. ✆ *Municipal Art Society: 212 935 3960*

3 Boat Tours

Circle Line offers two- or three-hour cruises around Manhattan, as well as Harbor Lights evening cruises and one-hour sails from South Street Seaport. New York Waterways has 90-minute harbor trips. ✆ *South Street Seaport: Pier 16 & Pier 83, 212 563 3200 • New York Waterways: 800 53 FERRY*

4 Bus Tours

Gray Line offers two- to ten-hour double-decker and motorcoach Manhattan sightseeing trips with multilingual guides, plus Brooklyn tours and Harlem gospel tours. An all-day tour costs $84, which includes a 1-hour Statue of Liberty boat cruise and Top of the Rock ticket. ✆ *Gray Line Bus Tours: 212 397 2620*

5 Backstage Tours

Among the insider's offerings are Lincoln Center (see p139), the Metropolitan Opera, Radio City Music Hall (see p13), NBC Studios (see p13), Carnegie Hall (see p125), Madison Square Garden, Grand Central Terminal (see p123), Gracie Mansion (see p135), and the New York Public Library (see p124). ✆ *Lincoln Center: 212 875 5350 • Metropolitan Opera: 212 769 7020 • Radio City Music Hall: 212 307 7171 • NBC Studios: 212 664 3700 • Carnegie Hall: 212 903 9600 • Madison Square Garden: 212 465 6080 • Grand Central Terminal: 212 340 2345 • Gracie Mansion: 212 639 9675 • New York Public Library: 212 340 0849*

6 Park Tours

See the glories and splendor of Central Park under the expert guidance of Urban Park Rangers or volunteer guides from the Park Conservancy. Free programs are held most weekends and some Wednesdays. ✆ *Park Conservancy schedules, 212-310-6600 • Urban Park Rangers, 311*

7 Bicycle Tours

A leisurely, two-hour spin around Central Park takes in all the important sights, with a break for refreshments. Tours cost $49 with bike rental. ✆ *203 West 58th St • Map H2 • 212 541 8759*

8 Garden Tours

The New York Botanical Garden (718 817 8700) holds various tours. ✆ *Call for tour schedule • Tickets are free with garden admission • Tram tours run every 20 minutes ($2 adults, $1 children, see p151)*

9 Museum Tours

The Metropolitan Museum of Art (see p133) offers 20 different guided tours daily in several languages, covering the highlights of the museum as well as specific galleries; tours are included with the price of admission. The Guggenheim Museum (see p133) offers family tours of museum highlights, also free with the price of admission.

10 Carriage Tours

Horse-drawn cabs take passengers on a short, old-fashioned ride through Central Park (see p26–7). Rides cost $34–54. ✆ *Central Park South at 59th St • Map H3*

Left **Givenchy** Center **Gourmet shopping** Right **Barnes & Noble bookstore**

Shopping Tips

Store Hours
Most stores operate 10am–7pm Mon–Sat, until 8pm Thu, and 11am or noon to 6pm or 7pm Sun. Many stay open on holidays but all close for Christmas and Easter.

Credit Cards
MasterCard and Visa are accepted everywhere; American Express and Discover in most places.

Women's Clothing
Department stores have the widest selections (see p64), Madison Avenue has the designer names (p136), and SoHo the best trendy fashions (see p65). For discounts, try Orchard Street (p91), Century 21, and Daffy's. ⊗ Century 21: 22 Cortlandt St , Map Q4 • Daffy's: 125 East 57th St & 111 5th Ave, Map H4 & L3

Men's Clothing
For designer fashion go to Barneys, traditional styles Brooks Brothers or Paul Stuart, and Thomas Pink for hipper designs; John Varvatos is sporty. ⊗ Barneys: 660 Madison Ave, Map K4 • Brooks Brothers: 346 Madison Ave, Map L4 • Paul Stuart: 350 Madison Ave at 45th St, Map J4 • Thomas Pink: 520 Madison Ave, Map H4 • John Varvatos: 122 Spring St, Map N3

Books
Barnes & Noble carries a huge range; Rizzoli specializes in photography and art; Books of Wonder is the place to go for children's books; and the Strand has a wide range of used books. ⊗ Barnes & Noble: 1972 Broadway, Map G2 • Rizzoli: 31 West 57th St, Map H3 • Books of Wonder: 18 West 18th St, Map M3 • Strand Book Store: 828 Broadway, Map M4

Gourmet Food
Among the city's gastronomic palaces, Zabar's is the best known (see p141), but Dean & DeLuca, the Gourmet Garage, Citarella, and Whole Foods have their devotees as well as multiple outlets. ⊗ Dean & DeLuca: 560 Broadway, Map M4 • Gourmet Garage: 2567 Broadway, Map E2 • Citarella: 2135 Broadway, Map G2 • Whole Foods: 10 Columbus Circle, Map H2

Crafts and Antiques
Manhattan Art & Antiques and Chelsea Antiques carry a little of everything. For American folk, try Kelter–Malce. Accessories abound at Archangel Antiques; Doyle & Doyle has vintage jewelry; while Iris Brown stocks antique dolls. ⊗ Manhattan Art & Antiques: 1050 2nd Ave, Map G4 • Chelsea Antiques: 110 West 25th St, Map L2 • Kelter–Malce: 74 Jane St, Map M2 • Archangel Antiques: 334 East 9th St, Map M4 • Doyle & Doyle: 189 Orchard St, Map N5 • Iris Brown: 205 East 63rd St, Map H4

Toys and Children's Clothes
F. A. O. Schwarz (see p66) and Toys 'R' Us are amazing but less overwhelming is the Children's General Store. Beautiful clothes are at Bonpoint, cool choices at Space Kiddets, and affordable outfits at Children's Place. ⊗ Toys 'R' Us: 1514 Broadway, Map J3 • Children's General Store: Grand Central Terminal, Map J4 • Bonpoint: 1269 & 810 Madison Ave, Map E4 • Space Kiddets: 26 East 22nd St, Map L4 • Children's Place: 1460 Broadway, Map K3

Music
Opera lovers should head for the Metropolitan Opera Shop, while vintage collectors should seek out the House of Oldies. For jazz and funk hit Bleecker St Records, and for house, Other Music. ⊗ Metropolitan Opera Shop: 136 West 65 St, Map G2 • House of Oldies: 35 Carmine St, Map N3 • Bleecker St Records: 239 Bleecker St, Map N3 • Other Music: 15 East 4th St, Map M4

Perfumes and Cosmetics
Fresh specializes in bodycare and perfumes. Kiehl's has quality skin products. Aveda features natural products made from plant extracts. ⊗ Fresh: 57 Spring St, Map N4 • Kiehl's: 109 3rd Ave, Map L4 • Aveda: 233 Spring St, Map N3

For New York stores **See pp64–5**

Left **TKTS booth** Right **Venue for open-air theater, Central Park**

New York on a Budget

1 TKTS Booths
Tickets for Broadway and off-Broadway shows are sold at a 25 to 50 percent discount (plus a small service charge) on the day of the show at TKTS booths. Arrive early as queues can be long.
⊗ *47th St & Broadway • Map J3 • Open 3–8pm daily, 10am–2pm for Wed & Sat matinees, 11am–7:30pm Sun • www.tdf.org*

2 Free TV Shows
Watch your favorite show for free – if you can get in a request early enough. For more information, call the individual networks. Same-day tickets are sometimes available at the Tourist Information Center *(see p162)* or from the NBC lobby desk.
⊗ *ABC: 212 456 3054 • CBS: 212 975 2476 • NBC: 212 664 3056, www.shopnbc.com*

3 Free Events
There are regular free drama performances and concerts in Central Park in July and August. Contact Summerstage (212 360 2777). Excellent concerts are also held by faculty and talented students at the Julliard School (212 799 5000).

4 Free Summer Venues
Metropolitan Opera performances, New York Philharmonic concerts, Shakespeare in the Park at the Delacorte Theater in Central Park, and outdoor performances at Lincoln Center's Damrosch Park – all free – are among the reasons why New Yorkers love summer. Contact NYC & Company (212 484 1222) for a current schedule.

5 Saving on Transit
The best transit deal is the $8.25 Fun Pass, a Metrocard that allows unlimited subway and bus rides from the first ride until 3am the next morning. If you are staying in the city longer, put $8 or more on a pay-per-ride Metrocard and get 15 percent extra credit, while a $27 card will buy you unlimited rides for one full week ($51.50 for 14 days).

6 Cheap Eats
Pre-theater prix-fixe dinners are good value, but lunch menus are usually better. During Restaurant Week, for two weeks in January and again in June, New York's best restaurants offer three-course lunches priced at $24, and dinners for $35. Book ahead through www.opentable.com

7 Changing Money
You can save money by using your bank card at ATMs (Automated Teller Machines). Many accept Plus or Cirrus network cards and will debit your account and pay you in dollars. The transaction fees are less than those at Currency Exchanges, and you get the wholesale exchange rate used between banks *(see p169)*.

8 Bargain Buys
CityPass will buy you admission to six top attractions for $79 ($59 for ages 6–17), half the price. You can buy it at participating sites such as the Empire State Building and the Guggenheim Museum. The New York Pass costs $75 for one day and is valid at 55 attractions. Longer passes are also available.
• *www.citypass.com*
• *www.newyorkpass.com*

9 Sale Periods
White sales on linens are held in January and August, coat sales are featured during the week of Veteran's Day in November and in February. Bathing suits go on sale after the 4th of July and everything is on sale before and after Christmas.

10 Discount Malls
Round trips are available seven times a day to Woodbury Common Premium Outlets, a one-hour drive to a mall of 220 discount outlets carrying top name brands such as Armani, Gucci, and Burberry. Tickets cost $40 ($32 if bought online). ⊗ *Short Line Bus Tours: Port Authority Bus Terminal, 800 631 8405 • www.coachusa.com/shortline*

New York Subway

🔟 Things to Avoid

1 Unlicensed Cabs
Unregulated cars whose drivers solicit passengers at airports or in front of hotels have no safety regulations and no metered limits on what they can charge you. Be patient, and stand in line for a licensed yellow cab instead. (For tips on taxi know-how see p163.)

2 "Going Out of Business" Signs
The "lost our lease" or "going out of business" signs you might see in shops – particularly along 5th Avenue or on Broadway – have been up there for years. The signs are intended to lure unwary customers into stores with, typically, overpriced electronics.

3 Pickpockets
Just as in most large cities around the world, New York has its share of pickpockets hoping to take advantage of distracted visitors. Be especially alert in crowds and when getting on and off crowded buses and subway trains. Even better, use hidden travel wallets to keep your money secure at all times. Leave your valuable jewelry at home or back at the hotel, and never stop to count your money on the street.

4 Ticket Scalpers
You may be more than happy to pay the extra price for tickets to sold-out sporting events or shows, but be aware of the risk you run; sometimes the tickets peddled by scalpers turn out to be counterfeit, and you could wind up with no money and no seat.

5 Three-card Monte Games
You'll see these card games on the street, especially around Broadway. Sometimes it seems as though a player has won big, but be warned – the winner is usually an assistant. You will only win these games if the dealer wants you to.

6 Rush Hour on the Subway
Most workers have no choice and have to ride the subway at its busiest hours. But you do not need to get caught in the crush; avoid the rush hours between 7am and 9am, and between 4.30pm and 6.30pm, and you'll have a much pleasanter ride. (For information on subway routes see p163.)

7 Hotel Phone Charges
Unfortunately there is no regulation on what hotels can charge for telephone calls made by their guests. Read carefully the card that explains your hotel's phone surcharges, since they can be hefty, even if you use a credit card. You can save money by patronizing the telephone booth in the lobby or sometimes by buying a phone card (see p169).

8 Hotel Breakfasts
Hotels notoriously overcharge for their breakfasts, counting on the fact that their guests will find it easier and pleasanter to stay in. But you can save more than half – and often have a better breakfast – just by seeking out a coffee shop down the block.

9 Luggage Hassles
One tip that might help you to avoid luggage hassles: Discourage break-ins by making it harder for thieves; use tape to seal your bags shut and make any tampering obvious. You can also put your travel itinerary inside any bags, so that if they go astray, the airline will be able to track you down. ✪ Lost and Found for bus and subway services: 212 712 4500 • Lost and Found for taxis: 311

10 Jaywalking
It may seem tempting to save a few minutes by cutting across traffic in the middle of the street rather than crossing at the traffic lights on the corner, but it could cost you dearly if a speeding, inattentive New York driver comes along. It is much better to follow the city slogan, "Cross at the green, not in-between."

Left **New York city bus "kneeling" to help the elderly** Center **Wheelchair access** Right **Tour bus**

🔟 Special Needs

1 Information Sources

Hospital Audiences, Inc. publishes Access for All ($5), a guide to available resources at all New York's cultural institutions. The Mayor's Office for People with Disabilities provides services to residents and also has information on city facilities. ◈ *Hospital Audiences, Inc.: 212 575 7676 • People with Disabilities: 212 788 2830*

2 Accommodation for the Disabled

New York city law requires that all facilities built after 1987 provide entrances and accessible restroom facilities for the disabled. All city buses now have steps that can be lowered to allow wheelchair access, and most street corners also have curb cuts for wheelchairs.

3 Special Tours

Hands On is an organization devoted to the hearing-impaired, and publishes a calendar of information on museum and backstage tours, performances, films, and other events available with sign language interpretation. ◈ *Hands On: 212 740 3087*

4 Aids for the Hearing-Impaired

All Broadway shows have free amplification devices for the hearing-impaired, and sign language interpretation can be arranged with the Theater Access Project or Hands On.

◈ *Theater Development Fund: 212 912 9770 • Hands On: 212 740 3087*

5 Aids for the Sight-impaired

Lighthouse International is an organization devoted to enabling the vision-impaired to cope through rehabilitation and education. It offers tips for travelers, and also lends receivers so that you can hear the new talking traffic signs at 59th Street and Lexington Avenue. ◈ *Lighthouse International: 111 East 59th St, between Park & Lexington Aves • Map H4 • 800 829 0500*

6 Facilities for Infants and Toddlers

Department stores are equipped with diaper changing stations (*see p64*); because space is so tight in New York, other facilities tend to be scarce. Most restaurants do have highchairs these days, but it is always wise to call and check what facilities they have for children before you set out.

7 Babysitting

The Babysitter's Guild, established over 60 years ago, is a reliable source for babysitting. Staff can accommodate 16 different languages, and rates start at $25 per hour, for a four-hour minimum, plus $4.50 for transportation ($10 after midnight). ◈ *The Babysitter's Guild: 212 682 0227*

8 Legal Assistance

The Legal Aid Society offers free advice and referrals; Legal Services for New York City, a non-profit referral service, also offers assistance to those with legal problems. ◈ *The Legal Aid Society: 212 577 3300 • Legal Services for New York City: 212 431 7200*

9 Other Useful Numbers

Help is at hand in the city for various eventualities. ◈ Clothing repairs: *Ramon's Tailor Shop 212 226 0747*. All-night drugstores: *Duane Reade 212 541 9708, Eckerd 212 772 0104*. Emergency car repairs: *Citywide Towing 866 TOWING 2*. Lost and found for buses and subways: *212 712 4500*. Lost and found for taxis: *311*. General New York queries: *311*.

10 Student Identification

Foreign students will benefit from having an International Student Identity Card (ISIC) which can help to secure discounts on transportation, rental cars, hotels, and various attractions in New York and across the U.S. The cards cost $22 and are available from STA Travel, CTS Travel U.S.A. or Travel Cuts. ◈ *STA Travel: 205 East 42nd St. Map K4. 212 822 2700 • CTS Travel U.S.A: Empire State Building, 350 5th Ave. Map K3. 212 760 1287 • Travel Cuts: 124 MacDougal St. Map N3.*

For New York's Top 10 places for children See pp66–7

Left **Standard mailbox** Center **Automated teller machine** Right **Currency exchange counter**

🔟 Banking and Communications

Banking Hours

Most New York banks open 9am–4pm Monday–Friday, though individual branches may have longer opening hours, including weekends. Only larger banks are equipped to exchange foreign currency. Be prepared to show a passport or other photo identification when changing currency.

Currency Exchange Locations

People's Foreign Exchange offers currency exchange with no commission charge. Travelex Currency Services charge a fee. 🖎 *People's Foreign Exchange: 575 5th Ave at 47th St. Map K3. 212 883 0550 • Travelex Currency Services: 1590 Broadway at 48th St. Map J3. 212 265 6049*

Automated Teller Machines (ATMs)

ATMs can be found at almost all banks and are open 24 hours a day. They accept most common bank cards and credit cards, although they usually charge a small service fee. 🖎 *For banks accepting Cirrus bank cards: 800 622 7747 • Plus cards: 800 843 7587*

Credit Cards

Cash advances can be obtained from ATMs using MasterCard and Visa cards; Banks accepting Cirrus (see ATM section) take

MasterCard; Plus card banks (see ATM section) accept Visa. American Express members can also withdraw cash with their credit card at American Express offices.

Cashing Checks

Travelers' checks in dollars issued by well-known organizations such as American Express or Travelex are widely accepted in the U.S. in restaurants, banks, and stores, although personal checks on a foreign bank are not. American Express offices will also cash checks for their cardholders.

Telephones

Public telephones are found in hotel lobbies, and in restaurants and department stores. It's no longer common to find a phone outside. You will need 25 cents in coins to make a local three-minute call, and more if you talk longer. You can buy prepaid telephone cards at many newsstands, which conveniently eliminate the need for coins.

Internet Access

Many hotels now have free dataport connections for laptop Internet access. In addition, free access to the Internet is available for members of the public at the Science and Business branch of the

New York Public Library. 🖎 *188 Madison Ave at 34th St • Map K4 • 212 592 7000*

Sending Mail

Postage for letters sent within the U.S. costs 44 cents for the first ounce, and 17 cents for additional ounces; stamps for postcards cost 27 cents. To send mail internationally, postcards cost 90 cents, and letters start at 90 cents for the first half-ounce.

Post Office Hours

All city post offices are open from 9am to 5pm Monday to Friday; some are open on Saturday; the General Post Office stays open 24 hours a day. Most hotels sell stamps and will mail letters for their guests. 🖎 *General Post Office: 421 8th Ave at 33rd St. Map K2. 800 ASK USPS*

Express and Courier Delivery

The U.S. Post Office Express Mail next-day delivery service starts at $17.50 for up to 8 ounces; global 2- to 3-day delivery costs from $49. Next-day delivery is also available from Federal Express, DHL (international only), and United Parcel Service; all include pick-up services in their charges. 🖎 *Federal Express: 800 GO FEDEX • DHL: 800 CALL DHL • UPS: 800 742 5877*

Left **Sign for public payphones** Center **Kaufman's Pharmacy** Right **New York ambulance**

Security and Health

1 Discouraging Thieves

Pickpockets are on the lookout for tourists, who usually have substantial amounts of cash on them. Don't flaunt jewelry or advertise your status by wearing a waistpack and sporting your camera around your neck. A local grocery store bag is a good, inconspicuous place for cameras.

2 Avoiding Scams

Beware of distractions in front of you when boarding buses or subways; a pickpocket's accomplice behind you may be after your wallet. If you buy electronics from street peddlers for next to nothing, you may find next to nothing of value inside the box when you open it.

3 Locations to Avoid

New York's crime rate is way down, but it makes little sense to take chances. Most city parks are delightful during the day, but after dark are not safe places to explore. Likewise, some neighborhoods (generally, anywhere on the edges of the city) are best avoided late at night.

4 Hotel Room Safety

Don't advertise your empty hotel room by putting out the "please make up this room" sign. Leave the lights on

if you think you will be returning late. Other than the maids, don't admit strangers to your room; if necessary, phone the desk to verify someone who claims to be an employee of the hotel.

5 Walk-in Medical Clinics

The D.O.C.S clinics, affiliated with the Beth Israel Medical Center, offer convenient by appointment or walk-in services for adults and children. ✪ 55 East 34th St, between Madison & Park Aves. Map K4. 212 252 6000. Open 8am–8pm Mon–Thu; 8am–7pm Fri; 9am–3pm Sat; 9am–2pm Sun • 202 West 23rd St at 7th Ave. Map L3. 212 352 2600

6 Hospital Emergency Rooms

Emergency treatment is available 24 hours a day; if you are able, call the number on your policy first, and check which hospitals your insurance company deals with. ✪ Roosevelt Hospital: 428 West 59th St at 9th Ave. Map H2. 212 523 4000 • St. Vincent's Hospital: 153 West 11th St at 7th Ave. Map M3. 212 604 7000

7 Dental Emergencies

For dental crises, D.O.C.S has walk-in clinics. You can also contact N.Y.U. Dental Care for urgent treatment. ✪ N.Y.U. Dental Care: 345 East 24th St, between

1st & 2nd Aves • Map L4 • 212 998 9800, 212 998 9828 weekend & out of hours

8 Travel Insurance

Most U.S. insurance is effective throughout the country, but those with foreign insurance coverage should take out comprehensive medical travel insurance before arriving in the U.S. Should you need any treatment, you will be expected to pay for it at the time of service and the bill can be an extremely steep one.

9 Smoking

Smoking is illegal in almost all public places in New York, including subways, movie theaters, restaurants and bars. The fines are stiff, $100 and up.

10 Telephone Helplines

Various helplines are available to call in a crisis. ✪ Suicide Help Line: 800 543 3638 • Sex Crimes Report Line: 212 267 7273 • Victim Services Agency: 212 577 7777 • Travelers' Aid: 212 944 0013

Emergency Numbers

Police, fire, and Medical Emergencies
911

N.Y. Hotel Urgent Medical Services
212 737 1212

Sunbathers basking at Jones Beach

ᵒ10 Excursions from New York

1 Jones Beach State Park

Miles of ocean beaches, pools, a boardwalk with games, miniature golf, and entertainment are all part of this exceptional recreational center on Long Island's south shore. A great day's outing from the city. ◈ *Long Island Railroad connects with buses • LIRR: 718 217 5477 • 90 mins from Manhattan*

2 Fire Island

An escapist's dream. No cars are allowed on this tranquil island off Long Island, rimmed with 26 miles (42 km) of beach. Visitors get around on foot or bike, and shop or dine in tiny, village centers. ◈ *Long Island Railroad to Bayshore ferry boats • LIRR: 718 217 5477 • 2 hrs, 30 mins from Manhattan*

3 The Hamptons

Celebrity-watching is a favorite sport in the sophisticated Hamptons on eastern Long Island, where society and entertainment names gather to enjoy the miles of beach and beautiful old colonial towns such as Southampton and Easthampton. ◈ *Long Island Railroad • LIRR: 718 217 5477 • 2 hrs, 30 mins from Manhattan*

4 New Jersey Shore

With the Atlantic Ocean beaches stretching the length of the state, the New Jersey shore is ideal for families. It offers lively boardwalks, laidback beach escapes, and Victorian towns like Spring Lake and Cape May, filled with romantic inns. ◈ *New Jersey Transit trains: 973 275 5555 • 90 mins from Manhattan*

5 Hyde Park

F. D. Roosevelt's estate and presidential library, the lavish Vanderbilt mansion, a chance to preview the work of future great chefs at the Culinary Institute of America, and scenic river views are among the lures of this Hudson River valley town. By car, Rhinebeck, 10 miles (16 km) away, is a good overnight base. ◈ *Metro North trains: 212 532 4900 • Short Line buses: 800 631 8405 • 2 hrs from Manhattan*

6 Buck's County, PA

This bucolic enclave of hills, streams, covered bridges, and mellow stone farmhouses offers visitors cozy, country inns, fine dining, choice antiquing, and gallery hopping. New Hope, a charming art colony, is the place to stay. ◈ *Trans-Bridge Line buses: 610 868 6001 • 2 hrs from Manhattan*

7 Princeton, NJ

Home to one of the oldest and most elite universities in America, Princeton is also a lovely town filled with fine 18th-century homes. On campus are Nassau Hall, the 1783 U.S. Capitol, and a museum of sculpture.

◈ *New Jersey Transit trains to Princeton: 973 275 5555 • 90 mins from Manhattan*

8 Philadelphia, PA

Boasting Independence Hall, colonial neighborhoods, a lively riverfront, and more than 100 museums, Philadelphia is a great addition to a visit to New York. ◈ *Amtrak trains. 800 USA RAIL. 1 hr, 45 mins from Manhattan • Boltbus: 1 877 BOLTBUS. 3 hrs from Manhattan*

9 Caramoor, Katonah

The 100-acre Caramoor estate, in northern Westchester County, includes a museum of room settings brought from European palaces, and a Venetian theater that hosts an outdoor summer music festival. ◈ *Metro North "Caramoor Specials": 212 532 4900 • 75 mins from Manhattan*

10 Tarrytown Mansions

Kykuit, the Rockefeller mansion overlooking the Hudson River, is the major draw, but Tarrytown also offers Philipsburg Manor, a restored Dutch farm estate. A little farther south in Irvington is Sunnyside, home of author Washington Irving, and Lyndhurst, palace of financier Jay Gould. ◈ *Metro North trains: 212 532 4900. 1 hr from Manhattan • New York Waterway river cruises to Kykuit: 800 533 3779*

Left **The Four Seasons** Center **The Carlyle** Right **The Pierre**

Best Hotels in New York

1 Four Seasons
For luxury in a modern mode, this dramatic, pale-hued tower by I.M. Pei is the ultimate, with rooms among the city's largest, and has every amenity. The bar and restaurant draws the city's elite.
◈ 57 East 57th St, New York, NY 10022 • Map H4 • 212 758 5700 • www. fourseasons.com • $$$$$

2 Carlyle
Antiques set the stage for an uptown, luxury lair that has long attracted the famous with its hushed European ambience and spacious quarters in understated good taste. Café Carlyle is the city's poshest cabaret.
◈ 35 East 76th St, New York, NY 10021 • Map G4 • 212 744 1600 • www. thecarlyle.com • $$$$$

3 New York Palace
This legendary hotel incorporates the opulent 1882 Villard Houses and a 55-story tower, with a choice of traditional or contemporary room decor. The hotel is also home to the lavish Gilt restaurant.
◈ 455 Madison Ave at 50th St, New York, NY 10022 • Map J4 • 212 888 7000 • www.newyorkpalace.com • $$$$$

4 Trump International Hotel and Towers
High ceilings and tall windows mean fabulous city and Central Park views, and the amenities are equally bountiful – Jacuzzis, personal business cards, room service from Jean Georges (see p68), or a chef to cook for you.
◈ 1 Central Park West, New York, NY 10023 • Map H2 • 212 299 1000 • www. trumpintl.com • $$$$$

5 Peninsula
The Hong Kong hotel group has done itself proud, turning a 1905 classic into a state-of-the-art luxury lodging. Rooms are contemporary with Art Nouveau accents and bedside controls for the many gadgets. The health club with pool is superb.
◈ 700 5th Ave, New York, NY 10019 • Map H3 • 212 956 2888 • www.peninsula. com • $$$$$

6 Pierre
A landmark opposite Central Park since the 1930s, the Pierre, part of the Taj Hotel group, is a bastion of old-world elegance. Personal service is a hallmark that draws many of the elite. The hotel reopened in 2009 after a $100-million facelift. ◈ 2 East 61st St, New York, NY 10021 • Map H3 • 212 838 8000 • www. tajhotels.com/pierre • $$$$$

7 St. Regis
Rooms come with Louis XVI furnishings, silk wall coverings, chandeliers, and a butler tending to your every need at this Beaux Arts beauty. Alain Ducasse's Adour restaurant and the famed King Cole bar are attached. ◈ 2 East 55th St, New York, NY 10022 • Map H4 • 212 753 4500 • www. stregis.com • $$$$$

8 The Mark
Discretely elegant, this member of the prestigious Mandarin group is a contemporary sanctuary. It draws an international clientele who appreciate the Biedemeier furnishings, antique prints, and luxury linens. ◈ 25 East 77th St, New York, NY 10021 • Map F3 • 212 744 4300 • www. themarkhotel.com • $$$$$

9 Hotel Plaza Athénée
An intimate, 152-room Parisian outpost located on a quiet upper East Side street. Modern facilities include a fitness center and staff waiting to attend to your every need. ◈ 37 East 64th St, New York, NY 10021 • Map H4 • 212 734 9100 • www.plaza-athenee. com • $$$$$

10 Mandarin Oriental
If your credit card can take it, there is no better way to spoil yourself than to stay at this luxurious hotel with views over Central Park and the city skyline. Rooms come with flat-screen TVs and high-speed Internet access; the spa is world-class. ◈ 80 Columbus Circle, New York, NY 10023 • Map H2 • 212 805 8800 • www.mandarin oriental.com • $$$$$

Note: Unless otherwise stated, all hotels accept credit cards, and have en-suite bathrooms and air conditioning

Price Categories

For a standard, double room per night (with breakfast if included), taxes, and extra charges.

$	under $150
$$	$150–$250
$$$	$250–$350
$$$$	$350–$450
$$$$$	over $450

Left **Exterior of The Plaza** Center **Renaissance New York** Right **Le Parker Meridien**

🔟 Deluxe Hotels

1 Sherry Netherland
Dating from 1927, this ornate hotel features a spectacular marble-and-bronze lobby and a signature clock marking the 5th Avenue entrance. The rooms are spacious, and most have glorious views over Central Park. ⊗ 781 5th Ave, New York, NY 10022 • Map H3 • 877 743 7710 • www.sherry netherland.com • $$$$$

2 Renaissance New York
An upscale oasis in the Theater District, with an elegant lobby, handsome traditional furnishings, and deep tubs in the bathrooms. The hotel's restaurant offers a dazzling Times Square view. ⊗ 714 7th Ave, New York, NY 10026 • Map J3 • 212 765 7676 • www. renaissance hotels.com • $$$–$$$$

3 Michelangelo
A handsome, New York outpost of an Italian hotel, with unusually spacious rooms in a choice of Art Deco, French Country, or Neo-Classical styles. ⊗ 152 West 51st St, New York, NY 10019 • Map J3 • 212 765 0505 • www. michelangelohotel.com • $$$$

4 The London NYC
Refurbished as a luxury retreat in 2007, this 54-story skyscraper is comprised of 564 well-appointed suites with bay windowed living rooms. Michelin-starred UK chef Gordon Ramsay has an intimate 45 seat restaurant at the hotel. ⊗ 151 West 54th St, New York, NY 10019 • Map H3 • 866 690 2029 • www. TheLondonNYC.com • $$$$–$$$$$

5 Regency Hotel
A gilt and mirrored sanctuary favored by show business moguls, the hotel has Regency decor that inspired the name and oversize suites. The restaurant, 540 Park, a power breakfast favorite, turns into Feinstein's club (see p56) at night. ⊗ 540 Park Ave, New York, NY 10021 • Map H4 • 212 759 4100 • www.loews hotels.com/regency • $$$$–$$$$$

6 Le Parker Meridien
The soaring public spaces, fitness facilities, and rooftop pool are assets of this lively hotel. Sleek, compact guest rooms offer ergonomic chairs, giant TVs, and DVD/CD players. ⊗ 118 West 57th St, New York, NY 10019 • Map H3 • 212 245 5000 • www.parker meridien.com • $$$$

7 70 Park Avenue
A small, sophisticated haven, with smart decor of Neo-Classical furnishings and a rich, gold and green color scheme. Other features include guest privileges at the well-equipped nearby spa. ⊗ 70 Park Ave, New York, NY 10016 • Map K4 • 212 973 2400 • www.70parkave.com • $$$

8 The Plaza
The grande dame of New York hotels, this 19-story, French Renaissance building opened in 1907 as a residence for the wealthy and is now a National Historic Landmark. The hotel has a champagne bar and tranquil gardens. ⊗ 5th Ave at Central Park South, New York, NY 10019 • Map H3 • 212 759 3000 • www. fairmont.com/theplaza • $$$$–$$$$$

9 Sofitel
Although it is just over ten years old, this hotel boasts a distinct old-world elegance. Rooms are comfortable, adorned with art, and soundproofed. The gift shop stocks hard-to-find French products. ⊗ 45 West 44th St, New York, NY 10036 • Map J3 • 212 354 8844 • www. sofitel.com • $$$–$$$$$

10 Waldorf-Astoria
An Art Deco landmark with a magnificent lobby, the 1,416-room Waldorf offers a variety of rooms, some quite grand. ⊗ 301 Park Ave, New York NY 10017 • Map J4 • 212 355 3000 • www.waldorfastoria. com • $$$$–$$$$$

Left **The Warwick Hotel** Center **The Mansfield Hotel** Right **Roger Williams Hotel**

Mid-Range Hotels

1 San Carlos Hotel
All the extra touches – from the morning newspaper and night-time chocolates on your pillow, to Aveda toiletries and flat-screen TVs – make the San Carlos seem like a four-star hotel. The decor is modern, and there is also a 24-hour fitness center. ✆ 150 East 50th St, New York, NY 10022 • Map J4 • 800 722 2012 • www.sancarloshotel. com • $$$

2 Warwick Hotel
William Randolph Hearst built the hotel in 1927, with large rooms and ample closets, and celebrities have been coming ever since. Rates have gone up since renovation added elegant decor and Italian marble bathrooms. ✆ 65 West 54th St, New York, NY 10019 • Map J3 • 212 247 2700 • www.warwick hotelny.com • $$$–$$$$

3 Mansfield Hotel
A distinctive Theater District hotel, the Mansfield features a soaring lobby, copper-domed salon (M Bar), and free continental breakfast and afternoon tea. Rooms have the feel of private apartments. ✆ 12 West 44th St, New York, NY 10036 • Map J4 • 212 277 8700 • www.mansfieldhotel. com • $$$

4 Algonquin Hotel
A literary landmark, famous for the literary clique known as the "Round Table," the Algonquin remains an oasis of civility, with antique lighting fixtures and New Yorker cartoon wallpaper in the halls. Rooms are small and charming. ✆ 59 West 44th St, New York, NY 10019 • Map J3 • 212 840 6800 • www.algonquinhotel.com • $$$

5 Salisbury Hotel
Well-placed for visits to Carnegie Hall, shops, and theaters, the Salisbury was once an apartment-hotel and still has a quiet, low-key, ambience, with traditional American decor, good-sized accommodations, and a pleasant breakfast room. ✆ 123 West 57th St, New York, NY 10019 • Map H3 • 212 246 1300 • www.nycsalisbury.com • $$$

6 Hotel Roger Williams
An atrium with floor-to-ceiling windows, fluted zinc columns, maple furniture, and a mezzanine lounge for complimentary breakfast are among the hotel's modern features, but rooms are styled more cozily. ✆ 131 Madison Ave, New York, NY 10016 • Map L4 • 212 448 7000 • www. hotelrogerwilliams.com • $$$

7 Hotel Elysée
The Elysée has the warmth of a small inn, serving not only breakfast, but wine and hors d'oeuvres in the evening. Room service is from the legendary Monkey Bar & Restaurant. ✆ 60 East 54th St, New York, NY 10022 • Map J4 • 212 753 1066 • www.elyseehotel.com • $$$–$$$$

8 Blakely New York
The cosmopolitan mood begins in the Art Deco lobby with clocks showing the time around the world. Contemporary rooms have cherry wood furnishings and kitchenettes. ✆ 136 West 55th St, New York, NY 10019 • Map H3 • 212 245 1800 • www.blakelynewyork.com • $$$

9 Shoreham
A thoroughly modern makeover has included custom cabinetry, creative use of light and textures, and guest rooms in pale tones. Complimentary breakfast and all-day refreshments included. ✆ 33 West 55th St, New York, NY 10019 • Map H3 • 212 247 6700 • www. shorehamhotel.com • $$$

10 Doubletree Guest Suites
The price of an ordinary hotel room will buy you two comfortable rooms (one with a sofabed), two TVs, and a kitchenette at this Theater District hotel. ✆ 1568 Broadway, New York, NY 10036 • Map J3 • 212 719 1600 • www.doubletreehotels. com • $$$

Note: Unless otherwise stated, all hotels accept credit cards, and have en-suite bathrooms and air conditioning

Price Categories

For a standard, double room per night (with breakfast if included), taxes, and extra charges.

$	under $150
$$	$150–$250
$$$	$250–$350
$$$$	$350–$450
$$$$$	over $450

Left **Hotel Edison** Right **Carlton Arms**

Budget Accommodations

1 Cosmopolitan Hotel

This budget gem in the heart of trendy TriBeCa has small but well-maintained rooms with equally tiny but clean bathrooms. There is easy access to public transport. ✆ 95 West Broadway, New York, NY 10007 • Map Q3 • 212 566 1900 • www.cosmohotel.com • $$

2 The Pod Hotel

Space is tight but the location is prime. Hip style and high tech features include free Wi-Fi and iPod connections. Rooms range from queens to bunk beds. Singles with shared baths can cost under $100. ✆ 230 East 51st, New York, NY 10022 • Map J4 • 212 355 0300 • www.thepodhotel.com • $

3 Gershwin Hotel

The bright red façade adorned with huge white abstract forms tells you that this is an arty, budget choice, popular with young visitors. Don't expect frills, but rooms do offer TV and private baths. ✆ 7 East 27th St, New York, NY 10016 • Map L3 • 212 545 8000 • www.gershwinhotel.com • $$

4 Herald Square Hotel

A tiny, budget hideaway renovated with taste. The small rooms have been nicely decorated, and baths are modern. The cherub over the front

door remains from the days when this Beaux Arts building was the first home of *LIFE* magazine. ✆ 19 West 31st St, New York, NY 10001 • Map K3 • 212 279 4017 • www.heraldsquarehotel.com • $

5 Hotel Edison

Built in 1931, this has long been one of the best-value hotels in the Theater District. It features a stunning Art Deco lobby and small but well-decorated rooms with updated bathrooms. The hotel's café is a favorite, inexpensive pre-theater dining choice. ✆ 228 West 47th St, New York, NY 10036 • Map J3 • 212 840 5000 • www.edisonhotelnyc.com • $$

6 La Quinta Manhattan

On a midtown block known for its Korean restaurants, this renovated building offers comfortable lodging, modern bathrooms, and first-class services at reasonable rates. ✆ 17 West 32nd St, New York, NY 10001 • Map K3 • 212 736 1600 • www.applecorehotels.com • $–$$$

7 Roomorama

Live like a local without spending like one. More than 1,800 listings for rooms and apartments citywide, staying with locals, available nightly, weekly, and monthly. The simple, transparent online payment system is

innovative and wallet-friendly. ✆ 1 877 750 7666 • www.roomorama.com • $–$$

8 Carlton Arms

There's no TV or phone, but this budget haven is popular with young visitors for its hip spirit and funky halls with walls painted by young artists. Private baths are available in 20 of the 54 colorful rooms. ✆ 160 East 25th St, New York, NY 10010 • Map L4 • 212 679 0680 • www.carltonarms.com • No air conditioning • $

9 Hostelling International

Although run by American Youth Hostels, all ages are welcome to share the clean, safe rooms, with 4 to 12 beds at budget prices. This 624-bed facility offers a coffee bar, cafeteria, and self-service kitchen. ✆ 891 Amsterdam Ave, New York, NY 10025 • Map D2 • 212 932 2300 • www.hinewyork.org • Most without en-suite bathrooms • $

10 Metro-Home

This company offers furnished studios to 3-bedroom apartments at a range of prices around the city. Refrigerators are stocked with breakfast fixings. Great value, but make sure that locations are near transit lines. ✆ 116 West 23rd St, 5th Floor, New York, NY 10011 • Map L3 • 646 274 1505 • www.metro-home.com • $–$$$

Left **The Muse** Center **Inn at Irving Place** Right **The Iroquois**

🔟 Boutique Hotels

1 Library Hotel
Books fill this 60-room themed hotel. Each floor is devoted to a Dewey Decimal System category, like the Arts or Philosophy, with appropriate volumes in each room. Includes a rooftop sitting room and terrace. ✆ 299 Madison Ave, New York, NY 10017 • Map K4 • 212 983 4500 • www.libraryhotel.com • $$$–$$$$

2 The Muse
A Theater District boutique, the Muse inspires with a smart lobby decorated with Matisse-like murals and good-size rooms done up in black and white. Offers personalized business cards for guests. ✆ 130 West 46th St, New York, NY 10036 • Map J3 • 212 485 2400 • www.themusehotel.com • $$$

3 Inn at Irving Place
Two Greek Revival townhouses form an elegant, 12-room inn straight from a Jane Austen novel. Rooms have fireplaces and antiques; only the VCRs and CD players bring them up to date. ✆ 56 Irving Place, New York, NY 10002 • Map M4 • 212 533 4600 • www.innatirving.com • $$$

4 Hotel Wales
There is a European feel to the genteel Wales. The renovated hotel has stylish, traditional furnishings and a panoramic, rooftop deck. Breakfast and tea are served in a room lined with illustrations from children's books. ✆ 1295 Madison Ave, New York, NY 10128 • Map E4 • 212 876 6000 • www.waleshotel.com • $$$

5 Lowell
Luxurious and intimate, the Lowell exudes old-world charm in rooms and suites with wood-burning fireplaces, libraries, flowers and marble baths. Decor is an eclectic mix of French, Deco, and Oriental. ✆ 28 East 63rd St, New York, NY 10021 • Map H4 • 212 838 1400 • www.lowellhotel.com • $$$$–$$$$$

6 Iroquois
A suite is named for James Dean, who lived here from 1951 to 1953; other Hollywood guests have included Sandra Bullock and Johnny Depp. Rooms are modestly sized but deluxe, with French decor. Packages offer excellent rates. ✆ 49 West 44th St, New York, NY 10036 • Map J3 • 212 840 3080 • www.iroquoisny.com • $$$

7 Casablanca
A Moroccan theme, complete with tiles, arches, and ceiling fans, sets this 48-room Theater District hotel apart. Rooms are small but well furnished. Continental breakfast is served in (where else?) Rick's Café. ✆ 147 West 43rd St, New York, NY 10036 • Map J3 • 212 869 1212 • www.casablancahotel.com • $$$

8 Hotel Giraffe
A sunny glass-walled lobby leads to this 73-room, award-winning hotel with stylish Retro decor and a delightful roof terrace. Indulgent rooms, just seven per floor, even feature bedside controls for the shades. Breakfast, snacks, evening cheese, wine, and champagne are all complimentary. ✆ 365 Park Ave South, New York, NY 10016 • Map L4 • 212 685 7700 • www.hotelgiraffe.com • $$$–$$$$

9 Dylan
Although the 1903 façade has been faithfully restored, the former Chemists' Club has been transformed with serene Zen decor. Carrara marble baths add to the quietly luxurious feel. ✆ 52 East 41st St, NY 10017 • Map K4 • 212 338 0500 • www.dylanhotel.com • $$$–$$$$$

10 Bryant Park
Raymond Hood's 1924 American Radiator Building has become an ultra-contemporary hotel, with giant glass windows, bold, red-lacquered lobby desks, and pale-hued rooms that are the last word in minimalist decor. ✆ 40 West 40th St, New York, NY 10018 • Map K3 • 212 869 0100 • www.bryantparkhotel.com • $$$$$

Note: Unless otherwise stated, all hotels accept credit cards, and have en-suite bathrooms and air conditioning

Price Categories

For a standard, double room per night (with breakfast if included), taxes, and extra charges.

$	under $150
$$	$150–$250
$$$	$250–$350
$$$$	$350–£450
$$$$$	over $450

Left **TriBeCa Grand Hotel** Right **Soho Grand Hotel**

🔟 Hip Hotels

Soho Grand Hotel
Perfectly suited to its artistic neighborhood, the hotel is housed in a landmark cast-iron building. The surroundings are dramatic and contemporary, and the Grand Bar is always hopping. ⊗ *310 West Broadway, New York, NY 10013 • Map P3 • 212 965 3000 • www.sohogrand. com • $$$$–$$$$$*

TriBeCa Grand Hotel
TriBeCa's first hotel is a hit. All the neighborhood gathers at the Church Lounge, the dramatic lobby/bar with 70 translucent columns of light. Rooms are a calm counterpoint with an array of high-tech toys. ⊗ *2 6th Ave, New York, NY 10013 • Map P3 • 212 519 6600 • www.tribecagrand. com • $$$$–$$$$$*

W Union Square
Designer David Rockwell has turned a Beaux Arts building into a contemporary showstopper, complete with floating staircase. Trademark W features include a lobby with books and chess sets, and rooms with pillow-top beds. ⊗ *201 Park Ave South, New York, NY 10003 • Map M4 • 212 253 9119 • www. whotels.com • $$$–$$$$$*

Morgans Hotel
Ian Schrager's understated first New York hotel, redesigned in 2008, still has loyal fans for its clean, uncluttered look and clever, functional built-ins in the small but trendy rooms. Celebrity favorite restaurant Asia de Cuba adjoins the lobby. ⊗ *237 Madison Ave, New York, NY 10016 • Map K4 • 212 686 0300 • www.morganshotel. com • $$–$$$*

Hotel on Rivington
Somewhat structurally out of place in the low-slung Lower East Side, the hotel does its best to tap the area's popularity. Rooms (some with balconies) are sensuous and modern and feature fab city panoramas. ⊗ *107 Rivington St, New York, NY 10002 • Map N5 • 212 475 2600 • $$$$*

The Standard
This outpost of L.A.'s hip crash pad has its own style. Just off the meatpacking district, The Standard has a happening 18th floor bar. The 337 rooms, with floor to ceiling windows and great views are airy and open. If modest, beware the glass-enclosed showers. ⊗ *848 Washington St, New York, NY 10014 • Map M2 • 212 645 4646 • www. standardhotels.com • $$$*

Hudson Hotel
The Schrager-Starck team pulled out all the stops for this 1,000 room extravaganza, a melting pot of styles described as "organized chaos". Tiny rooms were billed low-budget, but rates went up when the hotel became a hit. ⊗ *356 West 58th St, New York, NY 10019 • Map H2 • 212 554 6000 • www. hudsonhotel.com • $$*

Time Hotel
Bold red, bright yellow, or blue? Each of the 200 rooms in this hotel is awash in color, courtesy of hot designer Adam Tihany. Take the glass and chrome elevator to the peaceful second-floor bar. ⊗ *224 West 49th St, New York, NY 10036 • Map J3 • 212 246 5252 • www.thetimeny.com • $$$*

Mercer Hotel
A hit from day one with Hollywood luminaries, the Mercer is housed in an 1890 structure built for John Jacob Astor II, and makes good use of lofty spaces and a voguish, shabby-chic look. ⊗ *147 Mercer St, New York, NY 10012 • Map N4 • 212 966 6060 • www.mercer hotel.com • $$$$–$$$$$*

Cooper Square Hotel
Built in 2009, this 145-room hotel with sleek interiors by Antonio Citterio has vast windows overlooking the heart of downtown. Designer touches include myriad electronics and a signature fragrance. ⊗ *25 Cooper Square, New York, NY 10013 • 212 475 5700 • Map M4 • www.thecoopersquare hotel.com • $$–$$$$*

Left **Benjamin** Center **Hilton New York** Right **Hotel Metro**

🔟 Business Hotels

1 Hilton New York
The quintessential business hotel, the 2,040-room Hilton has a central location, huge ballroom, and extensive meeting facilities. A re-design has transformed the lobby, upgraded rooms, and added a large fitness club and spa. ✪ 1335 6th Ave, New York, NY 10019 • Map J3 • 212 586 7000 • www.hilton.com • $$$–$$$$

2 Millennium Broadway
A postmodern skyscraper, encompassing a theater, the Millennium is sleek and streamlined. Compact rooms are well appointed with high-tech features that include voicemail in four languages. ✪ 145 West 44th St, New York, NY 10036 • Map J3 • 212 768 4400 • www.millenniumhotels.com • $$$$

3 Benjamin
A 1927 landmark by Emery Roth has been converted to an all-suite hotel designed for executives, with all the requisite high-tech gadgetry and the popular An American Place restaurant. ✪ 125 East 50th St, New York, NY 10022 • Map J4 • 212 715 2500 • www.thebenjamin.com • $$$–$$$$

4 Beekman Tower Hotel
The Beekman is an Art Deco gem. Suites are roomy and provide kitchenettes; the 26th floor Top of the Tower lounge is the perfect unwinding place. ✪ 3 Mitchell Place, 49th St, New York, NY 10017 • Map J5 • 212 355 7300 • www.affinia.com • $$$–$$$$

5 Metropolitan
Built in 1961, this mid-range property offers 755 comfortable rooms and good value suites. Amenities include a fitness center and business facilities. ✪ 569 Lexington Ave, New York, NY 10022 • Map J4 • 212 752 7000 & 800 836 6471 • www.metropolitanhotelnyc.com • $$$

6 Hotel Metro
Popular with the fashion industry, and good value, the Metro has a sophisticated Deco feel and good-sized rooms. Public spaces include a library, rooftop terrace, and spacious dining room. ✪ 45 West 35th St, New York, NY 10001 • Map K3 • 212 947 2500 • www.hotelmetronyc • $$

7 Millennium U.N. Plaza Hotel
Kevin Roche's soaring tower attracts an international clientele, who enjoys panoramic views from rooms beginning on the 28th floor, a glass-enclosed swimming pool, and New York's only indoor hotel tennis court. ✪ U.N. Plaza, 44th St between 1st & 2nd Ave, New York, NY 10017 • Map J5 • 212 758 1234 • www.unplaza.com • $$$$

8 Sheraton Manhattan
An indoor pool, sauna, and free continental breakfast are among the features of this 22-story hotel, a quieter sibling and neighbor of the Sheraton New York, a major convention venue. The theater district is steps away. ✪ 790 7th Ave, New York, NY 10019 • Map J3 • 212 581 3300 • www.sheraton.com • $$$–$$$$$

9 Gild Hall
Combining luxury with business in the heart of the Financial District, the Gild Hall is a venture from the Thompson Hotels Group. The sleek rooms are well-equipped and the hotel features a library, champagne bar, and restaurant by Todd English. ✪ 15 Gold St, New York, NY 10038 • Map Q4 • 212 232 7700 • www.thompsonhotels.com • $$$–$$$$

10 Ritz Carlton Battery Park
This luxury hotel has stunning views of the harbor and impressive attention to detail. Special touches include telescopes in rooms, feather beds, and a "bath butler." Kids will enjoy the Skyscraper Museum close by. ✪ 2 West St, New York, NY • Map Q3 • 212 344 0800 • www.ritzcarlton.com • $$$$

Note: *Unless otherwise stated, all hotels accept credit cards, and have en-suite bathrooms and air conditioning*

Price Categories

For a standard, double room per night (with breakfast if included), taxes, and extra charges.

$	under $150
$$	$150–$250
$$$	$250–$350
$$$$	$350–£450
$$$$$	over $450

Left **The Lucerne** Right **Excelsior**

🔟 Neighborhood Hotels

1 Lucerne
The Upper West Side offers excellent value, and the Lucerne, housed in a terracotta-trimmed 1903 building, is top of the list. It has a comfortable lobby, business and fitness centers, a rooftop terrace, and tasteful rooms with many amenities. 🕲 201 West 79th St, New York, NY 10024 • Map F2 • 212 875 1000 • www. thelucernehotel.com • $$$

2 Excelsior
A lavish, old-world lobby fronts a refurbished, well-appointed hotel with traditional decor, many suites, in-room computers and Wi-Fi. A breakfast room, a library, outdoor decks, and a media room are among other features. 🕲 45 West 81st St, New York, NY 10024 • Map F2 • 212 362 9200 • www.excelsior hotelny.com • $$

3 Hotel Beacon
Named for the famous theater next door (see p52), the Beacon is a relaxed, comfortable hotel, with generous rooms with standard decor, and, a big plus: kitchenettes with refrigerators and microwaves. 🕲 2130 Broadway, New York, NY 10023 • Map G2 • 212 787 1100 • www. beaconhotel.com • $$

4 Belleclaire Hotel
The rooms in this renovated property are sparse, but well-designed and stylish. Bathrooms are small, and some rooms have a shared bath. Ask for a one-bath family suite if kids are in tow. Right in the heart of the Upper West Side, making it a great base for exploring. 🕲 250 West 77th St, New York, NY 10024 • Map F2 • 212 362 7700 • www. hotelbelleclaire.com • $$

5 The Inn on 23rd
One of New York's best-kept secrets. This charming B&B has 14 spacious rooms. Breakfast is served in the library, which also has an honor bar where you can whip up a cocktail before your night on the town. 🕲 131 West 23rd St, New York, NY 10011 • Map L3 • 212 463 0330 • www. innon23rd.com • $$–$$$

6 Franklin
An affordable lodging on the Upper East Side, the Franklin offers style rather than size, with sleek furnishings and compact rooms. Breakfast is complimentary, and hot drinks are served all day. 🕲 164 East 87th St, New York, NY 10128 • Map F4 • 212 369 1000 • www. franklinhotel.com • $$$

7 Chelsea Savoy
An excellent neighborhood lodging, close to Chelsea's shops, flea markets, cafés, and galleries. Pleasantly furnished rooms are a decent size, with all the necessary amenities. Choose rooms that face away from 23rd Street. 🕲 204 West 23rd St, New York, NY 10011 • Map L2 • 212 929 9353 • www. chelseasavoynyc.com • $$

8 Best Western Seaport Inn
Close to South Street Seaport, this restored 19th-century building has the predictable rooms of a chain hotel, but a cozy lobby. All 72 rooms have MP3 player alarm clocks and refrigerators. Breakfast is included. 🕲 33 Peck Slip, New York, NY 10038 • Map Q4 • 212 766 6600 • www. bestwestern.com • $$

9 Washington Square Hotel
A haven in the heart of Greenwich Village. Rooms are tiny, hallways painfully narrow, but the decor pleasant. Continental breakfast is included, and you can say you stayed where Bob Dylan and Joan Baez once hung out. 🕲 103 Waverly Place, New York, NY 10011 • Map N3 • 212 777 9515 • www. wshotel.com • $$

10 60 Thompson
SoHo's 12-story luxury hotel has 100 rooms, elegantly decked out with custom furnishings. Guests can enjoy the view from the roof garden lounge or watch the neighborhood scene from the sidewalk café. 🕲 60 Thompson St, New York, NY 10012 • Map N3 • 877 431 0400 • www. 60thompson.com • $$$$

General Index

Acknowledgments

The Author

Eleanor Berman is a widely published travel writer who has visited six continents. A long-time New Yorker, she is New York correspondent for the Expedia travel web site, main contributor to the *DK Eyewitness New York Travel Guide* (winner, Wanderlust Travel Guide Award 2009), and author of *New York Neighborhoods* (winner, Independent Publishers award, 2000) and nine other travel guides.

Project Editors Felicity Crowe, Marianne Petrou
Art Editor Gillian Andrews
Senior Editor Marcus Hardy
Senior Art Editor Marisa Renzullo
Senior Publishing Manager Louise Lang
Publishing Manager Scarlett O'Hara, Kate Poole
Art Director Gillian Allan
Photographers David King, Tim Knox
Illustrator Chris Orr & Associates
Cartography Casper Morris
Maps John Plumer
Editor Caroline Taverne
Researcher Vivienne Foley
Picture Research Jenny Silkstone, Lilly Sellar
Proofreader Stephanie Driver
Indexer Hilary Bird
DTP Jason Little

Production

Joanna Bull, Marie Ingledew

Design and Editorial Assistance

Emma Anacootee, Lydia Baillie, Sonal Bhatt, Tessa Bindloss, Rebecca Carman, Sherry Collins, Nicola Erdpresser, Gadi Farfour, Anna Freiberger, Jo Gardner, James Hall, Rose Hudson, Claire Jones, Todd Obolsky, Marianne Petrou, Pollyanna Poulter, Collette Sadler, David Saldanha, Sands Publishing Solutions, Melanie Simmonds, Hayley Smith, Brett Steel, Rachel Symons, Andrew Szudek, Shawn Thomas, Karen Villabona, Ros Walford.

Additional Photography

Rebecca Carman, Tony Foo, Andrew Holigan, Edvard Huember, Dave King, Norman McGrath, Michael Moran, Rough Guides/Angus Oborn, Susan Sayler, Paul Solomon, Chuck Spang, Chris Stevens, Shawn Thomas, Robert Wright.

Picture Credits

t-top, tl-top left, tlc-top left centre, tc-top centre, tr-top right, cla-centre left above, ca- centre above, cra- centre right above, cl-centre left, c-centre, cr-centre right, clb-centre left below, cb-centre below, crb-centreright below, bl-bottom left, b-bottom, bc-bottom centre, bcl-bottom centre left, br-bottom right, d-detail.

Artworks have been reproduced with permission of the following copyright holders: *'Untitled'* Christian Boltanski © ADAGP, Paris and DACS, London 2006 99bl; *'Group of Four Trees'* Jean Dubuffet © ADAGP, London 2006 76tr; *'Five in One'* Tony Rosenthal, © DACS London 2006 78tr.

The publishers would like to thank the following individuals, companies and picture libraries for their kind permission to reproduce their photographs.

ALAMY IMAGES: Black Star/Jochen Tack/Das Fotoarchiv 60tc; *Charging Bull* © Arturo Di Modica, photo Kevin Foy 75tl; Martyn Vickery 108tc; AMERICAN FOLK ART MUSEUM, New York: John Parnell 19c; AMERICAN MUSEUM OF NATURAL HISTORY, Courtesy Department of Library Services: 35c, 35b, 35t, 37c, 37b, 138cr; D. Finnin 36tl, 36tc, 36tr, 36c; AMT PUBLIC RELATIONS: Jazz Standard 53cla; ANDREA ROSEN GALLERY: *'The Universal Cell'* Matthew Ritchie, photo Tom Powel 120tr; ASSOCIATED PRESS AP: Stephen J Boitano 49b; BIG ONION WALKING TOURS: 162tr; MARY BOONE GALLERY: *Eric Fischl Installation* (1999) ZINDMAN/FREMONT, N.Y.C. 42tl; THE BOUTIQUE HOTEL GROUP: 174tc, 174tr; BROOKLYN MUSEUM, NEW YORK: 154tl; Adam Husted 40tr; CENTRAL PARK CONSERVANCY: Sara Cedar Miller 26b, 27b; CHANTERELLE: 103tc; CHILDREN'S MUSEUM OF THE ARTS: 99bl; COACH USA: 164tc; COLORIFIC: Black Star 18b; PAULA COOPER GALLERY: *Prospective Retrospective* by Carl Andre 43c, Adam Reich 42tr; CORBIS: 17cr, 48c, 48ca, 158-159; Nathan Benn 45cl; Bettman 19t, 20tl, 20c, 20b; 25t, 48tl, 49t; ChromoSohm Inc 4-5; Duomo 63c, Duomo/Chris Trotman 63t; Patrik Giardino 167t; Lynn Goldsmith 10-11c; Dave Houser 62c; David Katzenstein 62b; Kit Kittle 128tr; Bob Krist 168tr; Lawrence 70-71, 104c; James Marshall 157t; Gail Mooney 9t; 18cl, 22c, 64b, 128tc; Kelly Mooney 116cr, 119t; 74br; Museum of the City of New York 48tc; Charles O'Rear 38-39; Bill Ross 16t; Lee Snider 10cl, Visions of America/Joseph Sohm 162tc; Michael S. Yamashita 3bl, 131; DANIEL RESTAURANT: Peter Medliek 137tl; DEPARTMENT: 170TR; EDELMAN PR: New York Road Runners 9bl; HOTEL EDISON: 175tl; EXCELSIOR HOTEL: 179tc; FAIRMONT HOTELS & RESORTS 173tl; FLUTE CHAMPAGNE LOUNGE 54tl; FOUR SEASONS: Jennifer Calais Smith 68tl; GLADSTONE GALLERY: *'Dereconstruction'* curated by Matthew Higgs, photo David Regen 120tl; THE SOLOMON R. GUGGENHEIM FOUNDATION, NEW YORK: *'Before the Mirror'* Edouard Manet, 1876, Thannhauser Collection, Gift Justin K Thannhauser 1978, photo David Heald 33t; *'Black Lines'* Wassily Kandinsky, 1913, Gift Solomon R. Guggenheim 1937, photo David Heald © ADAGP, Paris and DACS, London 2006 33b; *'Haere Mai'* Paul Gauguin, Thannhauser Collection, Gift Justin K. Thannhauser 1978 33r; *'The Hermitage at Pontoise'* Camille Pissaro, Thannhauser Collection, Gift Justin K Thannhauser 1978 32c; *'Woman with Yellow Hair'* Pablo Picasso, December 1931, Thannhauser Collection, Gift Justin K Thannhauser, photo David Heald © Succession Picasso/DACS 2006 32b; HARRIS LEVY: 94tr; HILTONS OF NEW YORK CITY: 178tc; HULTON GETTY ARCHIVE: 20tr; Ernst Haas 20tc. THE IMAGE BANK/GETTY IMAGES: 59cl; IMAGE STATE: AGE Fotostock 96-97; THE IRVING PLACE: Roy J. Wright 176tc; JAZZ PROMO SERVICES: 52tr;

Acknowledgments

JOAN MARCUS: 23b, 25c, 25b; LUCKY CHENG'S: 60tl; THE METROPOLITAN MUSEUM OF ART, NY: The Metropolitan Museum of Art, New York: 28b, 29cb; *'Autumn Landscape'*, Louis Comfort Tiffany (American Tiffany Studios), gift of Robert W. de Forest, 1925 (25.173) 29tl; *'Cypresses'* Vincent van Gogh, 1889, Rogers Fund 1949 30b; *'Gertrude Stein'*, Pablo Picasso, 1905-6, Bequest of Gertrude Stein 1946 © Succession Picasso/DACS 2006 30tr; *'The Card Players'*, Paul Cezanne, Bequest of Stephen C. Clark 1960 30tl; *'Young Woman with Water Jug'*, Johannes Vermeer, 1664-5, Marquand Collection, Gift of Henry G. Marquand 1889 7c and 30c; *'Garden at Sainte-Adresse'* Claude Monet, 1867, Monet Purchase, special contributions and funds given or bequeathed by friends of the Museum 30tc; The Cloisters Collection/Mick Hales 31crb; Purchase The Costume Institute Fund in memory of Polaire Weissman 1989 29ca; *'Triptych with Annunciation'*, Robert Campin, 1425, The Cloisters Collection 1956 31b; The Cloisters Collection 1937 31t; The Cloisters Collection Gift of John D. Rockefeller 1937 31cl; MISS LONELYHEARTS: 94tl; MISS MAMIE'S SPOONBREAD TOO: 149tl; THE MUSE HOTEL: 176tl; MUSEUM OF MODERN ART: ©2004 Photo Elizabeth Felicella, architectural rendering Kohn Pedersen Fox Associates, digital composite Robert Bowen 40c; NEW YORK CITY FIRE DEPARTMENT: 170tr; PACE WILDENSTEIN: Ellen Page Wilson *'Cornflake Girl'*, Mel Ramos © DACS, London/VAGA, New York 2006 42c; PHOTOLIBRARY: Ambient Images/ Peter Bennett 118br; PRADA: 99br; THE PENINSULA NEW YORK: 54tc; REGENT HOTELS: 178tc; RENAISSANCE NEW YORK: 173tc; ROCKEFELLER CENTER ARCHIVE: 14tr, 15c, 15t, John D Rockefeller Jr 48tr; SOHO GRAND HOTEL: 177tr; SOUTH STREET SEAPORT MUSEUM: 82tc; ST. MAGGIE'S CAFE: 77tl; THEATRE DEVELOPMENT FUND: 166tl; TISHMAN SPEYER: Rockerfeller Center/Christine Roussel *'Winged Mercury'* 1933 by Lee Lawrie 14tl; TOP OF THE ROCK OBSERVATION DECK: 13bl; TRIBECA GRAND HOTEL: Michael Kleinberg 177tl.

All other images are © Dorling Kindersley. For further information see www.dkimages.com.

Special Editions of DK Travel Guides

DK Travel Guides can be purchased in bulk quantities at discounted prices for use in promotions or as premiums. We are also able to offer special editions and personalized jackets, corporate imprints, and excerpts from all of our books, tailored specifically to meet your own needs.

To find out more, please contact:

(in the US) **SpecialSales@dk.com**

(in the UK) **TravelSpecialSales@uk.dk. com**

(in Canada) DK Special Sales at **general@tourmaline.ca**

(in Australia) **business.development@ pearson.com.au**

DK Discover **traveldk.com**

Explore 1000s of destinations

NICO'S ... TO NEW... | LAURE... TO PAR... | SUE'S EXTREME SCUBA DIVING

Made by Ni... | Made by La... | Made by Sue

Create your own guide

Share views with fellow travellers

> View highlight

Comments

Leave a comment

Gemma's Paris G...
★★★★★ 4.2/5 (...

Yeah, what a nice idea ...
about 10 months ago

Great guide! When w...
and thought-provoki...
museum in Prinsen...

Clare

Faser

What a great idea! I might d...
about 10 months ago

traveldk.com • guides your way

Dear Jess,

The festive season is almost upon us and it's time to shop! Check out our top ten lists for hunting out bargains around the world and find out why New York's our perfect pick for Christmas gifts. If shopping's not your bag, get away to spend Christmas abroad this year - we'll help you plan your escape with what's on across the globe.

Receive exclusive offers

Search destinations> | Online travel guides> | City audio tours> | Competitions> | Make bookings>

In this issue:
● Christmas in New York
● Free Christmas shopping guide
● Plan your festive break

● Christmas shopping ideas
● Win a DAB digital radio
● 3 for 2 on travel guides

Advertisement

DISNEYLAND RESORT PARIS

Pick a ...

6 FAMOUS ATTRACTIONS
ONE AMAZING PRICE
SKIP MOST TICKET LINES

New York City PASS
ADMIT ONE · ADMIT ONE

Empire State Building Observatory

American Museum of Natural History

The Museum of Modern Art (MoMA)

The Metropolitan Museum of Art

Your choice of **Guggenheim Museum**
or **Top of the Rock™**

Your choice of **Statue of Liberty & Ellis
Island** or **Circle Line Sightseeing Cruise**

VALID UP TO **9** DAYS

SOLD AT THESE ATTRACTIONS
BUY IT AT THE FIRST ONE YOU VISIT
citypass.com
(888) 330-5008

Only **$84.00**
A $153.10 Value
(Youth 6 -17 $59.00)

CityPASS is also available in **Atlanta   Boston   Chicago   Hollywood   Houston
Philadelphia   San Francisco   Seattle   Southern California   Toronto**